# PUBLIC OPINION

WALTER LIPPMANN

DOVER PUBLICATIONS, INC.
Mineola, New York

*Bibliographical Note*

This Dover edition, published in 2004, is a newly reset, unabridged republication of the work originally published by Harcourt, Brace and Company, New York, in 1922.

*Library of Congress Cataloging-in-Publication Data*

Lippmann, Walter, 1889–1974.
    Public opinion / Walter Lippmann.
        p. cm.
    Originally published: New York, Harcourt, Brace and Company, [c1922].
    Includes index.
    ISBN 0-486-43703-5 (pbk.)
    1. Public opinion. 2. Public opinion—United States. 3. Social psychology. 4. Social psychology—United States. 5. United States—Politics and government. I. Title.

HM261.L75 2004
303.3'8—dc22

                                                        2004050241

Manufactured in the United States of America
Dover Publications, Inc., 31 East 2nd Street, Mineola, N.Y. 11501

TO
FAYE LIPPMANN

Wading River,
Long Island.
1921.

"Behold! human beings living in a sort of underground den, which has a mouth open towards the light and reaching all across the den; they have been here from their childhood, and have their legs and necks chained so that they cannot move, and can only see before them; for the chains are arranged in such a manner as to prevent them from turning round their heads. At a distance above and behind them the light of a fire is blazing, and between the fire and the prisoners there is a raised way; and you will see, if you look, a low wall built along the way, like the screen which marionette players have before them, over which they show the puppets.

I see, he said.

And do you see, I said, men passing along the wall carrying vessels, which appear over the wall; also figures of men and animals, made of wood and stone and various materials; and some of the prisoners, as you would expect, are talking, and some of them are silent?

This is a strange image, he said, and they are strange prisoners.

Like ourselves, I replied; and they see only their own shadows, or the shadows of one another, which the fire throws on the opposite wall of the cave?

True, he said: how could they see anything but the shadows if they were never allowed to move their heads?

And of the objects which are being carried in like manner they would see only the shadows?

Yes, he said.

And if they were able to talk with one another, would they not suppose that they were naming what was actually before them?"—The Republic of Plato, Book Seven. (Jowett Translation.)

# Contents

PART I.   INTRODUCTION

CHAPTER                                                          PAGE
I.   The World Outside and the Pictures in Our Heads. . . . .    1

PART II. APPROACHES TO THE WORLD OUTSIDE

II.    Censorship and Privacy . . . . . . . . . . . . . . . . . . . . . . . . . . .    18
III.   Contact and Opportunity  . . . . . . . . . . . . . . . . . . . . . . .    24
IV.    Time and Attention . . . . . . . . . . . . . . . . . . . . . . . . . . . . .    31
V.     Speed, Words, and Clearness  . . . . . . . . . . . . . . . . . . . . .    35

PART III.   STEREOTYPES

VI.     Stereotypes  . . . . . . . . . . . . . . . . . . . . . . . . . . . . . . . . .    43
VII.    Stereotypes as Defense  . . . . . . . . . . . . . . . . . . . . . . . .    52
VIII.   Blind Spots and Their Value . . . . . . . . . . . . . . . . . . . . .    57
IX.     Codes and Their Enemies . . . . . . . . . . . . . . . . . . . . . . .    63
X.      The Detection of Stereotypes  . . . . . . . . . . . . . . . . . . . .    71

PART IV.   INTERESTS

XI.    The Enlisting of Interest  . . . . . . . . . . . . . . . . . . . . . . . .    87
XII.   Self-Interest Reconsidered . . . . . . . . . . . . . . . . . . . . . . .    93

PART V.   THE MAKING OF A COMMON WILL

XIII.   The Transfer of Interest . . . . . . . . . . . . . . . . . . . . . . . .    105
XIV.    Yes or No . . . . . . . . . . . . . . . . . . . . . . . . . . . . . . . . . . .    119
XV.     Leaders and the Rank and File  . . . . . . . . . . . . . . . . . . .    127

PART VI.   THE IMAGE OF DEMOCRACY

XVI.   The Self-Centered Man  . . . . . . . . . . . . . . . . . . . . . . . . .    137

# Contents

XVII. The Self-Contained Community . . . . . . . . . . . . . . . . . . . . 142
XVIII. The Role of Force, Patronage and Privilege . . . . . . . . . . 150
XIX. The Old Image in a New Form: Guild Socialism . . . . . . 159
XX. A New Image . . . . . . . . . . . . . . . . . . . . . . . . . . . . . . . . . 169

## PART VII. NEWSPAPERS

XXI. The Buying Public . . . . . . . . . . . . . . . . . . . . . . . . . . . . 172
XXII. The Constant Reader . . . . . . . . . . . . . . . . . . . . . . . . . . 178
XXIII. The Nature of News . . . . . . . . . . . . . . . . . . . . . . . . . . . 183
XXIV. News, Truth, and a Conclusion . . . . . . . . . . . . . . . . . . . 194

## PART VIII. ORGANIZED INTELLIGENCE

XXV. The Entering Wedge . . . . . . . . . . . . . . . . . . . . . . . . . . . 198
XXVI. Intelligence Work . . . . . . . . . . . . . . . . . . . . . . . . . . . . . 203
XXVII. The Appeal to the Public . . . . . . . . . . . . . . . . . . . . . . . 213
XXVIII. The Appeal to Reason . . . . . . . . . . . . . . . . . . . . . . . . . . 220

Index . . . . . . . . . . . . . . . . . . . . . . . . . . . . . . . . . . . . . . . 225

# I. The World Outside and the Pictures in Our Heads

1

THERE is an island in the ocean where in 1914 a few Englishmen, Frenchmen, and Germans lived. No cable reaches that island, and the British mail steamer comes but once in sixty days. In September it had not yet come, and the islanders were still talking about the latest newspaper which told about the approaching trial of Madame Caillaux for the shooting of Gaston Calmette. It was, therefore, with more than usual eagerness that the whole colony assembled at the quay on a day in mid-September to hear from the captain what the verdict had been. They learned that for over six weeks now those of them who were English and those of them who were French had been fighting in behalf of the sanctity of treaties against those of them who were Germans. For six strange weeks they had acted as if they were friends, when in fact they were enemies.

But their plight was not so different from that of most of the population of Europe. They had been mistaken for six weeks, on the continent the interval may have been only six days or six hours. There was an interval. There was a moment when the picture of Europe on which men were conducting their business as usual, did not in any way correspond to the Europe which was about to make a jumble of their lives. There was a time for each man when he was still adjusted to an environment that no longer existed. All over the world as late as July 25th men were making goods that they would not be able to ship, buying goods they would not be able to import, careers were being planned, enterprises contemplated, hopes and expectations entertained, all in the belief that the world as known was the world as it was. Men were writing books describing that world. They trusted the picture in their heads. And then over four years later, on a Thursday morning, came the news of an armistice, and people gave vent to their unutterable relief that the slaughter was over. Yet in the five days before the real armistice came, though the end of the war had been celebrated, several thousand young men died on the battlefields.

Looking back we can see how indirectly we know the environment in which nevertheless we live. We can see that the news of it comes to us now fast, now slowly; but that whatever we believe to be a true picture, we treat as if it were the environment itself. It is harder to remember that about the beliefs upon which we are now acting, but in respect to other peoples and other ages we flatter ourselves that it is easy to see when they were in deadly earnest about ludicrous pictures of the world. We insist, because of our superior hindsight, that the world as they needed to know it, and the world as they did know it, were often two quite contradictory things. We can see, too, that while they governed and fought, traded and reformed in the world as they imagined it to be, they produced results, or failed to produce any, in the world as it was. They started for the Indies and found America. They diagnosed evil and hanged old women. They thought they could grow rich by always selling and never buying. A caliph, obeying what he conceived to be the Will of Allah, burned the library at Alexandria.

Writing about the year 389, St. Ambrose stated the case for the prisoner in Plato's cave who resolutely declines to turn his head. "To discuss the nature and position of the earth does not help us in our hope of the life to come. It is enough to know what Scripture states. 'That He hung up the earth upon nothing' (Job xxvi. 7). Why then argue whether He hung it up in air or upon the water, and raise a controversy as to how the thin air could sustain the earth; or why, if upon the waters, the earth does not go crashing down to the bottom? . . . Not because the earth is in the middle, as if suspended on even balance, but because the majesty of God constrains it by the law of His will, does it endure stable upon the unstable and the void."[1]

It does not help us in our hope of the life to come. It is enough to know what Scripture states. Why then argue? But a century and a half after St. Ambrose, opinion was still troubled, on this occasion by the problem of the antipodes. A monk named Cosmas, famous for his scientific attainments, was therefore deputed to write a Christian Topography, or "Christian Opinion concerning the World."[2] It is clear that he knew exactly what was expected of him, for he based all his conclusions on the Scriptures as he read them. It appears, then, that the world is a flat parallelogram, twice as broad from east to west as it is long from north to south. In the center is the earth surrounded by ocean, which is in turn surrounded by another earth, where men lived

---

[1] Hexaëmeron, i. cap 6, quoted in *The Mediæval Mind*, by Henry Osborn Taylor, Vol. I, p. 73.
[2] Lecky, *Rationalism in Europe*, Vol. I, pp. 276–8.

before the deluge. This other earth was Noah's port of embarkation. In the north is a high conical mountain around which revolve the sun and moon. When the sun is behind the mountain it is night. The sky is glued to the edges of the outer earth. It consists of four high walls which meet in a concave roof, so that the earth is the floor of the universe. There is an ocean on the other side of the sky, constituting the "waters that are above the firmament." The space between the celestial ocean and the ultimate roof of the universe belongs to the blest. The space between the earth and sky is inhabited by the angels. Finally, since St. Paul said that all men are made to live upon the "face of the earth" how could they live on the back where the Antipodes are supposed to be? "With such a passage before his eyes, a Christian, we are told, should not 'even speak of the Antipodes.'"[3]

Far less should he go to the Antipodes; nor should any Christian prince give him a ship to try; nor would any pious mariner wish to try. For Cosmas there was nothing in the least absurd about his map. Only by remembering his absolute conviction that this was the map of the universe can we begin to understand how he would have dreaded Magellan or Peary or the aviator who risked a collision with the angels and the vault of heaven by flying seven miles up in the air. In the same way we can best understand the furies of war and politics by remembering that almost the whole of each party believes absolutely in its picture of the opposition, that it takes as fact, not what is, but what it supposes to be the fact. And that therefore, like Hamlet, it will stab Polonius behind the rustling curtain, thinking him the king, and perhaps like Hamlet add:

> "Thou wretched, rash, intruding fool, farewell!
> I took thee for thy better; take thy fortune."

## 2

Great men, even during their lifetime, are usually known to the public only through a fictitious personality. Hence the modicum of truth in the old saying that no man is a hero to his valet. There is only a modicum of truth, for the valet, and the private secretary, are often immersed in the fiction themselves. Royal personages are, of course, constructed personalities. Whether they themselves believe in their public character, or whether they merely permit the chamberlain to stage-manage it, there are at least two distinct selves, the public and regal self, the private and human. The biographies of great people fall

---

[3] *Id.*

more or less readily into the histories of these two selves. The official biographer reproduces the public life, the revealing memoir the other. The Charnwood Lincoln, for example, is a noble portrait, not of an actual human being, but of an epic figure, replete with significance, who moves on much the same level of reality as Aeneas or St. George. Oliver's Hamilton is a majestic abstraction, the sculpture of an idea, "an essay" as Mr. Oliver himself calls it, "on American union." It is a formal monument to the state-craft of federalism, hardly the biography of a person. Sometimes people create their own façade when they think they are revealing the interior scene. The Repington diaries and Margot Asquith's are a species of self-portraiture in which the intimate detail is most revealing as an index of how the authors like to think about themselves.

But the most interesting kind of portraiture is that which arises spontaneously in people's minds. When Victoria came to the throne, says Mr. Strachey,[4] "among the outside public there was a great wave of enthusiasm. Sentiment and romance were coming into fashion; and the spectacle of the little girl-queen, innocent, modest, with fair hair and pink cheeks, driving through her capital, filled the hearts of the beholders with raptures of affectionate loyalty. What, above all, struck everybody with overwhelming force was the contrast between Queen Victoria and her uncles. The nasty old men, debauched and selfish, pigheaded and ridiculous, with their perpetual burden of debts, confusions, and disreputabilities—they had vanished like the snows of winter and here at last, crowned and radiant, was the spring."

M. Jean de Pierrefeu[5] saw hero-worship at first hand, for he was an officer on Joffre's staff at the moment of that soldier's greatest fame:

"For two years, the entire world paid an almost divine homage to the victor of the Marne. The baggage-master literally bent under the weight of the boxes, of the packages and letters which unknown people sent him with a frantic testimonial of their admiration. I think that outside of General Joffre, no commander in the war has been able to realize a comparable idea of what glory is. They sent him boxes of candy from all the great confectioners of the world, boxes of champagne, fine wines of every vintage, fruits, game, ornaments and utensils, clothes, smoking materials, inkstands, paperweights. Every territory sent its specialty. The painter sent his picture, the sculptor his statuette, the dear old lady a comforter or socks, the shepherd in his hut carved a pipe for his sake. All the manufacturers of the world who were hostile to Germany shipped their products, Havana its cigars, Portugal its port wine. I have known a hairdresser who had nothing better to do than to make a portrait of the

---

[4] Lytton Strachey, *Queen Victoria*, p. 72.
[5] Jean de Pierrefeu, G. Q. G. *Trois ans au Grand Quartier Général*, pp 94–95.

General out of hair belonging to persons who were dear to him; a professional penman had the same idea, but the features were composed of thousands of little phrases in tiny characters which sang the praise of the General. As to letters, he had them in all scripts, from all countries, written in every dialect, affectionate letters, grateful, overflowing with love, filled with adoration. They called him Savior of the World, Father of his Country, Agent of God, Benefactor of Humanity, etc. . . . And not only Frenchmen, but Americans, Argentinians, Australians, etc. etc. . . . Thousands of little children, without their parents' knowledge, took pen in hand and wrote to tell him their love: most of them called him Our Father. And there was poignancy about their effusions, their adoration, these sighs of deliverance that escaped from thousands of hearts at the defeat of barbarism. To all these naif little souls, Joffre seemed like St. George crushing the dragon. Certainly he incarnated for the conscience of mankind the victory of good over evil, of light over darkness.

Lunatics, simpletons, the half-crazy and the crazy turned their darkened brains toward him as toward reason itself. I have read the letter of a person living in Sydney, who begged the General to save him from his enemies; another, a New Zealander, requested him to send some soldiers to the house of a gentleman who owed him ten pounds and would not pay.

Finally, some hundreds of young girls, overcoming the timidity of their sex, asked for engagements, their families not to know about it; others wished only to serve him."

This ideal Joffre was compounded out of the victory won by him, his staff and his troops, the despair of the war, the personal sorrows, and the hope of future victory. But beside hero-worship there is the exorcism of devils. By the same mechanism through which heroes are incarnated, devils are made. If everything good was to come from Joffre, Foch, Wilson, or Roosevelt, everything evil originated in the Kaiser Wilhelm, Lenin, and Trotsky. They were as omnipotent for evil as the heroes were omnipotent for good. To many simple and frightened minds there was no political reverse, no strike, no obstruction, no mysterious death or mysterious conflagration anywhere in the world of which the causes did not wind back to these personal sources of evil.

### 3

Worldwide concentration of this kind on a symbolic personality is rare enough to be clearly remarkable, and every author has a weakness for the striking and irrefutable example. The vivisection of war reveals such examples, but it does not make them out of nothing. In a more normal public life, symbolic pictures are no less governant of behavior, but each symbol is far less inclusive because there are so many competing ones. Not only is each symbol charged with less feeling because at most it represents only a part of the population, but even within that part there is infinitely less suppression of individual difference. The symbols of public opinion, in times of moderate security, are subject to check and comparison and argument. They come and go, coalesce and are forgotten, never organizing perfectly the emotion of the whole group. There is, after all, just one human activity left in which whole populations accomplish the union sacrée. It occurs in those middle phases of a war when fear, pugnacity, and hatred have secured complete dominion of the spirit, either to crush every other instinct or to enlist it, and before weariness is felt.

At almost all other times, and even in war when it is deadlocked, a sufficiently greater range of feelings is aroused to establish conflict, choice, hesitation, and compromise. The symbolism of public opinion usually bears, as we shall see,[6] the marks of this balancing of interest. Think, for example, of how rapidly, after the armistice, the precarious and by no means successfully established symbol of Allied Unity disappeared, how it was followed almost immediately by the breakdown of each nation's symbolic picture of the other: Britain the Defender of Public Law, France watching at the Frontier of Freedom, America the Crusader. And think then of how within each nation the symbolic picture of itself frayed out, as party and class conflict and personal ambition began to stir postponed issues. And then of how the symbolic pictures of the leaders gave way, as one by one, Wilson, Clemenceau, Lloyd George, ceased to be the incarnation of human hope, and became merely the negotiators and administrators for a disillusioned world.

Whether we regret this as one of the soft evils of peace or applaud it as a return to sanity is obviously no matter here. Our first concern with fictions and symbols is to forget their value to the existing social order, and to think of them simply as an important part of the machinery of human communication. Now in any society that is not completely self-contained in its interests and so small that everyone can know all about everything that happens, ideas deal with events that are out of sight and hard to grasp. Miss Sherwin of Gopher Prairie,[7] is aware that a war is raging in France and tries to conceive it. She has never been to France, and certainly she has never been along what is now the battlefront. Pictures of French and German soldiers she has seen, but it is impossible for her to imagine three million men. No one, in fact, can imagine them, and the professionals do not try. They think of them as, say, two hundred divisions. But Miss Sherwin has no access to the order of battle maps, and so if she is to think about the war, she fastens upon

---

[6] Part V.
[7] See Sinclair Lewis, *Main Street*.

Joffre and the Kaiser as if they were engaged in a personal duel. Perhaps if you could see what she sees with her mind's eye, the image in its composition might be not unlike an Eighteenth Century engraving of a great soldier. He stands there boldly unruffled and more than life size, with a shadowy army of tiny little figures winding off into the landscape behind. Nor it seems are great men oblivious to these expectations. M. de Pierrefeu tells of a photographer's visit to Joffre. The General was in his "middle class office, before the worktable without papers, where he sat down to write his signature. Suddenly it was noticed that there were no maps on the walls. But since according to popular ideas it is not possible to think of a general without maps, a few were placed in position for the picture, and removed soon afterwards."[8]

The only feeling that anyone can have about an event he does not experience is the feeling aroused by his mental image of that event. That is why until we know what others think they know, we cannot truly understand their acts. I have seen a young girl, brought up in a Pennsylvania mining town, plunged suddenly from entire cheerfulness into a paroxysm of grief when a gust of wind cracked the kitchen window-pane. For hours she was inconsolable, and to me incomprehensible. But when she was able to talk, it transpired that if a window-pane broke it meant that a close relative had died. She was, therefore, mourning for her father, who had frightened her into running away from home. The father was, of course, quite thoroughly alive as a telegraphic inquiry soon proved. But until the telegram came, the cracked glass was an authentic message to that girl. Why it was authentic only a prolonged investigation by a skilled psychiatrist could show. But even the most casual observer could see that the girl, enormously upset by her family troubles, had hallucinated a complete fiction out of one external fact, a remembered superstition, and a turmoil of remorse, and fear and love for her father.

Abnormality in these instances is only a matter of degree. When an Attorney-General, who has been frightened by a bomb exploded on his doorstep, convinces himself by the reading of revolutionary literature that a revolution is to happen on the first of May 1920, we recognize that much the same mechanism is at work. The war, of course, furnished many examples of this pattern: the casual fact, the creative imagination, the will to believe, and out of these three elements, a counterfeit of reality to which there was a violent instinctive response. For it is clear enough that under certain conditions men respond as powerfully to fictions as they do to realities, and that in many cases they help to create the very fictions to which they respond. Let him cast the

---

[8] *Op. cit.*, p. 99.

first stone who did not believe in the Russian army that passed through England in August, 1914, did not accept any tale of atrocities without direct proof, and never saw a plot, a traitor, or a spy where there was none. Let him cast a stone who never passed on as the real inside truth what he had heard someone say who knew no more than he did.

In all these instances we must note particularly one common factor. It is the insertion between man and his environment of a pseudo-environment. To that pseudo-environment his behavior is a response. But because it *is* behavior, the consequences, if they are acts, operate not in the pseudo-environment where the behavior is stimulated, but in the real environment where action eventuates. If the behavior is not a practical act, but what we call roughly thought and emotion, it may be a long time before there is any noticeable break in the texture of the fictitious world. But when the stimulus of the pseudo-fact results in action on things or other people, contradiction soon develops. Then comes the sensation of butting one's head against a stone wall, of learning by experience, and witnessing Herbert Spencer's tragedy of the murder of a Beautiful Theory by a Gang of Brutal Facts, the discomfort in short of a maladjustment. For certainly, at the level of social life, what is called the adjustment of man to his environment takes place through the medium of fictions.

By fictions I do not mean lies. I mean a representation of the environment which is in lesser or greater degree made by man himself. The range of fiction extends all the way from complete hallucination to the scientists' perfectly self-conscious use of a schematic model, or his decision that for his particular problem accuracy beyond a certain number of decimal places is not important. A work of fiction may have almost any degree of fidelity, and so long as the degree of fidelity can be taken into account, fiction is not misleading. In fact, human culture is very largely the selection, the rearrangement, the tracing of patterns upon, and the stylizing of, what William James called "the random irradiations and resettlements of our ideas."[9] The alternative to the use of fictions is direct exposure to the ebb and flow of sensation. That is not a real alternative, for however refreshing it is to see at times with a perfectly innocent eye, innocence itself is not wisdom, though a source and corrective of wisdom.

For the real environment is altogether too big, too complex, and too fleeting for direct acquaintance. We are not equipped to deal with so much subtlety, so much variety, so many permutations and combinations. And although we have to act in that environment, we have to reconstruct it on a simpler model before we can manage with it. To tra-

---

[9] James, *Principles of Psychology*, Vol. II, p. 638.

verse the world men must have maps of the world. Their persistent difficulty is to secure maps on which their own need, or someone else's need, has not sketched in the coast of Bohemia.

### 4

The analyst of public opinion must begin then, by recognizing the triangular relationship between the scene of action, the human picture of that scene, and the human response to that picture working itself out upon the scene of action. It is like a play suggested to the actors by their own experience, in which the plot is transacted in the real lives of the actors, and not merely in their stage parts. The moving picture often emphasizes with great skill this double drama of interior motive and external behavior. Two men are quarreling, ostensibly about some money, but their passion is inexplicable. Then the picture fades out and what one or the other of the two men sees with his mind's eye is reënacted. Across the table they were quarreling about money. In memory they are back in their youth when the girl jilted him for the other man. The exterior drama is explained: the hero is not greedy; the hero is in love.

A scene not so different was played in the United States Senate. At breakfast on the morning of September 29, 1919, some of the Senators read a news dispatch in the *Washington Post* about the landing of American marines on the Dalmatian coast. The newspaper said:

### FACTS NOW ESTABLISHED

"The following important facts appear already *established*. The orders to Rear Admiral Andrews commanding the American naval forces in the Adriatic, came from the British Admiralty via the War Council and Rear Admiral Knapps in London. The approval or disapproval of the American Navy Department was not asked. . . .

### WITHOUT DANIELS' KNOWLEDGE

"Mr. Daniels was admittedly placed in a peculiar position when cables reached here stating that the forces over which he is presumed to have exclusive control were carrying on what amounted to naval warfare without his knowledge. It was fully realized that the *British Admiralty might desire to issue orders to Rear Admiral Andrews* to act on behalf of Great Britain and her Allies, because the situation required sacrifice on the part of some nation if D'Annunzio's followers were to be held in check.

"It was further realized that *under the new league of nations plan foreigners would be in a position to direct American Naval forces in emergencies* with or without the consent of the American Navy Department. . . ." etc. (Italics mine).

The first Senator to comment is Mr. Knox of Pennsylvania. Indignantly he demands investigation. In Mr. Brandegee of Connecticut, who spoke next, indignation has already stimulated credulity. Where Mr. Knox indignantly wishes to know if the report is true, Mr. Brandegee, a half a minute later, would like to know what would have happened if marines had been killed. Mr. Knox, interested in the question, forgets that he asked for an inquiry, and replies. If American marines had been killed, it would be war. The mood of the debate is still conditional. Debate proceeds. Mr. McCormick of Illinois reminds the Senate that the Wilson administration is prone to the waging of small unauthorized wars. He repeats Theodore Roosevelt's quip about "waging peace." More debate. Mr. Brandegee notes that the marines acted "under orders of a Supreme Council sitting somewhere," but he cannot recall who represents the United States on that body. The Supreme Council is unknown to the Constitution of the United States. Therefore Mr. New of Indiana submits a resolution calling for the facts.

So far the Senators still recognize vaguely that they are discussing a rumor. Being lawyers they still remember some of the forms of evidence. But as red-blooded men they already experience all the indignation which is appropriate to the fact that American marines have been ordered into war by a foreign government and without the consent of Congress. Emotionally they want to believe it, because they are Republicans fighting the League of Nations. This arouses the Democratic leader, Mr. Hitchcock of Nebraska. He defends the Supreme Council: it was acting under the war powers. Peace has not yet been concluded because the Republicans are delaying it. Therefore the action was necessary and legal. Both sides now assume that the report is true, and the conclusions they draw are the conclusions of their partisanship. Yet this extraordinary assumption is in a debate over a resolution to investigate the truth of the assumption. It reveals how difficult it is, even for trained lawyers, to suspend response until the returns are in. The response is instantaneous. The fiction is taken for truth because the fiction is badly needed.

A few days later an official report showed that the marines were not landed by order of the British Government or of the Supreme Council. They had not been fighting the Italians. They had been landed at the request of the Italian Government to protect Italians, and the American commander had been officially thanked by the Italian authorities. The marines were not at war with Italy. They had acted according to an established international practice which had nothing to do with the League of Nations.

The scene of action was the Adriatic. The picture of that scene in the Senators' heads at Washington was furnished, in this case probably with intent to deceive, by a man who cared nothing about the Adriatic, but much about defeating the League. To this picture the Senate responded by a strengthening of its partisan differences over the League.

## 5

Whether in this particular case the Senate was above or below its normal standard, it is not necessary to decide. Nor whether the Senate compares favorably with the House, or with other parliaments. At the moment, I should like to think only about the world-wide spectacle of men acting upon their environment, moved by stimuli from their pseudo-environments. For when full allowance has been made for deliberate fraud, political science has still to account for such facts as two nations attacking one another, each convinced that it is acting in self-defense, or two classes at war each certain that it speaks for the common interest. They live, we are likely to say, in different worlds. More accurately, they live in the same world, but they think and feel in different ones.

It is to these special worlds, it is to these private or group, or class, or provincial, or occupational, or national, or sectarian artifacts, that the political adjustment of mankind in the Great Society takes place. Their variety and complication are impossible to describe. Yet these fictions determine a very great part of men's political behavior. We must think of perhaps fifty sovereign parliaments consisting of at least a hundred legislative bodies. With them belong at least fifty hierarchies of provincial and municipal assemblies, which with their executive, administrative and legislative organs, constitute formal authority on earth. But that does not begin to reveal the complexity of political life. For in each of these innumerable centers of authority there are parties, and these parties are themselves hierarchies with their roots in classes, sections, cliques and clans; and within these are the individual politicians, each the personal center of a web of connection and memory and fear and hope.

Somehow or other, for reasons often necessarily obscure, as the result of domination or compromise or a logroll, there emerge from these political bodies commands, which set armies in motion or make peace, conscript life, tax, exile, imprison, protect property or confiscate it, encourage one kind of enterprise and discourage another, facilitate immigration or obstruct it, improve communication or censor it, establish schools, build navies, proclaim "policies," and "destiny," raise economic barriers, make property or unmake it, bring one people under the rule of another, or favor one class as against another. For each of these decisions some view of the facts is taken to be conclusive, some view of the circumstances is accepted as the basis of inference and as the stimulus of feeling. What view of the facts, and why that one?

And yet even this does not begin to exhaust the real complexity. The formal political structure exists in a social environment, where there are innumerable large and small corporations and institutions, voluntary and semi-voluntary associations, national, provincial, urban and neighborhood groupings, which often as not make the decision that the political body registers. On what are these decisions based?

"Modern society," says Mr. Chesterton, "is intrinsically insecure because it is based on the notion that all men will do the same thing for different reasons. . . . And as within the head of any convict may be the hell of a quite solitary crime, so in the house or under the hat of any suburban clerk may be the limbo of a quite separate philosophy. The first man may be a complete Materialist and feel his own body as a horrible machine manufacturing his own mind. He may listen to his thoughts as to the dull ticking of a clock. The man next door may be a Christian Scientist and regard his own body as somehow rather less substantial than his own shadow. He may come almost to regard his own arms and legs as delusions like moving serpents in the dream of delirium tremens. The third man in the street may not be a Christian Scientist but, on the contrary, a Christian. He may live in a fairy tale as his neighbors would say; a secret but solid fairy tale full of the faces and presences of unearthly friends. The fourth man may be a theosophist, and only too probably a vegetarian; and I do not see why I should not gratify myself with the fancy that the fifth man is a devil worshiper. . . . Now whether or not this sort of variety is valuable, this sort of unity is shaky. To expect that all men for all time will go on thinking different things, and yet doing the same things, is a doubtful speculation. It is not founding society on a communion, or even on a convention, but rather on a coincidence. Four men may meet under the same lamp post; one to paint it pea green as part of a great municipal reform; one to read his breviary in the light of it; one to embrace it with accidental ardour in a fit of alcoholic enthusiasm; and the last merely because the pea green post is a conspicuous point of rendezvous with his young lady. But to expect this to happen night after night is unwise. . . . "[10]

For the four men at the lamp post substitute the governments, the parties, the corporations, the societies, the social sets, the trades and professions, universities, sects, and nationalities of the world. Think of the legislator voting a statute that will affect distant peoples, a statesman coming to a decision. Think of the Peace Conference reconstituting the frontiers of Europe, an ambassador in a foreign country trying to discern the intentions of his own government and of the foreign government, a promoter working a concession in a backward country, an editor

---

[10] G. K. Chesterton, "The Mad Hatter and the Sane Householder," *Vanity Fair*, January, 1921, p. 54.

demanding a war, a clergyman calling on the police to regulate amuse-
ment, a club lounging-room making up its mind about a strike, a sewing
circle preparing to regulate the schools, nine judges deciding whether a
legislature in Oregon may fix the working hours of women, a cabinet
meeting to decide on the recognition of a government, a party convention choosing a candidate and writing a platform, twenty-seven million
voters casting their ballots, an Irishman in Cork thinking about an
Irishman in Belfast, a Third International planning to reconstruct the
whole of human society, a board of directors confronted with a set of
their employees' demands, a boy choosing a career, a merchant estimat-
ing supply and demand for the coming season, a speculator predicting
the course of the market, a banker deciding whether to put credit behind
a new enterprise, the advertiser, the reader of advertisments. . . . Think
of the different sorts of Americans thinking about their notions of "The
British Empire" or "France" or "Russia" or "Mexico." It is not so different from Mr. Chesterton's four men at the pea green lamp post.

## 6

And so before we involve ourselves in the jungle of obscurities about
the innate differences of men, we shall do well to fix our attention
upon the extraordinary differences in what men know of the world.[11]
I do not doubt that there are important biological differences. Since
man is an animal it would be strange if there were not. But as rational
beings it is worse than shallow to generalize at all about comparative
behavior until there is a measurable similarity between the environments to which behavior is a response.

The pragmatic value of this idea is that it introduces a much needed
refinement into the ancient controversy about nature and nurture,
innate quality and environment. For the pseudo-environment is a
hybrid compounded of "human nature" and "conditions." To my mind
it shows the uselessness of pontificating about what man is and always
will be from what we observe man to be doing, or about what are the
necessary conditions of society. For we do not know how men would
behave in response to the facts of the Great Society. All that we really
know is how they behave in response to what can fairly be called a most
inadequate picture of the Great Society. No conclusion about man or
the Great Society can honestly be made on evidence like that.

This, then, will be the clue to our inquiry. We shall assume that
what each man does is based not on direct and certain knowledge,

[11] Cf. Wallas, *Our Social Heritage*, pp. 77 *et seq.*

but on pictures made by himself or given to him! If his atlas tells him that the world is flat he will not sail near what he believes to be the edge of our planet for fear of falling off. If his maps include a fountain of eternal youth, a Ponce de Leon will go in quest of it. If someone digs up yellow dirt that looks like gold, he will for a time act exactly as if he had found gold. The way in which the world is imagined determines at any particular moment what men will do. It does not determine what they will achieve. It determines their effort, their feelings, their hopes, not their accomplishments and results. The very men who most loudly proclaim their "materialism" and their contempt for "ideologues," the Marxian communists, place their entire hope on what? On the formation by propaganda of a class-conscious group. But what is propaganda, if not the effort to alter the picture to which men respond, to substitute one social pattern for another? What is class consciousness but a way of realizing the world? National consciousness but another way? And Professor Giddings' consciousness of kind, but a process of believing that we recognize among the multitude certain ones marked as our kind?

Try to explain social life as the pursuit of pleasure and the avoidance of pain. You will soon be saying that the hedonist begs the question, for even supposing that man does pursue these ends, the crucial problem of why he thinks one course rather than another likely to produce pleasure, is untouched. Does the guidance of man's conscience explain? How then does he happen to have the particular conscience which he has? The theory of economic self-interest? But how do men come to conceive their interest in one way rather than another? The desire for security, or prestige, or domination, or what is vaguely called self-realization? How do men conceive their security, what do they consider prestige, how do they figure out the means of domination, or what is the notion of self which they wish to realize? Pleasure, pain, conscience, acquisition, protection, enhancement, mastery, are undoubtedly names for some of the ways people act. There may be instinctive dispositions which work toward such ends. But no statement of the end, or any description of the tendencies to seek it, can explain the behavior which results. The very fact that men theorize at all is proof that their pseudo-environments, their interior representations of the world, are a determining element in thought, feeling, and action. For if the connection between reality and human response were direct and immediate, rather than indirect and inferred, indecision and failure would be unknown, and (if each of us fitted as snugly into the world as the child in the womb), Mr. Bernard Shaw would not have been able to say that except for the first nine months of its existence no human being manages its affairs as well as a plant.

The chief difficulty in adapting the psychoanalytic scheme to political thought arises in this connection. The Freudians are concerned with the maladjustment of distinct individuals to other individuals and to concrete circumstances. They have assumed that if internal derangements could be straightened out, there would be little or no confusion about what is the obviously normal relationship. But public opinion deals with indirect, unseen, and puzzling facts, and there is nothing obvious about them. The situations to which public opinions refer are known only as opinions. The psychoanalyst, on the other hand, almost always assumes that the environment is knowable, and if not knowable then at least bearable, to any unclouded intelligence. This assumption of his is the problem of public opinion. Instead of taking for granted an environment that is readily known, the social analyst is most concerned in studying how the larger political environment is conceived, and how it can be conceived more successfully. The psychoanalyst examines the adjustment to an X, called by him the environment; the social analyst examines the X, called by him the pseudo-environment.

He is, of course, permanently and constantly in debt to the new psychology, not only because when rightly applied it so greatly helps people to stand on their own feet, come what may, but because the study of dreams, fantasy and rationalization has thrown light on how the pseudo-environment is put together. But he cannot assume as his criterion either what is called a "normal biological career"[12] within the existing social order, or a career "freed from religious suppression and dogmatic conventions" outside.[13] What for a sociologist is a normal social career? Or one freed from suppressions and conventions? Conservative critics do, to be sure, assume the first, and romantic ones the second. But in assuming them they are taking the whole world for granted. They are saying in effect either that society is the sort of thing which corresponds to their idea of what is normal, or the sort of thing which corresponds to their idea of what is free. Both ideas are merely public opinions, and while the psychoanalyst as physician may perhaps assume them, the sociologist may not take the products of existing public opinion as criteria by which to study public opinion.

## 7

The world that we have to deal with politically is out of reach, out of sight, out of mind. It has to be explored, reported, and imagined. Man is no Aristotelian god contemplating all existence at one glance. He is

---

[12] Edward J. Kempf, *Psychopathology*, p. 116.
[13] *Id.*, p. 151.

the creature of an evolution who can just about span a sufficient portion of reality to manage his survival, and snatch what on the scale of
time are but a few moments of insight and happiness. Yet this same
creature has invented ways of seeing what no naked eye could see, of
hearing what no ear could hear, of weighing immense masses and
infinitesimal ones, of counting and separating more items than he can
individually remember. He is learning to see with his mind vast portions of the world that he could never see, touch, smell, hear, or
remember. Gradually he makes for himself a trustworthy picture inside
his head of the world beyond his reach.

Those features of the world outside which have to do with the behavior of other human beings, in so far as that behavior crosses ours, is
dependent upon us, or is interesting to us, we call roughly public affairs.
The pictures inside the heads of these human beings, the pictures of
themselves, of others, of their needs, purposes, and relationship, are
their public opinions. Those pictures which are acted upon by groups
of people, or by individuals acting in the name of groups, are Public
Opinion with capital letters. And so in the chapters which follow we
shall inquire first into some of the reasons why the picture inside so
often misleads men in their dealings with the world outside. Under this
heading we shall consider first the chief factors which limit their access
to the facts. They are the artificial censorships, the limitations of social
contact, the comparatively meager time available in each day for paying
attention to public affairs, the distortion arising because events have to
be compressed into very short messages, the difficulty of making a small
vocabulary express a complicated world, and finally the fear of facing
those facts which would seem to threaten the established routine of
men's lives.

The analysis then turns from these more or less external limitations
to the question of how this trickle of messages from the outside is
affected by the stored up images, the preconceptions, and prejudices
which interpret, fill them out, and in their turn powerfully direct the
play of our attention, and our vision itself. From this it proceeds to
examine how in the individual person the limited messages from outside, formed into a pattern of stereotypes, are identified with his own
interests as he feels and conceives them. In the succeeding sections it
examines how opinions are crystallized into what is called Public
Opinion, how a National Will, a Group Mind, a Social Purpose, or
whatever you choose to call it, is formed.

The first five parts constitute the descriptive section of the book.
There follows an analysis of the traditional democratic theory of public
opinion. The substance of the argument is that democracy in its original form never seriously faced the problem which arises because the

pictures inside people's heads do not automatically correspond with the world outside. And then, because the democratic theory is under criticism by socialist thinkers, there follows an examination of the most advanced and coherent of these criticisms, as made by the English Guild Socialists. My purpose here is to find out whether these reformers take into account the main difficulties of public opinion. My conclusion is that they ignore the difficulties, as completely as did the original democrats, because they, too, assume, and in a much more complicated civilization, that somehow mysteriously there exists in the hearts of men a knowledge of the world beyond their reach.

I argue that representative government, either in what is ordinarily called politics, or in industry, cannot be worked successfully, no matter what the basis of election, unless there is an independent, expert organization for making the unseen facts intelligible to those who have to make the decisions. I attempt, therefore, to argue that the serious acceptance of the principle that personal representation must be supplemented by representation of the unseen facts would alone permit a satisfactory decentralization, and allow us to escape from the intolerable and unworkable fiction that each of us must acquire a competent opinion about all public affairs. It is argued that the problem of the press is confused because the critics and the apologists expect the press to realize this fiction, expect it to make up for all that was not foreseen in the theory of democracy, and that the readers expect this miracle to be performed at no cost or trouble to themselves. The newspapers are regarded by democrats as a panacea for their own defects, whereas analysis of the nature of news and of the economic basis of journalism seems to show that the newspapers necessarily and inevitably reflect, and therefore, in greater or lesser measure, intensify, the defective organization of public opinion. My conclusion is that public opinions must be organized for the press if they are to be sound, not by the press as is the case today. This organization I conceive to be in the first instance the task of a political science that has won its proper place as formulator, in advance of real decision, instead of apologist, critic, or reporter after the decision has been made. I try to indicate that the perplexities of government and industry are conspiring to give political science this enormous opportunity to enrich itself and to serve the public. And, of course, I hope that these pages will help a few people to realize that opportunity more vividly, and therefore to pursue it more consciously.

# PART II.   APPROACHES TO THE WORLD OUTSIDE


# II.  Censorship and Privacy

## 1

THE picture of a general presiding over an editorial conference at the most terrible hour of one of the great battles of history seems more like a scene from The Chocolate Soldier than a page from life. Yet we know at first hand from the officer who edited the French communiqués that these conferences were a regular part of the business of war; that in the worst moment of Verdun, General Joffre and his cabinet met and argued over the nouns, adjectives, and verbs that were to be printed in the newspapers the next morning.

"The evening communiqué of the twenty-third (February 1916)" says M. de Pierrefeu,[1] "was edited in a dramatic atmosphere. M. Berthelot, of the Prime Minister's office, had just telephoned by order of the minister asking General Pellé to strengthen the report and to emphasize the proportions of the enemy's attack. It was necessary to prepare the public for the worst outcome in case the affair turned into a catastrophe. This anxiety showed clearly that neither at G. H. Q. nor at the Ministry of War had the Government found reason for confidence. As M. Berthelot spoke, General Pellé made notes. He handed me the paper on which he had written the Government's wishes, together with the order of the day issued by General von Deimling and found on some prisoners, in which it was stated that this attack was the supreme offensive to secure peace. Skilfully used, all this was to demonstrate that Germany was letting loose a gigantic effort, an effort without precedent, and that from its success she hoped for the end of the war. The logic of this was that nobody need be surprised at our withdrawal. When, a half hour later, I went down with my manuscript, I found gathered together in Colonel Claudel's office, he being away, the major-general, General Janin, Colonel Dupont, and Lieutenant-

---

[1] G. Q. G., pp. 126–129.

Colonel Renouard. Fearing that I would not succeed in giving the desired impression, General Pellé had himself prepared a proposed communiqué. I read what I had just done. It was found to be too moderate. General Pellé's, on the other hand, seemed too alarming. I had purposely omitted von Deimling's order of the day. To put it into the communiqué *would be to break with the formula to which the public was accustomed*, would be to transform it into a kind of pleading. It would seem to say: 'How do you suppose we can resist?' There was reason to fear that the public would be distracted by this change of tone and would believe that everything was lost. I explained my reasons and suggested giving Deimling's text to the newspapers in the form of a separate note.

"Opinion being divided, General Pellé went to ask General de Castelnau to come and decide finally. The General arrived smiling, quiet and good humored, said a few pleasant words about this new kind of literary council of war, and looked at the texts. He chose the simpler one, gave more weight to the first phrase, inserted the words 'as had been anticipated,' which supply a reassuring quality, and was flatly against inserting von Deimling's order, but was for transmitting it to the press in a special note . . ." General Joffre that evening read the communiqué carefully and approved it.

Within a few hours those two or three hundred words would be read all over the world. They would paint a picture in men's minds of what was happening on the slopes of Verdun, and in front of that picture people would take heart or despair. The shopkeeper in Brest, the peasant in Lorraine, the deputy in the Palais Bourbon, the editor in Amsterdam or Minneapolis had to be kept in hope, and yet prepared to accept possible defeat without yielding to panic. They are told, therefore, that the loss of ground is no surprise to the French Command. They are taught to regard the affair as serious, but not strange. Now, as a matter of fact, the French General Staff was not fully prepared for the German offensive. Supporting trenches had not been dug, alternative roads had not been built, barbed wire was lacking. But to confess that would have aroused images in the heads of civilians that might well have turned a reverse into a disaster. The High Command could be disappointed, and yet pull itself together; the people at home and abroad, full of uncertainties, and with none of the professional man's singleness of purpose, might on the basis of a complete story have lost sight of the war in a mêlée of faction and counter-faction about the competence of the officers. Instead, therefore, of letting the public act on all the facts which the generals knew, the authorities presented only certain facts, and these only in such a way as would be most likely to steady the people.

In this case the men who arranged the pseudo-environment knew what the real one was. But a few days later an incident occurred about which the French Staff did not know the truth. The Germans announced[2] that on the previous afternoon they had taken Fort Douaumont by assault. At French headquarters in Chantilly no one could understand this news. For on the morning of the twenty-fifth, after the engagement of the XXth corps, the battle had taken a turn for the better. Reports from the front said nothing about Douaumont. But inquiry showed that the German report was true, though no one as yet knew how the fort had been taken. In the meantime, the German communiqué was being flashed around the world, and the French had to say something. So headquarters explained. "In the midst of total ignorance at Chantilly about the way the attack had taken place, we imagined, in the evening communiqué of the 26th, a plan of the attack which certainly had a thousand to one chance of being true." The communiqué of this imaginary battle read:

> "A bitter struggle is taking place around Fort de Douaumont which is an advanced post of the old defensive organization of Verdun. The position taken this morning by the enemy, *after several unsuccessful assaults that cost him very heavy losses,* has been reached again and passed by our troops whom the enemy has not been able to drive back."[3]

What had actually happened differed from both the French and German accounts. While changing troops in the line, the position had somehow been forgotten in a confusion of orders. Only a battery commander and a few men remained in the fort. Some German soldiers, seeing the door open, had crawled into the fort, and taken everyone inside prisoner. A little later the French who were on the slopes of the hill were horrified at being shot at from the fort. There had been no battle at Douaumont and no losses. Nor had the French troops advanced beyond it as the communiqués seemed to say. They were beyond it on either side, to be sure, but the fort was in enemy hands.

Yet from the communiqué everyone believed that the fort was half surrounded. The words did not explicitly say so, but "the press, as usual,

---

[2] On February 26, 1916. Pierrefeu, G. Q. G., pp. 133 *et seq.*

[3] This is my own translation: the English translation from London published in the New York Times of Sunday, Feb. 27, is as follows:

London, Feb. 26 (1916). A furious struggle has been in progress around Fort de Douaumont which is an advance element of the old defensive organization of Verdun fortresses. The position captured this morning by the enemy after several fruitless assaults which cost him extremely heavy losses,* was reached again and gone beyond by our troops, which all the attempts of the enemy have not been able to push back."

(*) The French text says "pertes très élevées." Thus the English translation exaggerates the original text.

forced the pace." Military writers concluded that the Germans would
soon have to surrender. In a few days they began to ask themselves why
the garrison, since it lacked food, had not yet surrendered. "It was necessary through the press bureau to request them to drop the encir-
clement theme."[4]

## 2

The editor of the French communiqué tells us that as the battle
dragged out, his colleagues and he set out to neutralize the pertinacity
of the Germans by continual insistence on their terrible losses. It is
necessary to remember that at this time, and in fact until late in 1917,
the orthodox view of the war for all the Allied peoples was that it would
be decided by "attrition." Nobody believed in a war of movement. It
was insisted that strategy did not count, or diplomacy. It was simply a
matter of killing Germans. The general public more or less believed
the dogma, but it had constantly to be reminded of it in face of spec-
tacular German successes.

"Almost no day passed but the communiqué. . . . ascribed to the
Germans with some appearance of justice heavy losses, extremely
heavy, spoke of bloody sacrifices, heaps of corpses, hecatombs.
Likewise the wireless constantly used the statistics of the intelligence
bureau at Verdun, whose chief, Major Cointet, had invented a method
of calculating German losses which obviously produced marvelous
results. Every fortnight the figures increased a hundred thousand or so.
These 300,000, 400,000, 500,000 casualties put out, divided into daily,
weekly, monthly losses, repeated in all sorts of ways, produced a striking effect. Our formulae varied little: 'according to prisoners the
German losses in the course of the attack have been considerable' . . .
'it is proved that the losses' . . . 'the enemy exhausted by his losses has
not renewed the attack' . . . Certain formulae, later abandoned because
they had been overworked, were used each day: 'under our artillery and
machine gun fire' . . . 'mowed down by our artillery and machine gun
fire' . . . Constant repetition impressed the neutrals and Germany itself,
and helped to create a bloody background in spite of the denials from
Nauen (the German wireless) which tried vainly to destroy the bad
effect of this perpetual repetition."[5]

The thesis of the French Command, which it wished to establish
publicly by these reports, was formulated as follows for the guidance of
the censors:

---

[4] Pierrefeu, *op. cit.*, pp. 134–5.
[5] *Op. cit.*, pp. 138–139.

"This offensive engages the active forces of our opponent whose manpower is declining. We have learned that the class of 1916 is already at the front. There will remain the 1917 class already being called up, and the resources of the third category (men above forty-five, or convalescents). In a few weeks, the German forces exhausted by this effort, will find themselves confronted with all the forces of the coalition (ten millions against seven millions)."[6]

According to M. de Pierrefeu, the French command had converted itself to this belief. "By an extraordinary aberration of mind, only the attrition of the enemy was seen; it appeared that our forces were not subject to attrition. General Nivelle shared these ideas. We saw the result in 1917."

We have learned to call this propaganda. A group of men, who can prevent independent access to the event, arrange the news of it to suit their purpose. That the purpose was in this case patriotic does not affect the argument at all. They used their power to make the Allied publics see affairs as they desired them to be seen. The casualty figures of Major Cointet which were spread about the world are of the same order. They were intended to provoke a particular kind of inference, namely that the war of attrition was going in favor of the French. But the inference is not drawn in the form of argument. It results almost automatically from the creation of a mental picture of endless Germans slaughtered on the hills about Verdun. By putting the dead Germans in the focus of the picture, and by omitting to mention the French dead, a very special view of the battle was built up. It was a view designed to neutralize the effects of German territorial advances and the impression of power which the persistence of the offensive was making. It was also a view that tended to make the public acquiesce in the demoralizing defensive strategy imposed upon the Allied armies. For the public, accustomed to the idea that war consists of great strategic movements, flank attacks, encirclements, and dramatic surrenders, had gradually to forget that picture in favor of the terrible idea that by matching lives the war would be won. Through its control over all news from the front, the General Staff substituted a view of the facts that comported with this strategy.

The General Staff of an army in the field is so placed that within wide limits it can control what the public will perceive. It controls the selection of correspondents who go to the front, controls their movements at the front, reads and censors their messages from the front, and operates the wires. The Government behind the army by its command of cables and passports, mails and custom houses and blockades

---

[6] *Op. cit.*, p. 147.

increases the control. It emphasizes it by legal power over publishers, over public meetings, and by its secret service. But in the case of an army the control is far from perfect. There is always the enemy's communiqué, which in these days of wireless cannot be kept away from neutrals. Above all there is the talk of the soldiers, which blows back from the front, and is spread about when they are on leave.[7] An army is an unwieldy thing. And that is why the naval and diplomatic censorship is almost always much more complete. Fewer people know what is going on, and their acts are more easily supervised.

### 3

Without some form of censorship, propaganda in the strict sense of the word is impossible. In order to conduct a propaganda there must be some barrier between the public and the event. Access to the real environment must be limited, before anyone can create a pseudo-environment that he thinks wise or desirable. For while people who have direct access can misconceive what they see, no one else can decide how they shall misconceive it, unless he can decide where they shall look, and at what. The military censorship is the simplest form of barrier, but by no means the most important, because it is known to exist, and is therefore in certain measure agreed to and discounted.

At different times and for different subjects some men impose and other men accept a particular standard of secrecy. The frontier between what is concealed because publication is not, as we say, "compatible with the public interest" fades gradually into what is concealed because it is believed to be none of the public's business. The notion of what constitutes a person's private affairs is elastic. Thus the amount of a man's fortune is considered a private affair, and careful provision is made in the income tax law to keep it as private as possible. The sale of a piece of land is not private, but the price may be. Salaries are generally treated as more private than wages, incomes as more private than inheritances. A person's credit rating is given only a limited circulation. The profits of big corporations are more public than those of small firms. Certain kinds of conversation, between man and wife, lawyer and client, doctor and patient, priest and communicant, are privileged. Directors' meetings are generally private. So are many political conferences. Most of what is said at a cabinet meeting, or by an ambassador to the Secretary of State, or at private interviews, or dinner tables, is private. Many people regard

---

[7] For weeks prior to the American attack at St. Mihiel and in the Argonne-Meuse, everybody in France told everybody else the deep secret.

the contract between employer and employee as private. There was a time when the affairs of all corporations were held to be as private as a man's theology is to-day. There was a time before that when his theology was held to be as public a matter as the color of his eyes. But infectious diseases, on the other hand, were once as private as the processes of a man's digestion. The history of the notion of privacy would be an entertaining tale. Sometimes the notions violently conflict, as they did when the bolsheviks published the secret treaties, or when Mr. Hughes investigated the life insurance companies, or when somebody's scandal exudes from the pages of Town Topics to the front pages of Mr. Hearst's newspapers.

Whether the reasons for privacy are good or bad, the barriers exist. Privacy is insisted upon at all kinds of places in the area of what is called public affairs. It is often very illuminating, therefore, to ask yourself how you got at the facts on which you base your opinion. Who actually saw, heard, felt, counted, named the thing, about which you have an opinion? Was it the man who told you, or the man who told him, or someone still further removed? And how much was he permitted to see? When he informs you that France thinks this and that, what part of France did he watch? How was he able to watch it? Where was he when he watched it? What Frenchmen was he permitted to talk to, what newspapers did he read, and where did they learn what they say? You can ask yourself these questions, but you can rarely answer them. They will remind you, however, of the distance which often separates your public opinion from the event with which it deals. And the reminder is itself a protection.

# III. Contact and Opportunity

## 1

WHILE censorship and privacy intercept much information at its source, a very much larger body of fact never reaches the whole public at all, or only very slowly. For there are very distinct limits upon the circulation of ideas.

A rough estimate of the effort it takes to reach "everybody" can be had by considering the Government's propaganda during the war. Remembering that the war had run over two years and a half before America entered it, that millions upon millions of printed pages had been circulated and untold speeches had been delivered, let us turn to Mr. Creel's account of his fight "for the minds of men, for the conquest of their convictions" in order that "the gospel of Americanism might be carried to every corner of the globe."[1]

Mr. Creel had to assemble machinery which included a Division of News that issued, he tells us, more than six thousand releases, had to enlist seventy-five thousand Four Minute Men who delivered at least seven hundred and fifty-five thousand, one hundred and ninety speeches to an aggregate of over three hundred million people. Boy scouts delivered annotated copies of President Wilson's addresses to the householders of America. Fortnightly periodicals were sent to six hundred thousand teachers. Two hundred thousand lantern slides were furnished for illustrated lectures. Fourteen hundred and thirty-eight different designs were turned out for posters, window cards, newspaper advertisements, cartoons, seals and buttons. The chambers of commerce, the churches, fraternal societies, schools, were used as channels of distribution. Yet Mr. Creel's effort, to which I have not begun to do justice, did not include Mr. McAdoo's stupendous organization for the Liberty Loans, nor Mr. Hoover's far reaching propaganda about food, nor the campaigns of the Red Cross, the Y. M. C. A., Salvation Army, Knights of Columbus, Jewish Welfare Board, not to mention the independent work of patriotic societies, like the League to Enforce Peace, the League of Free Nations Association, the National Security League, nor the activity of the publicity bureaus of the Allies and of the submerged nationalities.

Probably this is the largest and the most intensive effort to carry quickly a fairly uniform set of ideas to all the people of a nation. The older proselyting worked more slowly, perhaps more surely, but never so inclusively. Now if it required such extreme measures to reach everybody in time of crisis, how open are the more normal channels to men's minds? The Administration was trying, and while the war continued it very largely succeeded, I believe, in creating something that might almost be called one public opinion all over America. But think of the dogged work, the complicated ingenuity, the money and the personnel that were required. Nothing like that exists in time of peace, and as a corollary there are whole sections, there are vast groups, ghettoes, enclaves and classes that hear only vaguely about much that is going on.

They live in grooves, are shut in among their own affairs, barred out of larger affairs, meet few people not of their own sort, read little. Travel and trade, the mails, the wires, and radio, railroads, highways, ships,

---

[1] George Creel, *How We Advertised America.*

motor cars, and in the coming generation aeroplanes, are, of course, of the utmost influence on the circulation of ideas. Each of these affects the supply and the quality of information and opinion in a most intricate way. Each is itself affected by technical, by economic, by political conditions. Every time a government relaxes the passport ceremonies or the customs inspection, every time a new railway or a new port is opened, a new shipping line established, every time rates go up or down, the mails move faster or more slowly, the cables are uncensored and made less expensive, highways built, or widened, or improved, the circulation of ideas is influenced. Tariff schedules and subsidies affect the direction of commercial enterprise, and therefore the nature of human contracts. And so it may well happen, as it did for example in the case of Salem, Massachusetts, that a change in the art of ship-building will reduce a whole city from a center where international influences converge to a genteel provincial town. All the immediate effects of more rapid transit are not necessarily good. It would be difficult to say, for example, that the railroad system of France, so highly centralized upon Paris, has been an unmixed blessing to the French people.

It is certainly true that problems arising out of the means of communication are of the utmost importance, and one of the most constructive features of the program of the League of Nations has been the study given to railroad transit and access to the sea. The monopolizing of cables,[2] of ports, fuel stations, mountain passes, canals, straits, river courses, terminals, market places means a good deal more than the enrichment of a group of business men, or the prestige of a government. It means a barrier upon the exchange of news and opinion. But monopoly is not the only barrier. Cost and available supply are even greater ones, for if the cost of travelling or trading is prohibitive, if the demand for facilities exceeds the supply, the barriers exist even without monopoly.

2

The size of a man's income has considerable effect on his access to the world beyond his neighborhood. With money he can overcome almost every tangible obstacle of communication, he can travel, buy books and periodicals, and bring within the range of his attention almost any known fact of the world. The income of the individual, and the income of the community determine the amount of communica-

---

[2] Hence the wisdom of taking Yap seriously.

tion that is possible. But men's ideas determine how that income shall be spent, and that in turn affects in the long run the amount of income they will have. Thus also there are limitations, none the less real, because they are often self-imposed and self-indulgent.

There are portions of the sovereign people who spend most of their spare time and spare money on motoring and comparing motor cars, on bridge-whist and post-mortems, on moving-pictures and potboilers, talking always to the same people with minute variations on the same old themes. They cannot really be said to suffer from censorship, or secrecy, the high cost or the difficulty of communication. They suffer from anemia, from lack of appetite and curiosity for the human scene. Theirs is no problem of access to the world outside. Worlds of interest are waiting for them to explore, and they do not enter.

They move, as if on a leash, within a fixed radius of acquaintances according to the law and the gospel of their social set. Among men the circle of talk in business and at the club and in the smoking car is wider than the set to which they belong. Among women the social set and the circle of talk are frequently almost identical. It is in the social set that ideas derived from reading and lectures and from the circle of talk converge, are sorted out, accepted, rejected, judged and sanctioned. There it is finally decided in each phase of a discussion which authorities and which sources of information are admissible, and which not.

Our social set consists of those who figure as people in the phrase "people are saying"; they are the people whose approval matters most intimately to us. In big cities among men and women of wide interests and with the means for moving about, the social set is not so rigidly defined. But even in big cities, there are quarters and nests of villages containing self-sufficing social sets. In smaller communities there may exist a freer circulation, a more genuine fellowship from after breakfast to before dinner. But few people do not know, nevertheless, which set they really belong to, and which not.

Usually the distinguishing mark of a social set is the presumption that the children may intermarry. To marry outside the set involves, at the very least, a moment of doubt before the engagement can be approved. Each social set has a fairly clear picture of its relative position in the hierarchy of social sets. Between sets at the same level, association is easy, individuals are quickly accepted, hospitality is normal and unembarrassed. But in contact between sets that are "higher" or "lower," there is always reciprocal hesitation, a faint malaise, and a consciousness of difference. To be sure in a society like that of the United States, individuals move somewhat freely out of one set into another, especially where there is no racial barrier and where economic position changes so rapidly.

Economic position, however, is not measured by the amount of income. For in the first generation, at least, it is not income that determines social standing, but the character of a man's work, and it may take a generation or two before this fades out of the family tradition. Thus banking, law, medicine, public utilities, newspapers, the church, large retailing, brokerage, manufacture, are rated at a different social value from salesmanship, superintendence, expert technical work, nursing, school teaching, shop keeping; and those, in turn, are rated as differently from plumbing, being a chauffeur, dressmaking, subcontracting, or stenography, as these are from being a butler, lady's maid, a moving picture operator, or a locomotive engineer. And yet the financial return does not necessarily coincide with these gradations.

## 3

Whatever the tests of admission, the social set when formed is not a mere economic class, but something which more nearly resembles a biological clan. Membership is intimately connected with love, marriage and children, or, to speak more exactly, with the attitudes and desires that are involved. In the social set, therefore, opinions encounter the canons of Family Tradition, Respectability, Propriety, Dignity, Taste and Form, which make up the social set's picture of itself, a picture assiduously implanted in the children. In this picture a large space is tacitly given to an authorized version of what each set is called upon inwardly to accept as the social standing of the others. The more vulgar press for an outward expression of the deference due, the others are decently and sensitively silent about their own knowledge that such deference invisibly exists. But that knowledge, becoming overt when there is a marriage, a war, or a social upheaval, is the nexus of a large bundle of dispositions classified by Trotter[3] under the general term instinct of the herd.

Within each social set there are augurs like the van der Luydens and Mrs. Manson Mingott in *The Age of Innocence*, who are recognized as the custodians and the interpreters of its social pattern. You are made, they say, if the van der Luydens take you up. The invitations to their functions are the high sign of arrival and status. The elections to college societies, carefully graded and the gradations universally accepted, determine who is who in college. The social leaders, weighted with the ultimate eugenic responsibility, are peculiarly sensitive. Not only must they be watchfully aware of what makes for the integrity of their set, but

---

[3] W. Trotter, *Instincts of the Herd in War and Peace.*

they have to cultivate a special gift for knowing what other social sets are doing. They act as a kind of ministry of foreign affairs. Where most of the members of a set live complacently within the set, regarding it for all practical purposes as the world, the social leaders must combine an intimate knowledge of the anatomy of their own set with a persistent sense of its place in the hierarchy of sets.

The hierarchy, in fact, is bound together by the social leaders. At any one level there is something which might almost be called a social set of the social leaders. But vertically the actual binding together of society, in so far as it is bound together at all by social contact, is accomplished by those exceptional people, frequently suspect, who like Julius Beaufort and Ellen Olenska in *The Age of Innocence* move in and out. Thus there come to be established personal channels from one set to another, through which Tarde's laws of imitation operate. But for large sections of the population there are no such channels. For them the patented accounts of society and the moving pictures of high life have to serve. They may develop a social hierarchy of their own, almost unnoticed, as have the Negroes and the "foreign element," but among that assimilated mass which always considers itself the "nation," there is in spite of the great separateness of sets, a variety of personal contacts through which a circulation of standards takes place.

Some of the sets are so placed that they become what Professor Ross has called "radiant points of conventionality."[4] Thus the social superior is likely to be imitated by the social inferior, the holder of power is imitated by subordinates, the more successful by the less successful, the rich by the poor, the city by the country. But imitation does not stop at frontiers. The powerful, socially superior, successful, rich, urban social set is fundamentally international throughout the western hemisphere, and in many ways London is its center. It counts among its membership the most influential people in the world, containing as it does the diplomatic set, high finance, the upper circles of the army and the navy, some princes of the church, a few great newspaper proprietors, their wives and mothers and daughters who wield the scepter of invitation. It is at once a great circle of talk and a real social set. But its importance comes from the fact that here at last the distinction between public and private affairs practically disappears. The private affairs of this set are public matters, and public matters are its private, often its family affairs. The confinements of Margot Asquith like the confinements of royalty are, as the philosophers say, in much the same universe of discourse as a tariff bill or a parliamentary debate.

---

[4] Ross, *Social Psychology*, Ch. IX, X, XI.

There are large areas of governments in which this social set is not interested, and in America, at least, it has exercised only a fluctuating control over the national government. But its power in foreign affairs is always very great, and in war time its prestige is enormously enhanced. That is natural enough because these cosmopolitans have a contact with the outer world that most people do not possess. They have dined with each other in the capitals, and their sense of national honor is no mere abstraction; it is a concrete experience of being snubbed or approved by their friends. To Dr. Kennicott of Gopher Prairie it matters mighty little what Winston thinks and a great deal what Ezra Stowbody thinks, but to Mrs. Mingott with a daughter married to the Earl of Swithin it matters a lot when she visits her daughter, or entertains Winston himself. Dr. Kennicott and Mrs. Mingott are both socially sensitive, but Mrs. Mingott is sensitive to a social set that governs the world, while Dr. Kennicott's social set governs only in Gopher Prairie. But in matters that effect the larger relationships of the Great Society, Dr. Kennicott will often be found holding what he thinks is purely his own opinion, though, as a matter of fact, it has trickled down to Gopher Prairie from High Society, transmuted on its passage through the provincial social sets.

4

It is no part of our inquiry to attempt an account of the social tissue. We need only fix in mind how big is the part played by the social set in our spiritual contact with the world, how it tends to fix what is admissible, and to determine how it shall be judged. Affairs within its immediate competence each set more or less determines for itself. Above all it determines the detailed administration of the judgment. But the judgment itself is formed on patterns[5] that may be inherited from the past, transmitted or imitated from other social sets. The highest social set consists of those who embody the leadership of the Great Society. As against almost every other social set where the bulk of the opinions are first hand only about local affairs, in this Highest Society the big decisions of war and peace, of social strategy and the ultimate distribution of political power, are intimate experiences within a circle of what, potentially at least, are personal acquaintances.

Since position and contact play so big a part in determining what can be seen, heard, read, and experienced, as well as what it is permissible to see, hear, read, and know, it is no wonder that moral judgment

---

[5] *Cf.* Part III.

is so much more common than constructive thought. Yet in truly effective thinking the prime necessity is to liquidate judgments, regain an innocent eye, disentangle feelings, be curious and open-hearted. Man's history being what it is, political opinion on the scale of the Great Society requires an amount of selfless equanimity rarely attainable by any one for any length of time. We are concerned in public affairs, but immersed in our private ones. The time and attention are limited that we can spare for the labor of not taking opinions for granted, and we are subject to constant interruption.

# IV. Time and Attention

NATURALLY it is possible to make a rough estimate only of the amount of attention people give each day to informing themselves about public affairs. Yet it is interesting that three estimates that I have examined agree tolerably well, though they were made at different times, in different places, and by different methods.[1]

A questionnaire was sent by Hotchkiss and Franken to 1761 men and women college students in New York City, and answers came from all but a few. Scott used a questionnaire on four thousand prominent business and professional men in Chicago and received replies from twenty-three hundred. Between seventy and seventy-five percent of all those who replied to either inquiry thought they spent a quarter of an hour a day reading newspapers. Only four percent of the Chicago group guessed at less than this and twenty-five percent guessed at more. Among the New Yorkers a little over eight percent figured their newspaper reading at less than fifteen minutes, and seventeen and a half at more.

Very few people have an accurate idea of fifteen minutes, so the figures are not to be taken literally. Moreover, business men, professional people, and college students are most of them liable to a curious little bias against appearing to spend too much time over the newspapers, and perhaps also to a faint suspicion of a desire to be known as rapid

[1] July, 1900. D. F. Wilcox, *The American Newspaper: A Study in Social Psychology*, Annals of the American Academy of Political and Social Science, vol. xvi, p. 56. (The statistical tables are reproduced in James Edward Rogers', *The American Newspaper.*)

1916 (?). W. D. Scott, *The Psychology of Advertising*, pp. 226–248. See also Henry Foster Adams, *Advertising and its Mental Laws*, Ch. IV.

1920. *Newspaper Reading Habits of College Students*, by Prof. George Burton Hotchkiss and Richard B. Franken, published by the Association of National Advertisers, Inc., 15 East 26th Street, New York City.

readers. All that the figures can justly be taken to mean is that over three quarters of those in the selected groups rate rather low the attention they give to printed news of the outer world.

These time estimates are fairly well confirmed by a test which is less subjective. Scott asked his Chicagoans how many papers they read each day, and was told that

| | | |
|---|---|---|
| 14 percent read but one paper | | |
| 46 " " | | two papers |
| 21 " " | | three papers |
| 10 " " | | four papers |
| 3 " " | | five papers |
| 2 " " | | six papers |
| 3 " " | | all the papers (eight |

at the time of this inquiry).

The two- and three-paper readers are sixty-seven percent, which comes fairly close to the seventy-one percent in Scott's group who rate themselves at fifteen minutes a day. The omnivorous readers of from four to eight papers coincide roughly with the twenty-five percent who rated themselves at more than fifteen minutes.

## 2

It is still more difficult to guess how the time is distributed. The college students were asked to name "the five features which interest you most." Just under twenty percent voted for "general news," just under fifteen for editorials, just under twelve for "politics," a little over eight for finance, not two years after the armistice a little over six for foreign news, three and a half for local, nearly three for business, and a quarter of one percent for news about "labor." A scattering said they were most interested in sports, special articles, the theatre, advertisements, cartoons, book reviews, "accuracy," music, "ethical tone," society, brevity, art, stories, shipping, school news, "current news," print. Disregarding these, about sixty-seven and a half percent picked as the most interesting features news and opinion that dealt with public affairs.

This was a mixed college group. The girls professed greater interest than the boys in general news, foreign news, local news, politics, editorials, the theatre, music, art, stories, cartoons, advertisements, and "ethical tone." The boys on the other hand were more absorbed in finance, sports, business page, "accuracy" and "brevity." These discriminations correspond a little too closely with the ideals of what is cultured and moral, manly and decisive, not to make one suspect the utter objectivity of the replies.

Yet they agree fairly well with the replies of Scott's Chicago business and professional men. They were asked, not what features interested them most, but why they preferred one newspaper to another. Nearly seventy-one percent based their conscious preference on local news (17.8%), or political (15.8%) or financial (11.3%), or foreign (9.5%), or general (7.2%), or editorials (9%). The other thirty percent decided on grounds not connected with public affairs. They ranged from not quite seven who decided for ethical tone, down to one twentieth of one percent who cared most about humor.

How do these preferences correspond with the space given by newspapers to various subjects? Unfortunately there are no data collected on this point for the newspapers read by the Chicago and New York groups at the time the questionnaires were made. But there is an interesting analysis made over twenty years ago by Wilcox. He studied one hundred and ten newspapers in fourteen large cities, and classified the subject matter of over nine thousand columns.

Averaged for the whole country the various newspaper matter was found to fill:

| | | | | | |
|---|---|---|---|---|---|
| I. News | 55.3 | (a) War News | 17.9 | | |
| | | (b) General " | 21.8 | Foreign | 1.2 |
| | | | | Politics | 6.4 |
| | | | | Crime | 3.1 |
| | | | | Mis'c | 11.1 |
| | | c) Special " | 15.6 | Business | 8.2 |
| | | | | Sport | 5.1 |
| | | | | Society | 2.3 |
| II. Illustrations | 3.1 | | | | |
| III. Literature | 2.4 | | | | |
| IV. Opinion | 7.1 | (a) Editorials | 3.9 | | |
| | | (b) Letters & Exchange | 3.2 | | |
| V. Advertisements | 32.1 | | | | |

In order to bring this table into a fair comparison, it is necessary to exclude the space given to advertisements, and recompute the percentages. For the advertisements occupied only an infinitesimal part of the conscious preference of the Chicago group or the college group. I think this is justifiable for our purposes because the press prints what advertisements it can get,[2] whereas the rest of the paper is designed to the taste of its readers. The table would then read:

---

[2] Except those which it regards as objectionable, and those which, in rare instances, are crowded out.

| | | | | |
|---|---|---|---|---|
| | | War News | 26.4— | |
| I. News | 81.4+ | General News | 32.0+ | Foreign 1.8—<br>Political 9.4+<br>Crime 4.6—<br>Mis'c 16.3+ |
| | | Special " | 23.0— | Business 12.1—<br>Sporting 7.5+<br>Society 3.3— |
| II. Illustrations | 4.6— | | | |
| III. Literature | 3.5+ | | | |
| IV. Opinion | 10.5— | Editorials<br>Letters | 5.8—<br>4.7+ | |

In this revised table if you add up the items which may be supposed to deal with public affairs, that is to say war, foreign, political, miscellaneous, business news, and opinion, you find a total of 76.5% of the edited space devoted in 1900 to the 70.6% of reasons given by Chicago business men in 1916 for preferring a particular newspaper, and to the five features which most interested 67.5% of the New York college students in 1920.

This would seem to show that the tastes of business men and college students in big cities to-day still correspond more or less to the averaged judgments of newspaper editors in big cities twenty years ago. Since that time the proportion of features to news has undoubtedly increased, and so has the circulation and the size of newspapers. Therefore, if to-day you could secure accurate replies from more typical groups than college students or business and professional men, you would expect to find a smaller percentage of time devoted to public affairs, as well as a smaller percentage of space. On the other hand you would expect to find that the average man spends more than the quarter of an hour on his newspaper, and that while the percentage of space given to public affairs is less than twenty years ago the net amount is greater.

No elaborate deductions are to be drawn from these figures. They help merely to make somewhat more concrete our notions of the effort that goes day by day into acquiring the data of our opinions. The newspapers are, of course, not the only means, but they are certainly the principal ones. Magazines, the public forum, the chautauqua, the church, political gatherings, trade union meetings, women's clubs, and news serials in the moving picture houses supplement the press. But taking it all at the most favorable estimate, the time each day is small when any of us is directly exposed to information from our unseen environment.

# V. Speed, Words, and Clearness

## 1

THE unseen environment is reported to us chiefly by words. These words are transmitted by wire or radio from the reporters to the editors who fit them into print. Telegraphy is expensive, and the facilities are often limited. Press service news is, therefore, usually coded. Thus a dispatch which reads,—

"Washington, D. C. June 1.—The United States regards the question of German shipping seized in this country at the outbreak of hostilities as a closed incident,"

may pass over the wires in the following form:

"Washn 1. The Uni Stas rgds tq of Ger spg seized in ts cou at t outbk o hox as a clod incident."[1]

A news item saying:

"Berlin, June 1, Chancellor Wirth told the Reichstag to-day in outlining the Government's program that 'restoration and reconciliation would be the keynote of the new Government's policy.' He added that the Cabinet was determined disarmament should be carried out loyally and that disarmament would not be the occasion of the imposition of further penalties by the Allies."

may be cabled in this form:

"Berlin 1. Chancellor Wirth told t Reichstag tdy in outlining the gvts pgn tt qn restoration & reconciliation wd b the keynote f new gvts policy. qj He added ttt cabinet ws dtmd disarmament sd b carried out loyally & tt disarmament wd n b. the ocan f imposition of further penalties bi t alis."

In this second item the substance has been culled from a long speech in a foreign tongue, translated, coded, and then decoded. The operators who receive the messages transcribe them as they go along, and I am told that a good operator can write fifteen thousand or even more words per eight hour day, with a half an hour out for lunch and two ten minute periods for rest.

---

[1] Phillip's Code.

2

A few words must often stand for a whole succession of acts, thoughts, feelings and consequences. We read:

> "Washington, Dec. 23—A statement charging Japanese military authorities with deeds more 'frightful and barbarous' than anything ever alleged to have occurred in Belgium during the war was issued here to-day by the Korean Commission, based, the Commission said, on authentic reports received by it from Manchuria."

Here eyewitnesses, their accuracy unknown, report to the makers of 'authentic reports;' they in turn transmit these to a commission five thousand miles away. It prepares a statement, probably much too long for publication, from which a correspondent culls an item of print three and a half inches long. The meaning has to be telescoped in such a way as to permit the reader to judge how much weight to give to the news.

It is doubtful whether a supreme master of style could pack all the elements of truth that complete justice would demand into a hundred word account of what had happened in Korea during the course of several months. For language is by no means a perfect vehicle of meanings. Words, like currency, are turned over and over again, to evoke one set of images to-day, another to-morrow. There is no certainty whatever that the same word will call out exactly the same idea in the reader's mind as it did in the reporter's. Theoretically, if each fact and each relation had a name that was unique, and if everyone had agreed on the names, it would be possible to communicate without misunderstanding. In the exact sciences there is an approach to this ideal, and that is part of the reason why of all forms of world-wide coöperation, scientific inquiry is the most effective.

Men command fewer words than they have ideas to express, and language, as Jean Paul said, is a dictionary of faded metaphors.[2] The journalist addressing half a million readers of whom he has only a dim picture, the speaker whose words are flashed to remote villages and overseas, cannot hope that a few phrases will carry the whole burden of their meaning. "The words of Lloyd George, badly understood and badly transmitted," said M. Briand to the Chamber of Deputies,[3] "seemed to give the Pan-Germanists the idea that the time had come to start something." A British Prime Minister, speaking in English to the whole attentive world, speaks his own meaning in his own words to all kinds of

---

[2] Cited by White, *Mechanisms of Character Formation.*
[3] Special Cable to *The New York Times*, May 25, 1921, by Edwin L. James.

people who will see their meaning in those words. No matter how rich or subtle — or rather the more rich and the more subtle that which he has to say, the more his meaning will suffer as it is sluiced into standard speech and then distributed again among alien minds.[4]

Millions of those who are watching him can read hardly at all. Millions more can read the words but cannot understand them. Of those who can both read and understand, a good three-quarters we may assume have some part of half an hour a day to spare for the subject. To them the words so acquired are the cue for a whole train of ideas on which ultimately a vote of untold consequences may be based. Necessarily the ideas which we allow the words we read to evoke form the biggest part of the original data of our opinions. The world is vast, the situations that concern us are intricate, the messages are few, the biggest part of opinion must be constructed in the imagination.

When we use the word "Mexico" what picture does it evoke in a resident of New York? Likely as not, it is some composite of sand, cactus, oil wells, greasers, rum-drinking Indians, testy old cavaliers flourishing whiskers and sovereignty, or perhaps an idyllic peasantry à la Jean

---

[4] In May of 1921, relations between England and France were strained by the insurrection of M. Korfanty in Upper Silesia. The London Correspondence of the *Manchester Guardian* (May 20, 1921), contained the following item:

"The Franco-English Exchange in Words.

"In quarters well acquainted with French ways and character I find a tendency to think that undue sensibility has been shown by our press and public opinion in the lively and at times intemperate language of the French press through the present crisis. The point was put to me by a well-informed neutral observer in the following manner.

"Words, like money, are tokens of value. They represent meaning, therefore, and just as money, their representative value goes up and down. The French word 'etonnant' was used by Bossuet with a terrible weight of meaning which it has lost to-day. A similar thing can be observed with the English word 'awful.' Some nations constitutionally tend to understate, others to overstate. What the British Tommy called an unhealthy place could only be described by an Italian soldier by means of a rich vocabulary aided with an exuberant mimicry. Nations that understate keep their word-currency sound. Nations that overstate suffer from inflation in their language.

"Expressions such as 'a distinguished scholar,' 'a clever writer,' must be translated into French as 'a great savant,' 'an exquisite master.' It is a mere matter of exchange, just as in France one pound pays 46 francs, and yet one knows that that does not increase its value at home. Englishmen reading the French press should endeavour to work out a mental operation similar to that of the banker who puts back francs into pounds, and not forget in so doing that while in normal times the change was 25 it is now 46 on account of the war. For there is a war fluctuation on word exchanges as well as on money exchanges.

"The argument, one hopes, works both ways, and Frenchmen do not fail to realize that there is as much value behind English reticence as behind their own exuberance of expression."

Jacques, assailed by the prospect of smoky industrialism, and fighting
for the Rights of Man. What does the word "Japan" evoke? Is it a vague
horde of slant-eyed yellow men, surrounded by Yellow Perils, picture
brides, fans, Samurai, banzais, art, and cherry blossoms? Or the word
"alien"? According to a group of New England college students, writing in the year 1920, an alien was the following:[5]

> "A person hostile to this country."
> "A person against the government."
> "A person who is on the opposite side."
> "A native of an unfriendly country."
> "A foreigner at war."
> "A foreigner who tries to do harm to the country he is in."
> "An enemy from a foreign land."
> "A person against a country." etc. . . .

Yet the word alien is an unusually exact legal term, far more exact than
words like sovereignty, independence, national honor, rights, defense,
aggression, imperialism, capitalism, socialism, about which we so readily take sides "for" or "against."

## 3

The power to dissociate superficial analogies, attend to differences
and appreciate variety is lucidity of mind. It is a relative faculty. Yet the
differences in lucidity are extensive, say as between a newly born infant
and a botanist examining a flower. To the infant there is precious little
difference between his own toes, his father's watch, the lamp on the
table, the moon in the sky, and a nice bright yellow edition of Guy de
Maupassant. To many a member of the Union League Club there is no
remarkable difference between a Democrat, a Socialist, an anarchist,
and a burglar, while to a highly sophisticated anarchist there is a whole
universe of difference between Bakunin, Tolstoi, and Kropotkin. These
examples show how difficult it might be to secure a sound public opinion about de Maupassant among babies, or about Democrats in the
Union League Club.

A man who merely rides in other people's automobiles may not rise
to finer discrimination than between a Ford, a taxicab, and an automobile. But let that same man own a car and drive it, let him, as the
psychoanalysts would say, project his libido upon automobiles, and he
will describe a difference in carburetors by looking at the rear end of a

---

[5] *The New Republic:* December 29, 1920, p. 142.

car a city block away. That is why it is often such a relief when the talk turns from "general topics" to a man's own hobby. It is like turning from the landscape in the parlor to the ploughed field outdoors. It is a return to the three dimensional world, after a sojourn in the painter's portrayal of his own emotional response to his own inattentive memory of what he imagines he ought to have seen.

We easily identify, says Ferenczi, two only partially similar things:[6] the child more easily than the adult, the primitive or arrested mind more readily than the mature. As it first appears in the child, consciousness seems to be an unmanageable mixture of sensations. The child has no sense of time, and almost none of space, it reaches for the chandelier with the same confidence that it reaches for its mother's breast, and at first with almost the same expectation. Only very gradually does function define itself. To complete inexperience this is a coherent and undifferentiated world, in which, as someone has said of a school of philosophers, all facts are born free and equal. Those facts which belong together in the world have not yet been separated from those which happen to lie side by side in the stream of consciousness.

At first, says Ferenczi, the baby gets some of the things it wants by crying for them. This is "the period of magical hallucinatory omnipotence." In its second phase the child points to the things it wants, and they are given to it. "Omnipotence by the help of magic gestures." Later, the child learns to talk, asks for what it wishes, and is partially successful. "The period of magic thoughts and magic words." Each phase may persist for certain situations, though overlaid and only visible at times, as for example, in the little harmless superstitions from which few of us are wholly free. In each phase, partial success tends to confirm that way of acting, while failure tends to stimulate the development of another. Many individuals, parties, and even nations, rarely appear to transcend the magical organization of experience. But in the more advanced sections of the most advanced peoples, trial and error after repeated failure has led to the invention of a new principle. The moon, they learn, is not moved by baying at it. Crops are not raised from the soil by spring festivals or Republican majorities, but by sunlight, moisture, seeds, fertilizer, and cultivation.[7]

Allowing for the purely schematic value of Ferenczi's categories of response, the quality which we note as critical is the power to discriminate among crude perceptions and vague analogies. This power has

---

[6] Internat. Zeitschr. f. Ärztl. Psychoanalyse, 1913. Translated and republished by Dr. Ernest Jones in S. Ferenczi, *Contributions to Psychoanalysis*, Ch. VIII, *Stages in the Development of the Sense of Reality*.

[7] Ferenczi, being a pathologist, does not describe this maturer period where experience is organized as equations, the phase of realism on the basis of science.

been studied under laboratory conditions.[8] The Zurich Association Studies indicate clearly that slight mental fatigue, an inner disturbance of attention or an external distraction, tend to "flatten" the quality of the response. An example of the very "flat" type is the clang association (cat-hat), a reaction to the sound and not to the sense of the stimulant word. One test, for example, shows a 9% increase of clang in the second series of a hundred reactions. Now the clang is almost a repetition, a very primitive form of analogy.

4

If the comparatively simple conditions of a laboratory can so readily flatten out discrimination, what must be the effect of city life? In the laboratory the fatigue is slight enough, the distraction rather trivial. Both are balanced in measure by the subject's interest and self-consciousness. Yet if the beat of a metronome will depress intelligence, what do eight or twelve hours of noise, odor, and heat in a factory, or day upon day among chattering typewriters and telephone bells and slamming doors, do to the political judgments formed on the basis of newspapers read in street-cars and subways? Can anything be heard in the hubbub that does not shriek, or be seen in the general glare that does not flash like an electric sign? The life of the city dweller lacks solitude, silence, ease. The nights are noisy and ablaze. The people of a big city are assaulted by incessant sound, now violent and jagged, now falling into unfinished rhythms, but endless and remorseless. Under modern industrialism thought goes on in a bath of noise. If its discriminations are often flat and foolish, here at least is some small part of the reason. The sovereign people determines life and death and happiness under conditions where experience and experiment alike show thought to be most difficult. "The intolerable burden of thought" is a burden when the conditions make it burdensome. It is no burden when the conditions are favorable. It is as exhilarating to think as it is to dance, and just as natural.

Every man whose business it is to think knows that he must for part of the day create about himself a pool of silence. But in that helter-

---

[8] See, for example, *Diagnostische Assoziation Studien*, conducted at the Psychiatric University Clinic in Zurich under the direction of Dr. C. G. Jung. These tests were carried on principally under the so-called Kräpelin-Aschaffenburg classification. They show reaction time, classify response to the stimulant word as inner, outer, and clang, show separate results for the first and second hundred words, for reaction time and reaction quality when the subject is distracted by holding an idea in mind, or when he replies while beating time with a metronome. Some of the results are summarized in Jung, *Analytical Psychology*, Ch. II, transl. by Dr. Constance E. Long.

skelter which we flatter by the name of civilization, the citizen per-
forms the perilous business of government under the worst possible
conditions. A faint recognition of this truth inspires the movement for
a shorter work day, for longer vacations, for light, air, order, sunlight
and dignity in factories and offices. But if the intellectual quality of our
life is to be improved that is only the merest beginning. So long as so
many jobs are an endless and, for the worker, an aimless routine, a kind
of automatism using one set of muscles in one monotonous pattern, his
whole life will tend towards an automatism in which nothing is particularly to be distinguished from anything else unless it is announced
with a thunderclap. So long as he is physically imprisoned in crowds
by day and even by night his attention will flicker and relax. It will not
hold fast and define clearly where he is the victim of all sorts of pother,
in a home which needs to be ventilated of its welter of drudgery, shriek-
ing children, raucous assertions, indigestible food, bad air, and suffo-
cating ornament.

Occasionally perhaps we enter a building which is composed and
spacious; we go to a theatre where modern stagecraft has cut away distraction, or go to sea, or into a quiet place, and we remember how clut-
tered, how capricious, how superfluous and clamorous is the ordinary
urban life of our time. We learn to understand why our addled minds
seize so little with precision, why they are caught up and tossed about
in a kind of tarantella by headlines and catch-words, why so often they
cannot tell things apart or discern identity in apparent differences.

## 5

But this external disorder is complicated further by internal.
Experiment shows that the speed, the accuracy, and the intellectual
quality of association is deranged by what we are taught to call emotional conflicts. Measured in fifths of a second, a series of a hundred
stimuli containing both neutral and hot words may show a variation as
between 5 and 32 or even a total failure to respond at all.[9] Obviously
our public opinion is in intermittent contact with complexes of all
sorts; with ambition and economic interest, personal animosity, racial
prejudice, class feeling and what not. They distort our reading, our
thinking, our talking and our behavior in a great variety of ways.

And finally since opinions do not stop at the normal members of
society, since for the purposes of an election, a propaganda, a following, numbers constitute power, the quality of attention is still further

---

[9] Jung, *Clark Lectures.*

depressed. The mass of absolutely illiterate, of feeble-minded, grossly neurotic, undernourished and frustrated individuals, is very considerable, much more considerable, there is reason to think, than we generally suppose. Thus a wide popular appeal is circulated among persons who are mentally children or barbarians, people whose lives are a morass of entanglements, people whose vitality is exhausted, shut-in people, and people whose experience has comprehended no factor in the problem under discussion. The stream of public opinion is stopped by them in little eddies of misunderstanding, where it is discolored with prejudice and far fetched analogy.

A "broad appeal" takes account of the quality of association, and is made to those susceptibilities which are widely distributed. A "narrow" or a "special" appeal is one made to those susceptibilities which are uncommon. But the same individual may respond with very different quality to different stimuli, or to the same stimuli at different times. Human susceptibilities are like an alpine country. There are isolated peaks, there are extensive but separated plateaus, and there are deeper strata which are quite continuous for nearly all mankind. Thus the individuals whose susceptibilities reach the rarefied atmosphere of those peaks where there exists an exquisitive difference between Frege and Peano, or between Sassetta's earlier and later periods, may be good stanch Republicans at another level of appeal, and when they are starving and afraid, indistinguishable from any other starving and frightened person. No wonder that the magazines with the large circulations prefer the face of a pretty girl to any other trade mark, a face, pretty enough to be alluring, but innocent enough to be acceptable. For the "psychic level" on which the stimulus acts determines whether the public is to be potentially a large or a small one.

6

Thus the environment with which our public opinions deal is refracted in many ways, by censorship and privacy at the source, by physical and social barriers at the other end, by scanty attention, by the poverty of language, by distraction, by unconscious constellations of feeling, by wear and tear, violence, monotony. These limitations upon our access to that environment combine with the obscurity and complexity of the facts themselves to thwart clearness and justice of perception, to substitute misleading fictions for workable ideas, and to deprive us of adequate checks upon those who consciously strive to mislead.

# PART III.  STEREOTYPES

# VI.  Stereotypes

## 1

E ACH of us lives and works on a small part of the earth's surface, moves in a small circle, and of these acquaintances knows only a few intimately. Of any public event that has wide effects we see at best only a phase and an aspect. This is as true of the eminent insiders who draft treaties, make laws, and issue orders, as it is of those who have treaties framed for them, laws promulgated to them, orders given at them. Inevitably our opinions cover a bigger space, a longer reach of time, a greater number of things, than we can directly observe. They have, therefore, to be pieced together out of what others have reported and what we can imagine.

Yet even the eyewitness does not bring back a naïve picture of the scene.[1] For experience seems to show that he himself brings something to the scene which later he takes away from it, that oftener than not what he imagines to be the account of an event is really a transfigura-

---

[1] *Eg. cf.* Edmond Locard, *L'Enquête Criminelle et les Méthodes Scientifiques.* A great deal of interesting material has been gathered in late years on the credibility of the witness, which shows, as an able reviewer of Dr. Locard's book says in *The Times* (London) Literary Supplement (August 18, 1921), that credibility varies as to classes of witnesses and classes of events, and also as to type of perception. Thus, perceptions of touch, odor, and taste have low evidential value. Our hearing is defective and arbitrary when it judges the source and direction of sound, and in listening to the talk of other people "words which are not heard will be supplied by the witness in all good faith. He will have a theory of the purport of the conversation, and will arrange the sounds he heard to fit it." Even visual perceptions are liable to great error, as in identification, recognition, judgment of distance, estimates of numbers, for example, the size of a crowd. In the untrained observer, the sense of time is highly variable. All these original weaknesses are complicated by tricks of memory, and the incessant creative quality of the imagination. *Cf.* also Sherrington, *The Integrative Action of the Nervous System*, pp. 318–327.

The late Professor Hugo Münsterberg wrote a popular book on this subject called *On the Witness Stand.*

tion of it. Few facts in consciousness seem to be merely given. Most facts in consciousness seem to be partly made. A report is the joint product of the knower and known, in which the rôle of the observer is always selective and usually creative. The facts we see depend on where we are placed, and the habits of our eyes.

An unfamiliar scene is like the baby's world, "one great, blooming, buzzing confusion."[2] This is the way, says Mr. John Dewey,[3] that any new thing strikes an adult, so far as the thing is really new and strange. "Foreign languages that we do not understand always seem jibberings, babblings, in which it is impossible to fix a definite, clear-cut, individualized group of sounds. The countryman in the crowded street, the landlubber at sea, the ignoramus in sport at a contest between experts in a complicated game, are further instances. Put an inexperienced man in a factory, and at first the work seems to him a meaningless medley. All strangers of another race proverbially look alike to the visiting stranger. Only gross differences of size or color are perceived by an outsider in a flock of sheep, each of which is perfectly individualized to the shepherd. A diffusive blur and an indiscriminately shifting suction characterize what we do not understand. The problem of the acquisition of meaning by things, or (stated in another way) of forming habits of simple apprehension, is thus the problem of introducing (1) *definiteness* and *distinction* and (2) *consistency* or *stability* of meaning into what is otherwise vague and wavering."

But the kind of definiteness and consistency introduced depends upon who introduces them. In a later passage[4] Dewey gives an example of how differently an experienced layman and a chemist might define the word metal. "Smoothness, hardness, glossiness, and brilliancy, heavy weight for its size . . . the serviceable properties of capacity for being hammered and pulled without breaking, of being softened by heat and hardened by cold, of retaining the shape and form given, of resistance to pressure and decay, would probably be included" in the layman's definition. But the chemist would likely as not ignore these esthetic and utilitarian qualities, and define a metal as "any chemical element that enters into combination with oxygen so as to form a base."

For the most part we do not first see, and then define, we define first and then see. In the great blooming, buzzing confusion of the outer world we pick out what our culture has already defined for us, and we tend to perceive that which we have picked out in the form stereotyped for us by our culture. Of the great men who assembled at Paris to settle the affairs of mankind, how many were there who were able to see

[2] Wm. James, *Principles of Psychology*, Vol. I, p. 488.
[3] John Dewey, *How We Think*, p. 121.
[4] *Op. cit.*, p. 133.

much of the Europe about them, rather than their commitments about Europe? Could anyone have penetrated the mind of M. Clemenceau, would he have found there images of the Europe of 1919, or a great sediment of stereotyped ideas accumulated and hardened in a long and pugnacious existence? Did he see the Germans of 1919, or the German type as he had learned to see it since 1871? He saw the type, and among the reports that came to him from Germany, he took to heart those reports, and, it seems, those only, which fitted the type that was in his mind. If a junker blustered, that was an authentic German; if a labor leader confessed the guilt of the empire, he was not an authentic German.

At a Congress of Psychology in Göttingen an interesting experiment was made with a crowd of presumably trained observers.[5]

> "Not far from the hall in which the Congress was sitting there was a public fête with a masked ball. Suddenly the door of the hall was thrown open and a clown rushed in madly pursued by a negro, revolver in hand. They stopped in the middle of the room fighting; the clown fell, the negro leapt upon him, fired, and then both rushed out of the hall. The whole incident hardly lasted twenty seconds.
>
> "The President asked those present to write immediately a report since there was sure to be a judicial inquiry. Forty reports were sent in. Only one had less than 20% of mistakes in regard to the principal facts; fourteen had 20% to 40% of mistakes; twelve from 40% to 50%; thirteen more than 50%. Moreover in twenty-four accounts 10% of the details were pure inventions and this proportion was exceeded in ten accounts and diminished in six. Briefly a quarter of the accounts were false.
>
> "It goes without saying that the whole scene had been arranged and even photographed in advance. The ten false reports may then be relegated to the category of tales and legends; twenty-four accounts are half legendary, and six have a value approximating to exact evidence."

Thus out of forty trained observers writing a responsible account of a scene that had just happened before their eyes, more than a majority saw a scene that had not taken place. What then did they see? One would suppose it was easier to tell what had occurred, than to invent something which had not occurred. They saw their stereotype of such a brawl. All of them had in the course of their lives acquired a series of images of brawls, and these images flickered before their eyes. In one man these images displaced less than 20% of the actual scene, in thirteen men more than half. In thirty-four out of the forty observers the stereotypes preempted at least one-tenth of the scene.

---

[5] A. von Gennep, *La formation des légendes*, pp. 158–159. Cited F. van Langenhove, *The Growth of a Legend*, pp. 120–122.

A distinguished art critic has said[6] that "what with the almost numberless shapes assumed by an object. . . . What with our insensitiveness and inattention, things scarcely would have for us features and outlines so determined and clear that we could recall them at will, but for the stereotyped shapes art has lent them." The truth is even broader than that, for the stereotyped shapes lent to the world come not merely from art, in the sense of painting and sculpture and literature, but from our moral codes and our social philosophies and our political agitations as well. Substitute in the following passage of Mr. Berenson's the words 'politics,' 'business,' and 'society,' for the word 'art' and the sentences will be no less true: ". . . unless years devoted to the study of all schools of art have taught us also to see with our own eyes, we soon fall into the habit of moulding whatever we look at into the forms borrowed from the one art with which we are acquainted. There is our standard of artistic reality. Let anyone give us shapes and colors which we cannot instantly match in our paltry stock of hackneyed forms and tints, and we shake our heads at his failure to reproduce things as we know they certainly are, or we accuse him of insincerity."

Mr. Berenson speaks of our displeasure when a painter "does not visualize objects exactly as we do," and of the difficulty of appreciating the art of the Middle Ages because since then "our manner of visualizing forms has changed in a thousand ways."[7] He goes on to show how in regard to the human figure we have been taught to see what we do see. "Created by Donatello and Masaccio, and sanctioned by the Humanists, the new canon of the human figure, the new cast of features . . . presented to the ruling classes of that time the type of human being most likely to win the day in the combat of human forces. . . . Who had the power to break through this new standard of vision and, out of the chaos of things, to select shapes more definitely expressive of reality than those fixed by men of genius? No one had such power. People had perforce to see things in that way and in no other, and to see only the shapes depicted, to love only the ideals presented. . . ."[8]

---

[6] Bernard Berenson, *The Central Italian Painters of the Renaissance*, pp. 60, *et seq.*
[7] *Cf.* also his comment on *Dante's Visual Images, and his Early Illustrators* in *The Study and Criticism of Italian Art* (First Series), p. 13. "We cannot help dressing Virgil as a Roman, and giving him a 'classical profile' and 'statuesque carriage,' but Dante's visual image of Virgil was probably no less mediaeval, no more based on a critical reconstruction of antiquity, than his entire conception of the Roman poet. Fourteenth Century illustrators make Virgil look like a mediaeval scholar, dressed in cap and gown, and there is no reason why Dante's visual image of him should have been other than this."
[8] *The Central Italian Painters*, pp. 66–67.

2

If we cannot fully understand the acts of other people, until we know what they think they know, then in order to do justice we have to appraise not only the information which has been at their disposal, but the minds through which they have filtered it. For the accepted types, the current patterns, the standard versions, intercept information on its way to consciousness. Americanization, for example, is superficially at least the substitution of American for European stereotypes. Thus the peasant who might see his landlord as if he were the lord of the manor, his employer as he saw the local magnate, is taught by Americanization to see the landlord and employer according to American standards. This constitutes a change of mind, which is, in effect, when the inoculation succeeds, a change of vision. His eye sees differently. One kindly gentlewoman has confessed that the stereotypes are of such overweening importance, that when hers are not indulged, she at least is unable to accept the brotherhood of man and the fatherhood of God: "we are strangely affected by the clothes we wear. Garments create a mental and social atmosphere. What can be hoped for the Americanism of a man who insists on employing a London tailor? One's very food affects his Americanism. What kind of American consciousness can grow in the atmosphere of sauerkraut and Limburger cheese? Or what can you expect of the Americanism of the man whose breath always reeks of garlic?"[9]

This lady might well have been the patron of a pageant which a friend of mine once attended. It was called the Melting Pot, and it was given on the Fourth of July in an automobile town where many foreign-born workers are employed. In the center of the baseball park at second base stood a huge wooden and canvas pot. There were flights of steps up to the rim on two sides. After the audience had settled itself, and the band had played, a procession came through an opening at one side of the field. It was made up of men of all the foreign nationalities employed in the factories. They wore their native costumes, they were singing their national songs; they danced their folk dances, and carried the banners of all Europe. The master of ceremonies was the principal of the grade school dressed as Uncle Sam. He led them to the pot. He directed them up the steps to the rim, and inside. He called them out again on the other side. They came, dressed in derby hats, coats, pants, vest, stiff collar and polka-dot tie, undoubtedly, said my

---

[9] Cited by Mr. Edward Hale Bierstadt, *New Republic*, June 1, 1921, p. 21.

friend, each with an Eversharp pencil in his pocket, and all singing the
Star-Spangled Banner.

To the promoters of this pageant, and probably to most of the actors,
it seemed as if they had managed to express the most intimate difficulty
to friendly association between the older peoples of America and the
newer. The contradiction of their stereotypes interfered with the full
recognition of their common humanity. The people who change their
names know this. They mean to change themselves, and the attitude of
strangers toward them.

There is, of course, some connection between the scene outside and
the mind through which we watch it, just as there are some long-haired
men and short-haired women in radical gatherings. But to the hurried
observer a slight connection is enough. If there are two bobbed heads
and four beards in the audience, it will be a bobbed and bearded audience to the reporter who knows beforehand that such gatherings are
composed of people with these tastes in the management of their hair.
There is a connection between our vision and the facts, but it is often
a strange connection. A man has rarely looked at a landscape, let us say,
except to examine its possibilities for division into building lots, but he
has seen a number of landscapes hanging in the parlor. And from them
he has learned to think of a landscape as a rosy sunset, or as a country
road with a church steeple and a silver moon. One day he goes to the
country, and for hours he does not see a single landscape. Then the sun
goes down looking rosy. At once he recognizes a landscape and
exclaims that it is beautiful. But two days later, when he tries to recall
what he saw, the odds are that he will remember chiefly some landscape in a parlor.

Unless he has been drunk or dreaming or insane he did see a sunset,
but he saw in it, and above all remembers from it, more of what the oil
painting taught him to observe, than what an impressionist painter, for
example, or a cultivated Japanese would have seen and taken away with
him. And the Japanese and the painter in turn will have seen and
remembered more of the form they had learned, unless they happen to
be the very rare people who find fresh sight for mankind. In untrained
observation we pick recognizable signs out of the environment. The
signs stand for ideas, and these ideas we fill out with our stock of
images. We do not so much see this man and that sunset; rather we
notice that the thing is man or sunset, and then see chiefly what our
mind is already full of on those subjects.

3

There is economy in this. For the attempt to see all things freshly and
in detail, rather than as types and generalities, is exhausting, and

among busy affairs practically out of the question. In a circle of friends, and in relation to close associates or competitors, there is no shortcut through, and no substitute for, an individualized understanding. Those whom we love and admire most are the men and women whose consciousness is peopled thickly with persons rather than with types, who know us rather than the classification into which we might fit. For even without phrasing it to ourselves, we feel intuitively that all classification is in relation to some purpose not necessarily our own; that between two human beings no association has final dignity in which each does not take the other as an end in himself. There is a taint on any contact between two people which does not affirm as an axiom the personal inviolability of both.

But modern life is hurried and multifarious, above all physical distance separates men who are often in vital contact with each other, such as employer and employee, official and voter. There is neither time nor opportunity for intimate acquaintance. Instead we notice a trait which marks a well known type, and fill in the rest of the picture by means of the stereotypes we carry about in our heads. He is an agitator. That much we notice, or are told. Well, an agitator is this sort of person, and so *he* is this sort of person. He is an intellectual. He is a plutocrat. He is a foreigner. He is a "South European." He is from Back Bay. He is a Harvard Man. How different from the statement: he is a Yale Man. He is a regular fellow. He is a West Pointer. He is an old army sergeant. He is a Greenwich Villager: what don't we know about him then, and about her? He is an international banker. He is from Main Street.

The subtlest and most pervasive of all influences are those which create and maintain the repertory of stereotypes. We are told about the world before we see it. We imagine most things before we experience them. And those preconceptions, unless education has made us acutely aware, govern deeply the whole process of perception. They mark out certain objects as familiar or strange, emphasizing the difference, so that the slightly familiar is seen as very familiar, and the somewhat strange as sharply alien. They are aroused by small signs, which may vary from a true index to a vague analogy. Aroused, they flood fresh vision with older images, and project into the world what has been resurrected in memory. Were there no practical uniformities in the environment, there would be no economy and only error in the human habit of accepting foresight for sight. But there are uniformities sufficiently accurate, and the need of economizing attention is so inevitable, that the abandonment of all stereotypes for a wholly innocent approach to experience would impoverish human life.

What matters is the character of the stereotypes, and the gullibility with which we employ them. And these in the end depend upon those inclusive patterns which constitute our philosophy of life. If in that

philosophy we assume that the world is codified according to a code
which we possess, we are likely to make our reports of what is going on
describe a world run by our code. But if our philosophy tells us that
each man is only a small part of the world, that his intelligence catches
at best only phases and aspects in a coarse net of ideas, then, when we
use our stereotypes, we tend to know that they are only stereotypes, to
hold them lightly, to modify them gladly. We tend, also, to realize more
and more clearly when our ideas started, where they started, how they
came to us, why we accepted them. All useful history is antiseptic in
this fashion. It enables us to know what fairy tale, what school book,
what tradition, what novel, play, picture, phrase, planted one preconception in this mind, another in that mind.

## 4

Those who wish to censor art do not at least underestimate this influence. They generally misunderstand it, and almost always they are
absurdly bent on preventing other people from discovering anything
not sanctioned by them. But at any rate, like Plato in his argument
about the poets, they feel vaguely that the types acquired through fiction tend to be imposed on reality. Thus there can be little doubt that
the moving picture is steadily building up imagery which is then
evoked by the words people read in their newspapers. In the whole
experience of the race there has been no aid to visualization comparable to the cinema. If a Florentine wished to visualize the saints, he
could go to the frescoes in his church, where he might see a vision of
saints standardized for his time by Giotto. If an Athenian wished to
visualize the gods he went to the temples. But the number of objects
which were pictured was not great. And in the East, where the spirit of
the second commandment was widely accepted, the portraiture of concrete things was even more meager, and for that reason perhaps the faculty of practical decision was by so much reduced. In the western
world, however, during the last few centuries there has been an enormous increase in the volume and scope of secular description, the
word picture, the narrative, the illustrated narrative, and finally the
moving picture and, perhaps, the talking picture.

Photographs have the kind of authority over imagination to-day,
which the printed word had yesterday, and the spoken word before that.
They seem utterly real. They come, we imagine, directly to us without
human meddling, and they are the most effortless food for the mind
conceivable. Any description in words, or even any inert picture,
requires an effort of memory before a picture exists in the mind. But on
the screen the whole process of observing, describing, reporting, and
then imagining, has been accomplished for you. Without more trouble

than is needed to stay awake the result which your imagination is always aiming at is reeled off on the screen. The shadowy idea becomes vivid; your hazy notion, let us say, of the Ku Klux Klan, thanks to Mr. Griffiths, takes vivid shape when you see the Birth of a Nation. Historically it may be the wrong shape, morally it may be a pernicious shape, but it is a shape, and I doubt whether anyone who has seen the film and does not know more about the Ku Klux Klan than Mr. Griffiths, will ever hear the name again without seeing those white horsemen.

5

And so when we speak of the mind of a group of people, of the French mind, the militarist mind, the bolshevik mind, we are liable to serious confusion unless we agree to separate the instinctive equipment from the stereotypes, the patterns, and the formulae which play so decisive a part in building up the mental world to which the native character is adapted and responds. Failure to make this distinction accounts for oceans of loose talk about collective minds, national souls, and race psychology. To be sure a stereotype may be so consistently and authoritatively transmitted in each generation from parent to child that it seems almost like a biological fact. In some respects, we may indeed have become, as Mr. Wallas says,[10] biologically parasitic upon our social heritage. But certainly there is not the least scientific evidence which would enable anyone to argue that men are born with the political habits of the country in which they are born. In so far as political habits are alike in a nation, the first places to look for an explanation are the nursery, the school, the church, not in that limbo inhabited by Group Minds and National Souls. Until you have thoroughly failed to see tradition being handed on from parents, teachers, priests, and uncles, it is a solecism of the worst order to ascribe political differences to the germ plasm.

It is possible to generalize tentatively and with a decent humility about comparative differences within the same category of education and experience. Yet even this is a tricky enterprise. For almost no two experiences are exactly alike, not even of two children in the same household. The older son never does have the experience of being the younger. And therefore, until we are able to discount the difference in nurture, we must withhold judgment about differences of nature. As well judge the productivity of two soils by comparing their yield before

---

[10] Graham Wallas, *Our Social Heritage*, p. 17.

you know which is in Labrador and which in Iowa, whether they have been cultivated and enriched, exhausted, or allowed to run wild.

# VII. Stereotypes as Defense

## 1

THERE is another reason, besides economy of effort, why we so often hold to our stereotypes when we might pursue a more disinterested vision. The systems of stereotypes may be the core of our personal tradition, the defenses of our position in society.

They are an ordered, more or less consistent picture of the world, to which our habits, our tastes, our capacities, our comforts, and our hopes have adjusted themselves. They may not be a complete picture of the world, but they are a picture of a possible world to which we are adapted. In that world people and things have their well-known places, and do certain expected things. We feel at home there. We fit in. We are members. We know the way around. There we find the charm of the familiar, the normal, the dependable; its grooves and shapes are where we are accustomed to find them. And though we have abandoned much that might have tempted us before we creased ourselves into that mould, once we are firmly in, it fits as snugly as an old shoe.

No wonder, then, that any disturbance of the stereotypes seems like an attack upon the foundations of the universe. It is an attack upon the foundations of *our* universe, and, where big things are at stake, we do not readily admit that there is any distinction between our universe and the universe. A world which turns out to be one in which those we honor are unworthy, and those we despise are noble, is nerve-racking. There is anarchy if our order of precedence is not the only possible one. For if the meek should indeed inherit the earth, if the first should be last, if those who are without sin alone may cast a stone, if to Caesar you render only the things that are Caesar's, then the foundations of self-respect would be shaken for those who have arranged their lives as if these maxims were not true.

A pattern of stereotypes is not neutral. It is not merely a way of substituting order for the great blooming, buzzing confusion of reality. It is not merely a short cut. It is all these things and something more. It is the guarantee of our self-respect; it is the projection upon the world of our own sense of our own value, our own position and our own rights. The stereotypes are, therefore, highly charged with the feelings that are attached to them. They are the fortress of our tradition, and behind its defenses we can continue to feel ourselves safe in the position we occupy.

2

When, for example, in the fourth century B.C., Aristotle wrote his defense of slavery in the face of increasing skepticism,[1] the Athenian slaves were in great part indistinguishable from free citizens. Mr. Zimmern quotes an amusing passage from the Old Oligarch explaining the good treatment of the slaves. "Suppose it were legal for a slave to be beaten by a citizen, it would frequently happen that an Athenian might be mistaken for a slave or an alien and receive a beating;—since the Athenian people is not better clothed than the slave or alien, nor in personal appearance is there any superiority." This absence of distinction would naturally tend to dissolve the institution. If free men and slaves looked alike, what basis was there for treating them so differently? It was this confusion which Aristotle set himself to clear away in the first book of his Politics. With unerring instinct he understood that to justify slavery he must teach the Greeks a way of *seeing* their slaves that comported with the continuance of slavery.

So, said Aristotle, there are beings who are slaves by nature.[2] "He then is by nature formed a slave, who is fitted to become the chattel of another person, *and on that account is so.*" All this really says is that whoever happens to be a slave is by nature intended to be one. Logically the statement is worthless, but in fact it is not a proposition at all, and logic has nothing to do with it. It is a stereotype, or rather it is part of a stereotype. The rest follows almost immediately. After asserting that slaves perceive reason, but are not endowed with the use of it, Aristotle insists that "it is the intention of nature to make the bodies of slaves and free men different from each other, that the one should be robust for their necessary purposes, but the other erect; useless indeed for such servile labours, but fit for civil life. . . . It is clear then that some men are free by nature, and others are slaves. . . ."

If we ask ourselves what is the matter with Aristotle's argument, we find that he has begun by erecting a great barrier between himself and the facts. When he had said that those who are slaves are by nature intended to be slaves, he at one stroke excluded the fatal question whether those particular men who happened to be slaves were the particular men intended by nature to be slaves. For that question would have tainted each case of slavery with doubt. And since the fact of being a slave was not evidence that a man was destined to be one, no certain test would have remained. Aristotle, therefore, excluded entirely that destructive doubt. Those who are slaves are intended to be slaves. Each slave holder was to look upon his chattels as natural slaves.

---

[1] Zimmern: *Greek Commonwealth.* See his footnote, p. 383.
[2] *Politics*, Bk. I, Ch. 5.

When his eye had been trained to see them that way, he was to note as confirmation of their servile character the fact that they performed servile work, that they were competent to do servile work, and that they had the muscles to do servile work.

This is the perfect stereotype. Its hallmark is that it precedes the use of reason; is a form of perception, imposes a certain character on the data of our senses before the data reach the intelligence. The stereotype is like the lavender window-panes on Beacon Street, like the door-keeper at a costume ball who judges whether the guest has an appropriate masquerade. There is nothing so obdurate to education or to criticism as the stereotype. It stamps itself upon the evidence in the very act of securing the evidence. That is why the accounts of returning travellers are often an interesting tale of what the traveller carried abroad with him on his trip. If he carried chiefly his appetite, a zeal for tiled bathrooms, a conviction that the Pullman car is the acme of human comfort, and a belief that it is proper to tip waiters, taxicab drivers, and barbers, but under no circumstances station agents and ushers, then his Odyssey will be replete with good meals and bad meals, bathing adventures, compartment-train escapades, and voracious demands for money. Or if he is a more serious soul he may while on tour have found himself at celebrated spots. Having touched base, and cast one furtive glance at the monument, he buried his head in Baedeker, read every word through, and moved on to the next celebrated spot; and thus returned with a compact and orderly impression of Europe, rated one star, or two.

In some measure, stimuli from the outside, especially when they are printed or spoken words, evoke some part of a system of stereotypes, so that the actual sensation and the preconception occupy consciousness at the same time. The two are blended, much as if we looked at red through blue glasses and saw green. If what we are looking at corresponds successfully with what we anticipated, the stereotype is reinforced for the future, as it is in a man who knows in advance that the Japanese are cunning and has the bad luck to run across two dishonest Japanese.

If the experience contradicts the stereotype, one of two things happens. If the man is no longer plastic, or if some powerful interest makes it highly inconvenient to rearrange his stereotypes, he pooh-poohs the contradiction as an exception that proves the rule, discredits the witness, finds a flaw somewhere, and manages to forget it. But if he is still curious and open-minded, the novelty is taken into the picture, and allowed to modify it. Sometimes, if the incident is striking enough, and if he has felt a general discomfort with his established scheme, he may be shaken to such an extent as to distrust all accepted ways of looking at life, and to expect that normally a thing will not be what it is generally supposed to be. In the extreme case, especially if he is literary, he may develop a passion for inverting the moral canon by making Judas, Benedict Arnold, or Caesar Borgia the hero of his tale.

### 3

The rôle played by the stereotype can be seen in the German tales about Belgian snipers. Those tales curiously enough were first refuted by an organization of German Catholic priests known as Pax.[3] The existence of atrocity stories is itself not remarkable, nor that the German people gladly believed them. But it is remarkable that a great conservative body of patriotic Germans should have set out as early as August 16, 1914, to contradict a collection of slanders on the enemy, even though such slanders were of the utmost value in soothing the troubled conscience of their fellow countrymen. Why should the Jesuit order in particular have set out to destroy a fiction so important to the fighting morale of Germany?

I quote from M. van Langenhove's account:

"Hardly had the German armies entered Belgium when strange rumors began to circulate. They spread from place to place, they were reproduced by the press, and they soon permeated the whole of Germany. It was said that the Belgian people, *instigated by the clergy*, had intervened perfidiously in the hostilities; had attacked by surprise isolated detachments; had indicated to the enemy the positions occupied by the troops; that old men, and even children, had been guilty of horrible atrocities upon wounded and defenseless German soldiers, tearing out their eyes and cutting off fingers, nose or ears; *that the priests from their pulpits had exhorted the people to commit these crimes, promising them as a reward the kingdom of heaven, and had even taken the lead in this barbarity.*

"Public credulity accepted these stories. The highest powers in the state welcomed them without hesitation and endorsed them with their authority . . .

"In this way public opinion in Germany was disturbed and a lively indignation manifested itself, *directed especially against the priests* who were held responsible for the barbarities attributed to the Belgians . . . By a natural diversion *the anger* to which they were a prey *was directed* by the Germans *against the Catholic clergy generally.* Protestants allowed the old religious hatred to be relighted in their minds and delivered themselves to attacks against Catholics. A new *Kulturkampf* was let loose.

---

[3] Fernand van Langenhove, *The Growth of a Legend.* The author is a Belgian sociologist.

"The Catholics did not delay in taking action against this hostile attitude." (Italics mine)[4]

There may have been some sniping. It would be extraordinary if every angry Belgian had rushed to the library, opened a manual of international law, and had informed himself whether he had a right to take potshot at the infernal nuisance tramping through his streets. It would be no less extraordinary if an army that had never been under fire, did not regard every bullet that came its way as unauthorized, because it was inconvenient, and indeed as somehow a violation of the rules of the Kriegspiel, which then constituted its only experience of war. One can imagine the more sensitive bent on convincing themselves that the people to whom they were doing such terrible things must be terrible people. And so the legend may have been spun until it reached the censors and propagandists, who, whether they believed it or not, saw its value, and let it loose on the German civilians. They too were not altogether sorry to find that the people they were outraging were sub-human. And, above all, since the legend came from their heroes, they were not only entitled to believe it, they were unpatriotic if they did not.

But where so much is left to the imagination because the scene of action is lost in the fog of war, there is no check and no control. The legend of the ferocious Belgian priests soon tapped an old hatred. For in the minds of most patriotic protestant Germans, especially of the upper classes, the picture of Bismarck's victories included a long quarrel with the Roman Catholics. By a process of association, Belgian priests became priests, and hatred of Belgians a vent for all their hatreds. These German protestants did what some Americans did when under the stress of war they created a compound object of hatred out of the enemy abroad and all their opponents at home. Against this synthetic enemy, the Hun in Germany and the Hun within the Gate, they launched all the animosity that was in them.

The Catholic resistance to the atrocity tales was, of course, defensive. It was aimed at those particular fictions which aroused animosity against all Catholics, rather than against Belgian Catholics alone. The *Informations Pax*, says M. van Langenhove, had only an ecclesiastical bearing and "confined their attention almost exclusively to the reprehensible acts attributed to the priests." And yet one cannot help wondering a little about what was set in motion in the minds of German Catholics by this revelation of what Bismarck's empire meant in relation to them; and also whether there was any obscure connection between that knowledge and the fact that the prominent

---

[4] *Op. cit.*, pp. 5-7

German politician who was willing in the armistice to sign the death warrant of the empire was Erzberger,[5] the leader of the Catholic Centre Party.

# VIII. Blind Spots and Their Values

## 1

I HAVE been speaking of stereotypes rather than ideals, because the word ideal is usually reserved for what we consider the good, the true and the beautiful. Thus it carries the hint that here is something to be copied or attained. But our repertory of fixed impressions is wider than that. It contains ideal swindlers, ideal Tammany politicians, ideal jingoes, ideal agitators, ideal enemies. Our stereotyped world is not necessarily the world we should like it to be. It is simply the kind of world we expect it to be. If events correspond there is a sense of familiarity, and we feel that we are moving with the movement of events. Our slave must be a slave by nature, if we are Athenians who wish to have no qualms. If we have told our friends that we do eighteen holes of golf in 95, we tell them after doing the course in 110, that we are not ourselves to-day. That is to say, we are not acquainted with the duffer who foozled fifteen strokes.

Most of us would deal with affairs through a rather haphazard and shifting assortment of stereotypes, if a comparatively few men in each generation were not constantly engaged in arranging, standardizing, and improving them into logical systems, known as the Laws of Political Economy, the Principles of Politics, and the like. Generally when we write about culture, tradition, and the group mind, we are thinking of these systems perfected by men of genius. Now there is no disputing the necessity of constant study and criticism of these idealized versions, but the historian of people, the politician, and the publicity man cannot stop there. For what operates in history is not the systematic idea as a genius formulated it, but shifting imitations, replicas, counterfeits, analogies, and distortions in individual minds.

Thus Marxism is not necessarily what Karl Marx wrote in Das Kapital, but whatever it is that all the warring sects believe, who claim to be the faithful. From the gospels you cannot deduce the history of Christianity, nor from the Constitution the political history of America. It is Das Kapital as conceived, the gospels as preached and the preachment as understood, the Constitution as interpreted and administered,

---

[5] Since this was written, Erzberger has been assassinated.

to which you have to go. For while there is a reciprocating influence between the standard version and the current versions, it is these current versions as distributed among men which affect their behavior.[1]

"The theory of Relativity," says a critic whose eyelids, like the Lady Lisa's, are a little weary, "promises to develop into a principle as adequate to universal application as was the theory of Evolution. This latter theory, from being a technical biological hypothesis, became an inspiring guide to workers in practically every branch of knowledge: manners and customs, morals, religions, philosophies, arts, steam engines, electric tramways—everything had 'evolved.' 'Evolution' became a very general term; it also became imprecise until, in many cases, the original, definite meaning of the word was lost, and the theory it had been evoked to describe was misunderstood. We are hardy enough to prophesy a similar career and fate for the theory of Relativity. The technical physical theory, at present imperfectly understood, will become still more vague and dim. History repeats itself, and Relativity, like Evolution, after receiving a number of intelligible but somewhat inaccurate popular expositions in its scientific aspect, will be launched on a world-conquering career. We suggest that, by that time, it will probably be called *Relativismus*. Many of these larger applications will doubtless be justified; some will be absurd and a considerable number will, we imagine, reduce to truisms. And the physical theory, the mere seed of this mighty growth, will become once more the purely technical concern of scientific men."[2]

But for such a world-conquering career an idea must correspond, however imprecisely, to something. Professor Bury shows for how long a time the idea of progress remained a speculative toy. "It is not easy," he writes,[3] "for a new idea of the speculative order to penetrate and

---

[1] But unfortunately it is ever so much harder to know this actual culture than it is to summarize and to comment upon the works of genius. The actual culture exists in people far too busy to indulge in the strange trade of formulating their beliefs. They record them only incidentally, and the student rarely knows how typical are his data. Perhaps the best he can do is to follow Lord Bryce's suggestion [*Modern Democracies*, Vol. I, p. 156] that he move freely "among all sorts and conditions of men," to seek out the unbiassed persons in every neighborhood who have skill in sizing up. "There is a *flair* which long practise and 'sympathetic touch' bestow. The trained observer learns how to profit by small indications, as an old seaman discerns, sooner than the landsman, the signs of coming storm." There is, in short, a vast amount of guess work involved, and it is no wonder that scholars, who enjoy precision, so often confine their attentions to the neater formulations of other scholars.

[2] *The Times* (London), *Literary Supplement*, June 2, 1921, p. 352. Professor Einstein said when he was in America in 1921 that people tended to overestimate the influence of his theory, and to under-estimate its certainty.

[3] J. B. Bury, *The Idea of Progress*, p. 324.

inform the general consciousness of a community until it has assumed some external and concrete embodiment, or is recommended by some striking material evidence. In the case of Progress both these conditions were fulfilled (in England) in the period 1820–1850." The most striking evidence was furnished by the mechanical revolution. "Men who were born at the beginning of the century had seen, before they had passed the age of thirty, the rapid development of steam navigation, the illumination of towns and houses by gas, the opening of the first railway." In the consciousness of the average householder miracles like these formed the pattern of his belief in the perfectibility of the human race.

Tennyson, who was in philosophical matters a fairly normal person, tells us that when he went by the first train from Liverpool to Manchester (1830) he thought that the wheels ran in grooves. Then he wrote this line:

"Let the great world spin forever down the ringing grooves of change."[4]

And so a notion more or less applicable to a journey between Liverpool and Manchester was generalized into a pattern of the universe "for ever." This pattern, taken up by others, reinforced by dazzling inventions, imposed an optimistic turn upon the theory of evolution. That theory, of course, is, as Professor Bury says, neutral between pessimism and optimism. But it promised continual change, and the changes visible in the world marked such extraordinary conquests of nature, that the popular mind made a blend of the two. Evolution first in Darwin himself, and then more elaborately in Herbert Spencer, was a "progress towards perfection."

## 2

The stereotype represented by such words as "progress" and "perfection" was composed fundamentally of mechanical inventions. And mechanical it has remained, on the whole, to this day. In America more than anywhere else, the spectacle of mechanical progress has made so deep an impression, that it has suffused the whole moral code. An American will endure almost any insult except the charge that he is not progressive. Be he of long native ancestry, or a recent immigrant, the aspect that has always struck his eye is the immense physical growth

[4] Tennyson, *Memoir by his Son*, Vol. I, p. 195. Cited by Bury, *op. cit.*, p. 326.

of American civilization. That constitutes a fundamental stereotype through which he views the world: the country village will become the great metropolis, the modest building a skyscraper, what is small shall be big; what is slow shall be fast; what is poor shall be rich; what is few shall be many; whatever is shall be more so.

Not every American, of course, sees the world this way. Henry Adams didn't, and William Allen White doesn't. But those men do, who in the magazines devoted to the religion of success appear as Makers of America. They mean just about that when they preach evolution, progress, prosperity, being constructive, the American way of doing things. It is easy to laugh, but, in fact, they are using a very great pattern of human endeavor. For one thing it adopts an impersonal criterion; for another it adopts an earthly criterion; for a third it is habituating men to think quantitatively. To be sure the ideal confuses excellence with size, happiness with speed, and human nature with contraption. Yet the same motives are at work which have ever actuated any moral code, or ever will. The desire for the biggest, the fastest, the highest, or if you are a maker of wristwatches or microscopes the smallest; the love in short of the superlative and the "peerless," is in essence and possibility a noble passion.

Certainly the American version of progress has fitted an extraordinary range of facts in the economic situation and in human nature. It turned an unusual amount of pugnacity, acquisitiveness, and lust of power into productive work. Nor has it, until more recently perhaps, seriously frustrated the active nature of the active members of the community. They have made a civilization which provides them who made it with what they feel to be ample satisfaction in work, mating and play, and the rush of their victory over mountains, wildernesses, distance, and human competition has even done duty for that part of religious feeling which is a sense of communion with the purpose of the universe. The pattern has been a success so nearly perfect in the sequence of ideals, practice, and results, that any challenge to it is called un-American.

And yet, this pattern is a very partial and inadequate way of representing the world. The habit of thinking about progress as "development" has meant that many aspects of the environment were simply neglected. With the stereotype of "progress" before their eyes, Americans have in the mass seen little that did not accord with that progress. They saw the expansion of cities, but not the accretion of slums; they cheered the census statistics, but refused to consider overcrowding; they pointed with pride to their growth, but would not see the drift from the land, or the unassimilated immigration. They expanded industry furiously at reckless cost to their natural resources; they built up gigantic corporations without arranging for industrial relations. They grew to be one of the most powerful nations on earth without preparing their institutions or their minds for the ending of their isolation. They stumbled into the World War morally and physically unready, and they stumbled out again, much disillusioned, but hardly more experienced.

In the World War the good and the evil influence of the American stereotype was plainly visible. The idea that the war could be won by recruiting unlimited armies, raising unlimited credits, building an unlimited number of ships, producing unlimited munitions, and concentrating without limit on these alone, fitted the traditional stereotype, and resulted in something like a physical miracle.[5] But among those most affected by the stereotype, there was no place for the consideration of what the fruits of victory were, or how they were to be attained. Therefore, aims were ignored, or regarded as automatic, and victory was conceived, because the stereotype demanded it, as nothing but an annihilating victory in the field. In peace time you did not ask what the fastest motor car was for, and in war you did not ask what the completest victory was for. Yet in Paris the pattern did not fit the facts. In peace you can go on endlessly supplanting small things with big ones, and big ones with bigger ones; in war when you have won absolute victory, you cannot go on to a more absolute victory. You have to do something on an entirely different pattern. And if you lack such a pattern, the end of the war is to you what it was to so many good people, an anticlimax in a dreary and savorless world.

This marks the point where the stereotype and the facts, that cannot be ignored, definitely part company. There is always such a point, because our images of how things behave are simpler and more fixed than the ebb and flow of affairs. There comes a time, therefore, when the blind spots come from the edge of vision into the center. Then unless there are critics who have the courage to sound an alarm, and leaders capable of understanding the change, and a people tolerant by habit, the stereotype, instead of economizing effort, and focussing energy as it did in 1917 and 1918, may frustrate effort and waste men's energy by blinding them, as it did for those people who cried for a Carthaginian peace in 1919 and deplored the Treaty of Versailles in 1921.

### 3

Uncritically held, the stereotype not only censors out much that needs to be taken into account, but when the day of reckoning comes, and the stereotype is shattered, likely as not that which it did wisely take

[5] I have in mind the transportation and supply of two million troops overseas. Prof. Wesley Mitchell points out that the total production of goods after our entrance into the war did not greatly increase in volume over that of the year 1916; but that production for war purposes did increase.

into account is ship-wrecked with it. That is the punishment assessed by Mr. Bernard Shaw against Free Trade, Free Contract, Free Competition, Natural Liberty, Laissez-faire, and Darwinism. A hundred years ago, when he would surely have been one of the tartest advocates of these doctrines, he would not have seen them as he sees them to-day, in the Infidel Half Century,[6] to be excuses for "'doing the other fellow down' with impunity, all interference by a guiding government, all organization except police organization to protect legalized fraud against fisticuffs, all attempt to introduce human purpose and design and forethought into the industrial welter being 'contrary to the laws of political economy.'" He would have seen, then, as one of the pioneers of the march to the plains of heaven[7] that, of the kind of human purpose and design and forethought to be found in a government like that of Queen Victoria's uncles, the less the better. He would have seen, not the strong doing the weak down, but the foolish doing the strong down. He would have seen purposes, designs and forethoughts at work, obstructing invention, obstructing enterprise, obstructing what he would infallibly have recognized as the next move of Creative Evolution.

Even now Mr. Shaw is none too eager for the guidance of any guiding government he knows, but in theory he has turned a full loop against laissez-faire. Most advanced thinking before the war had made the same turn against the established notion that if you unloosed everything, wisdom would bubble up, and establish harmony. Since the war, with its definite demonstration of guiding governments, assisted by censors, propagandists, and spies, Roebuck Ramsden and Natural Liberty have been readmitted to the company of serious thinkers.

One thing is common to these cycles. There is in each set of stereotypes a point where effort ceases and things happen of their own accord, as you would like them to. The progressive stereotype, powerful to incite work, almost completely obliterates the attempt to decide what work and why that work. Laissez-faire, a blessed release from stupid officialdom, assumes that men will move by spontaneous combustion towards a pre-established harmony. Collectivism, an antidote to ruthless selfishness, seems, in the Marxian mind, to suppose an economic determinism towards efficiency and wisdom on the part of socialist officials. Strong government, imperialism at home and abroad, at its best deeply conscious of the price of disorder, relies at last on the notion that all that matters to the governed will be known by the governors. In each theory there is a spot of blind automatism.

---

[6] *Back to Methuselah*. Preface.
[7] *The Quintessence of Ibsenism*.

That spot covers up some fact, which if it were taken into account, would check the vital movement that the stereotype provokes. If the progressive had to ask himself, like the Chinaman in the joke, what he wanted to do with the time he saved by breaking the record, if the advocate of laissez-faire had to contemplate not only free and exuberant energies of men, but what some people call their human nature, if the collectivist let the center of his attention be occupied with the problem of how he is to secure his officials, if the imperialist dared to doubt his own inspiration, you would find more Hamlet and less Henry the Fifth. For these blind spots keep away distracting images, which with their attendant emotions, might cause hesitation and infirmity of purpose. Consequently the stereotype not only saves time in a busy life and is a defense of our position in society, but tends to preserve us from all the bewildering effect of trying to see the world steadily and see it whole.

# IX. Codes and Their Enemies

## 1

A NYONE who has stood at the end of a railroad platform waiting for a friend, will recall what queer people he mistook for him. The shape of a hat, a slightly characteristic gait, evoked the vivid picture in his mind's eye. In sleep a tinkle may sound like the pealing of a great bell; the distant stroke of a hammer like a thunderclap. For our constellations of imagery will vibrate to a stimulus that is perhaps but vaguely similar to some aspect of them. They may, in hallucination, flood the whole consciousness. They may enter very little into perception, though I am inclined to think that such an experience is extremely rare and highly sophisticated, as when we gaze blankly at a familiar word or object, and it gradually ceases to be familiar. Certainly for the most part, the way we see things is a combination of what is there and of what we expected to find. The heavens are not the same to an astronomer as to a pair of lovers; a page of Kant will start a different train of thought in a Kantian and in a radical empiricist; the Tahitian belle is a better looking person to her Tahitian suitor than to the readers of the *National Geographic Magazine*.

Expertness in any subject is, in fact, a multiplication of the number of aspects we are prepared to discover, plus the habit of discounting our expectations. Where to the ignoramus all things look alike, and life is just one thing after another, to the specialist things are highly individual. For a chauffeur, an epicure, a connoisseur, a member of the President's cabinet, or a professor's wife, there are evident distinctions and qualities, not at all evident to the casual person who discusses automobiles, wines, old masters, Republicans, and college faculties.

But in our public opinions few can be expert, while life is, as Mr. Bernard Shaw has made plain, so short. Those who are expert are so on only a few topics. Even among the expert soldiers, as we learned during the war, expert cavalrymen were not necessarily brilliant with trench-warfare and tanks. Indeed, sometimes a little expertness on a small topic may simply exaggerate our normal human habit of trying to squeeze into our stereotypes all that can be squeezed, and of casting into outer darkness that which does not fit.

Whatever we recognize as familiar we tend, if we are not very careful, to visualize with the aid of images already in our mind. Thus in the American view of Progress and Success there is a definite picture of human nature and of society. It is the kind of human nature and the kind of society which logically produce the kind of progress that is regarded as ideal. And then, when we seek to describe or explain actually successful men, and events that have really happened, we read back into them the qualities that are presupposed in the stereotypes.

These qualities were standardized rather innocently by the older economists. They set out to describe the social system under which they lived, and found it too complicated for words. So they constructed what they sincerely hoped was a simplified diagram, not so different in principle and in veracity from the parallelogram with legs and head in a child's drawing of a complicated cow. The scheme consisted of a capitalist who had diligently saved capital from his labor, an entrepreneur who conceived a socially useful demand and organized a factory, a collection of workmen who freely contracted, take it or leave it, for their labor, a landlord, and a group of consumers who bought in the cheapest market those goods which by the ready use of the pleasure-pain calculus they knew would give them the most pleasure. The model worked. The kind of people, which the model assumed, living in the sort of world the model assumed, invariably cooperated harmoniously in the books where the model was described.

With modification and embroidery, this pure fiction, used by economists to simplify their thinking, was retailed and popularized until for large sections of the population it prevailed as the economic mythology of the day. It supplied a standard version of capitalist, promoter, worker and consumer in a society that was naturally more bent on achieving success than on explaining it. The buildings which rose, and the bank accounts which accumulated, were evidence that the stereotype of how the thing had been done was accurate. And those who benefited most by success came to believe they were the kind of men they were supposed to be. No wonder that the candid friends of successful men, when they read the official biography and the obituary, have to restrain themselves from asking whether this is indeed their friend.

2

To the vanquished and the victims, the official portraiture was, of course, unrecognizable. For while those who exemplified progress did not often pause to inquire whether they had arrived according to the route laid down by the economists, or by some other just as creditable, the unsuccessful people did inquire. "No one," says William James,[1] "sees further into a generalization than his own knowledge of detail extends." The captains of industry saw in the great trusts monuments of (their) success; their defeated competitors saw the monuments of (their) failure. So the captains expounded the economies and virtues of big business, asked to be let alone, said they were the agents of prosperity, and the developers of trade. The vanquished insisted upon the wastes and brutalities of the trusts, and called loudly upon the Department of Justice to free business from conspiracies. In the same situation one side saw progress, economy, and a splendid development; the other, reaction, extravagance, and a restraint of trade. Volumes of statistics, anecdotes about the real truth and the inside truth, the deeper and the larger truth, were published to prove both sides of the argument.

For when a system of stereotypes is well fixed, our attention is called to those facts which support it, and diverted from those which contradict. So perhaps it is because they are attuned to find it, that kindly people discover so much reason for kindness, malicious people so much malice. We speak quite accurately of seeing through rose-colored spectacles, or with a jaundiced eye. If, as Philip Littell once wrote of a distinguished professor, we see life as through a class darkly, our stereotypes of what the best people and the lower classes are like will not be contaminated by understanding. What is alien will be rejected, what is different will fall upon unseeing eyes. We do not see what our eyes are not accustomed to take into account. Sometimes consciously, more often without knowing it, we are impressed by those facts which fit our philosophy.

3

This philosophy is a more or less organized series of images for describing the unseen world. But not only for describing it. For judging it as well. And, therefore, the stereotypes are loaded with preference, suffused with affection or dislike, attached to fears, lusts, strong wishes, pride, hope. Whatever invokes the stereotype is judged with the appropriate sentiment. Except where we deliberately keep prejudice in suspense, we do not study a man and judge him to be bad. We see a

---

[1] *The Letters of William James*, Vol. I, p. 65.

bad man. We see a dewy morn, a blushing maiden, a sainted priest, a humorless Englishman, a dangerous Red, a carefree bohemian, a lazy Hindu, a wily Oriental, a dreaming Slav, a volatile Irishman, a greedy Jew, a 100% American. In the workaday world that is often the real judgment, long in advance of the evidence, and it contains within itself the conclusion which the evidence is pretty certain to confirm. Neither justice, nor mercy, nor truth, enter into such a judgment, for the judgment has preceded the evidence. Yet a people without prejudices, a people with altogether neutral vision, is so unthinkable in any civilization of which it is useful to think, that no scheme of education could be based upon that ideal. Prejudice can be detected, discounted, and refined, but so long as finite men must compress into a short schooling preparation for dealing with a vast civilization, they must carry pictures of it around with them, and have prejudices. The quality of their thinking and doing will depend on whether those prejudices are friendly, friendly to other people, to other ideas, whether they evoke love of what is felt to be positively good, rather than hatred of what is not contained in their version of the good.

Morality, good taste and good form first standardize and then emphasize certain of these underlying prejudices. As we adjust ourselves to our code, we adjust the facts we see to that code. Rationally, the facts are neutral to all our views of right and wrong. Actually, our canons determine greatly what we shall perceive and how.

For a moral code is a scheme of conduct applied to a number of typical instances. To behave as the code directs is to serve whatever purpose the code pursues. It may be God's will, or the king's, individual salvation in a good, solid, three dimensional paradise, success on earth, or the service of mankind. In any event the makers of the code fix upon certain typical situations, and then by some form of reasoning or intuition, deduce the kind of behavior which would produce the aim they acknowledge. The rules apply where they apply.

But in daily living how does a man know whether his predicament is the one the law-giver had in mind? He is told not to kill. But if his children are attacked, may he kill to stop a killing? The Ten Commandments are silent on the point. Therefore, around every code there is a cloud of interpreters who deduce more specific cases. Suppose, then, that the doctors of the law decide that he may kill in self-defense. For the next man the doubt is almost as great; how does he know that he is defining self-defense correctly, or that he has not misjudged the facts, imagined the attack, and is really the aggressor? Perhaps he has provoked the attack. But what is a provocation? Exactly these confusions infected the minds of most Germans in August, 1914.

Far more serious in the modern world than any difference of moral code is the difference in the assumptions about facts to which the code is applied. Religious, moral and political formulae are nothing like so far apart as the facts assumed by their votaries. Useful discussion, then, instead of comparing ideals, reëxamines the visions of the facts. Thus the rule that you should do unto others as you would have them do unto you rests on the belief that human nature is uniform. Mr. Bernard Shaw's statement that you should not do unto others what you would have them do unto you, because their tastes may be different, rests on the belief that human nature is not uniform. The maxim that competition is the life of trade consists of a whole tome of assumptions about economic motives, industrial relations, and the working of a particular commercial system. The claim that America will never have a merchant marine, unless it is privately owned and managed, assumes a certain proved connection between a certain kind of profit-making and incentive. The justification by the bolshevik propagandist of the dictatorship, espionage, and the terror, because "every state is an apparatus of violence"[2] is an historical judgment, the truth of which is by no means self-evident to a non-communist.

At the core of every moral code there is a picture of human nature, a map of the universe, and a version of history. To human nature (of the sort conceived), in a universe (of the kind imagined), after a history (so understood), the rules of the code apply. So far as the facts of personality, of the environment and of memory are different, by so far the rules of the code are difficult to apply with success. Now every moral code has to conceive human psychology, the material world, and tradition some way or other. But in the codes that are under the influence of science, the conception is known to be an hypothesis, whereas in the codes that come unexamined from the past or bubble up from the caverns of the mind, the conception is not taken as an hypothesis demanding proof or contradiction, but as a fiction accepted without question. In the one case, man is humble about his beliefs, because he knows they are tentative and incomplete; in the other he is dogmatic, because his belief is a completed myth. The moralist who submits to the scientific discipline knows that though he does not know everything, he is in the way of knowing something; the dogmatist, using a myth, believes himself to share part of the insight of omniscience, though he lacks the criteria by which to tell truth from error. For the distinguishing mark of a myth is that truth and error, fact and fable, report and fantasy, are all on the same plane of credibility.

The myth is, then, not necessarily false. It might happen to be wholly true. It may happen to be partly true. If it has affected human conduct a long time, it is almost certain to contain much that is profoundly and

---

[2] See *Two Years of Conflict on the Internal Front*, published by the Russian Socialist Federated Soviet Republic, Moscow, 1920. Translated by Malcolm W. Davis for the *New York Evening Post*, January 15, 1921.

importantly true. What a myth never contains is the critical power to separate its truths from its errors. For that power comes only by realizing that
no human opinion, whatever its supposed origin, is too exalted for the
test of evidence, that every opinion is only somebody's opinion. And if
you ask why the test of evidence is preferable to any other, there is no
answer unless you are willing to use the test in order to test it.

4

The statement is, I think, susceptible of overwhelming proof, that
moral codes assume a particular view of the facts. Under the term
moral codes I include all kinds: personal, family, economic, professional, legal, patriotic, international. At the center of each there is a pattern of stereotypes about psychology, sociology, and history. The same
view of human nature, institutions or tradition rarely persists through
all our codes. Compare, for example, the economic and the patriotic
codes. There is a war supposed to affect all alike. Two men are partners
in business. One enlists, the other takes a war contract. The soldier sacrifices everything, perhaps even his life. He is paid a dollar a day, and
no one says, no one believes, that you could make a better soldier out
of him by any form of economic incentive. That motive disappears out
of his human nature. The contractor sacrifices very little, is paid a
handsome profit over costs, and few say or believe that he would produce the munitions if there were no economic incentive. That may be
unfair to him. The point is that the accepted patriotic code assumes
one kind of human nature, the commercial code another. And the
codes are probably founded on true expectations to this extent, that
when a man adopts a certain code he tends to exhibit the kind of
human nature which the code demands.

That is one reason why it is so dangerous to generalize about human
nature. A loving father can be a sour boss, an earnest municipal
reformer, and a rapacious jingo abroad. His family life, his business
career, his politics, and his foreign policy rest on totally different versions of what others are like and of how he should act. These versions
differ by codes in the same person, the codes differ somewhat among
persons in the same social set, differ widely as between social sets, and
between two nations, or two colors, may differ to the point where there
is no common assumption whatever. That is why people professing the
same stock of religious beliefs can go to war. The element of their belief
which determines conduct is that view of the facts which they assume.

That is where codes enter so subtly and so pervasively into the making of public opinion. The orthodox theory holds that a public opinion
constitutes a moral judgment on a group of facts. The theory I am
suggesting is that, in the present state of education, a public opinion is

primarily a moralized and codified version of the facts. I am arguing that the pattern of stereotypes at the center of our codes largely determines what group of facts we shall see, and in what light we shall see them. That is why, with the best will in the world, the news policy of a journal tends to support its editorial policy; why a capitalist sees one set of facts, and certain aspects of human nature, literally sees them; his socialist opponent another set and other aspects, and why each regards the other as unreasonable or perverse, when the real difference between them is a difference of perception. That difference is imposed by the difference between the capitalist and socialist pattern of stereotypes. "There are no classes in America," writes an American editor. "The history of all hitherto existing society is the history of class struggles," says the Communist Manifesto. If you have the editor's pattern in your mind, you will see vividly the facts that confirm it, vaguely and ineffectively those that contradict. If you have the communist pattern, you will not only look for different things, but you will see with a totally different emphasis what you and the editor happen to see in common.

## 5

And since my moral system rests on my accepted version of the facts, he who denies either my moral judgments or my version of the facts, is to me perverse, alien, dangerous. How shall I account for him? The opponent has always to be explained, and the last explanation that we ever look for is that he sees a different set of facts. Such an explanation we avoid, because it saps the very foundation of our own assurance that we have seen life steadily and seen it whole. It is only when we are in the habit of recognizing our opinions as a partial experience seen through our stereotypes that we become truly tolerant of an opponent. Without that habit, we believe in the absolutism of our own vision, and consequently in the treacherous character of all opposition. For while men are willing to admit that there are two sides to a "question," they do not believe that there are two sides to what they regard as a "fact." And they never do believe it until after long critical education, they are fully conscious of how second-hand and subjective is their apprehension of their social data.

So where two factions see vividly each its own aspect, and contrive their own explanations of what they see, it is almost impossible for them to credit each other with honesty. If the pattern fits their experience at a crucial point, they no longer look upon it as an interpretation. They look upon it as "reality." It may not resemble the reality, except that it culminates in a conclusion which fits a real experience. I may represent my trip from New York to Boston by a straight line on a map, just as a man may regard his triumph as the end of a straight and narrow path. The road by which I actually went to Boston may have involved many detours, much turning and twisting, just as his road may have involved much besides pure enterprise, labor and thrift. But provided I reach Boston and he succeeds, the airline and the straight path will serve as ready made charts. Only when somebody tries to follow them, and does not arrive, do we have to answer objections. If we insist on our charts, and he insists on rejecting them, we soon tend to regard him as a dangerous fool, and he to regard us as liars and hypocrites. Thus we gradually paint portraits of each other. For the opponent presents himself as the man who says, evil be thou my good. He is an annoyance who does not fit into the scheme of things. Nevertheless he interferes. And since that scheme is based in our minds on incontrovertible fact fortified by irresistible logic, some place has to be found for him in the scheme. Rarely in politics or industrial disputes is a place made for him by the simple admission that he has looked upon the same reality and seen another aspect of it. That would shake the whole scheme.

Thus to the Italians in Paris Fiume was Italian. It was not merely a city that it would be desirable to include within the Italian kingdom. It was Italian. They fixed their whole mind upon the Italian majority within the legal boundaries of the city itself. The American delegates, having seen more Italians in New York than there are in Fiume, without regarding New York as Italian, fixed their eyes on Fiume as a central European port of entry. They saw vividly the Jugoslavs in the suburbs and the non-Italian hinterland. Some of the Italians in Paris were therefore in need of a convincing explanation of the American perversity. They found it in a rumor which started, no one knows where, that an influential American diplomat was in the snares of a Jugoslav mistress. She had been seen. . . . He had been seen. . . . At Versailles just off the boulevard. . . . The villa with the large trees.

This is a rather common way of explaining away opposition. In their more libelous form such charges rarely reach the printed page, and a Roosevelt may have to wait years, or a Harding months, before he can force an issue, and end a whispering campaign that has reached into every circle of talk. Public men have to endure a fearful amount of poisonous clubroom, dinner table, boudoir slander, repeated, elaborated, chuckled over, and regarded as delicious. While this sort of thing is, I believe, less prevalent in America than in Europe, yet rare is the American official about whom somebody is not repeating a scandal.

Out of the opposition we make villains and conspiracies. If prices go up unmercifully the profiteers have conspired; if the newspapers misrepresent the news, there is a capitalist plot; if the rich are too rich, they have been stealing; if a closely fought election is lost, the electorate was corrupted; if a statesman does something of which you disapprove, he has been bought or influenced by some discreditable person. If workingmen are restless, they are the victims of agitators; if they are restless over wide areas, there is a conspiracy on foot. If you do not produce enough aeroplanes, it is the work of spies; if there is trouble in Ireland, it is German or Bolshevik "gold." And if you go stark, staring mad looking for plots, you see all strikes, the Plumb plan, Irish rebellion, Mohammedan unrest, the restoration of King Constantine, the League of Nations, Mexican disorder, the movement to reduce armaments, Sunday movies, short skirts, evasion of the liquor laws, Negro self-assertion, as sub-plots under some grandiose plot engineered either by Moscow, Rome, the Free Masons, the Japanese, or the Elders of Zion.

# X. The Detection of Stereotypes

## 1

SKILLED diplomatists, compelled to talk out loud to the warring peoples, learned how to use a large repertory of stereotypes. They were dealing with a precarious alliance of powers, each of which was maintaining its war unity only by the most careful leadership. The ordinary soldier and his wife, heroic and selfless beyond anything in the chronicles of courage, were still not heroic enough to face death gladly for all the ideas which were said by the foreign offices of foreign powers to be essential to the future of civilization. There were ports, and mines, rocky mountain passes, and villages that few soldiers would willingly have crossed No Man's Land to obtain for their allies.

Now it happened in one nation that the war party which was in control of the foreign office, the high command, and most of the press, had claims on the territory of several of its neighbors. These claims were called the Greater Ruritania by the cultivated classes who regarded Kipling, Treitschke, and Maurice Barrès as one hundred percent Ruritanian. But the grandiose idea aroused no enthusiasm abroad. So holding this finest flower of the Ruritanian genius, as their poet laureate said, to their hearts, Ruritania's statesmen went forth to divide and conquer. They divided the claim into sectors. For each piece they invoked that stereotype which some one or more of their allies found it difficult to resist, because that ally had claims for which it hoped to find approval by the use of this same stereotype.

The first sector happened to be a mountainous region inhabited by alien peasants. Ruritania demanded it to complete her natural geographical frontier. If you fixed your attention long enough on the ineffable value of what is natural, those alien peasants just dissolved into fog, and only the slope of the mountains was visible. The next sector was inhabited by Ruritanians, and on the principle that no people ought to live under alien rule, they were re-annexed. Then came a city of considerable commercial importance, not inhabited by Ruritanians. But until the Eighteenth Century it had been part of Ruritania, and on the principle of Historic Right it was annexed. Farther on there was a splendid mineral deposit owned by aliens and worked by aliens. On the principle of reparation for damage it was annexed. Beyond this there was a territory inhabited 97% by aliens, constituting the natural geographical frontier of another nation, never historically a part of Ruritania. But one of the provinces which had been federated into Ruritania had formerly traded in those markets, and the upper class culture was Ruritanian. On the principle of cultural superiority and the necessity of defending civilization, the lands were claimed. Finally, there was a port wholly disconnected from Ruritania geographically, ethnically, economically, historically, traditionally. It was demanded on the ground that it was needed for national defense.

In the treaties that concluded the Great War you can multiply examples of this kind. Now I do not wish to imply that I think it was possible to resettle Europe consistently on any one of these principles. I am certain that it was not. The very use of these principles, so pretentious and so absolute, meant that the spirit of accommodation did not prevail and that, therefore, the substance of peace was not there. For the moment you start to discuss factories, mines, mountains, or even political authority, as perfect examples of some eternal principle or other, you are not arguing, you are fighting. That eternal principle censors out all the objections, isolates the issue from its background and its context, and sets going in you some strong emotion, appropriate enough to the principle, highly inappropriate to the docks, warehouses, and real estate. And having started in that mood you cannot stop. A real danger exists. To meet it you have to invoke more absolute principles in order to defend what is open to attack. Then you have to defend the defenses, erect buffers, and buffers for the buffers, until the whole affair is so scrambled that it seems less dangerous to fight than to keep on talking.

There are certain clues which often help in detecting the false absolutism of a stereotype. In the case of the Ruritanian propaganda the principles blanketed each other so rapidly that one could readily see how the argument had been constructed. The series of contradictions showed that for each sector that stereotype was employed which would obliterate all the facts that interfered with the claim. Contradiction of this sort is often a good clue.

2

Inability to take account of space is another. In the spring of 1918, for example, large numbers of people, appalled by the withdrawal of

Russia, demanded the "reëstablishment of an Eastern Front." The war, as they had conceived it, was on two fronts, and when one of them disappeared there was an instant demand that it be recreated. The unemployed Japanese army was to man the front, substituting for the Russian. But there was one insuperable obstacle. Between Vladivostok and the eastern battleline there were five thousand miles of country, spanned by one broken down railway. Yet those five thousand miles would not stay in the minds of the enthusiasts. So overwhelming was their conviction that an eastern front was needed, and so great their confidence in the valor of the Japanese army, that, mentally, they had projected that army from Vladivostok to Poland on a magic carpet. In vain our military authorities argued that to land troops on the rim of Siberia had as little to do with reaching the Germans, as climbing from the cellar to the roof of the Woolworth building had to do with reaching the moon.

The stereotype in this instance was the war on two fronts. Ever since men had begun to imagine the Great War they had conceived Germany held between France and Russia. One generation of strategists, and perhaps two, had lived with that visual image as the starting point of all their calculations. For nearly four years every battle-map they saw had deepened the impression that this was the war. When affairs took a new turn, it was not easy to see them as they were then. They were seen through the stereotype, and facts which conflicted with it, such as the distance from Japan to Poland, were incapable of coming vividly into consciousness.

It is interesting to note that the American authorities dealt with the new facts more realistically than the French. In part, this was because (previous to 1914) they had no preconception of a war upon the continent; in part because the Americans, engrossed in the mobilization of their forces, had a vision of the western front which was itself a stereotype that excluded from *their* consciousness any very vivid sense of the other theatres of war. In the spring of 1918 this American view could not compete with the traditional French view, because while the Americans believed enormously in their own powers, the French at that time (before Cantigny and the Second Marne) had the gravest doubts. The American confidence suffused the American stereotype, gave it that power to possess consciousness, that liveliness and sensible pungency, that stimulating effect upon the will, that emotional interest as an object of desire, that congruity with the activity in hand, which James notes as characteristic of what we regard as "real."[1] The French in despair remained fixed on their accepted image. And when facts,

---

[1] *Principles of Psychology*, Vol. II, p. 300.

gross geographical facts, would not fit with the preconception, they were either censored out of mind, or the facts were themselves stretched out of shape. Thus the difficulty of the Japanese reaching the Germans five thousand miles away was, in measure, overcome by bringing the Germans more than half way to meet them. Between March and June 1918, there was supposed to be a German army operating in Eastern Siberia. This phantom army consisted of some German prisoners actually seen, more German prisoners thought about, and chiefly of the delusion that those five thousand intervening miles did not really exist.[2]

## 3

A true conception of space is not a simple matter. If I draw a straight line on a map between Bombay and Hong Kong and measure the distance, I have learned nothing whatever about the distance I should have to cover on a voyage. And even if I measure the actual distance that I must traverse, I still know very little until I know what ships are in the service, when they run, how fast they go, whether I can secure accommodation and afford to pay for it. In practical life space is a matter of available transportation, not of geometrical planes, as the old railroad magnate knew when he threatened to make grass grow in the streets of a city that had offended him. If I am motoring and ask how far it is to my destination, I curse as an unmitigated booby the man who tells me it is three miles, and does not mention a six mile detour. It does me no good to be told that it is three miles if you walk. I might as well be told it is one mile as the crow flies. I do not fly like a crow, and I am not walking either. I must know that it is nine miles for a motor car, and also, if that is the case, that six of them are ruts and puddles. I call the pedestrian a nuisance who tells me it is three miles and think evil of the aviator who told me it was one mile. Both of them are talking about the space they have to cover, not the space I must cover.

In the drawing of boundary lines absurd complications have arisen through failure to conceive the practical geography of a region. Under

---

[2] See in this connection Mr. Charles Grasty's interview with Marshal Foch, *New York Times*, February 26, 1918.

"Germany is walking through Russia. America and Japan, who are in a position to do so, should go to meet her in Siberia."

See also the resolution by Senator King of Utah, June 10, 1918, and Mr. Taft's statement in the *New York Times*, June 11, 1918, and the appeal to America on May 5, 1918, by Mr. A. J. Sack, Director of the Russian Information Bureau: "If Germany were in the Allied place . . . she would have 3,000,000 fighting on the East front within a year."

some general formula like self-determination statesmen have at various times drawn lines on maps, which, when surveyed on the spot, ran through the middle of a factory, down the center of a village street, diagonally across the nave of a church, or between the kitchen and bedroom of a peasant's cottage. There have been frontiers in a grazing country which separated pasture from water, pasture from market, and in an industrial country, railheads from railroad. On the colored ethnic map the line was ethnically just, that is to say, just in the world of that ethnic map.

4

But time, no less than space, fares badly. A common example is that of the man who tries by making an elaborate will to control his money long after his death. "It had been the purpose of the first William James," writes his great-grandson Henry James,[3] "to provide that his children (several of whom were under age when he died) should qualify themselves by industry and experience to enjoy the large patrimony which he expected to bequeath to them, and with that in view he left a will which was a voluminous compound of restraints and instructions. He showed thereby how great were both his confidence in his own judgment and his solicitude for the moral welfare of his descendants." The courts upset the will. For the law in its objection to perpetuities recognizes that there are distinct limits to the usefulness of allowing anyone to impose his moral stencil upon an unknown future. But the desire to impose it is a very human trait, so human that the law permits it to operate for a limited time after death.

The amending clause of any constitution is a good index of the confidence the authors entertained about the reach of their opinions in the succeeding generations. There are, I believe, American state constitutions which are almost incapable of amendment. The men who made them could have had but little sense of the flux of time: to them the Here and Now was so brilliantly certain, the Hereafter so vague or so terrifying, that they had the courage to say how life should run after they were gone. And then because constitutions are difficult to amend, zealous people with a taste for mortmain have loved to write on this imperishable brass all kinds of rules and restrictions that, given any decent humility about the future, ought to be no more permanent than an ordinary statute.

A presumption about time enters widely into our opinions. To one

---

[3] *The Letters of William James*, Vol. I, p. 6.

person an institution which has existed for the whole of his conscious life is part of the permanent furniture of the universe: to another it is ephemeral. Geological time is very different from biological time. Social time is most complex. The statesman has to decide whether to calculate for the emergency or for the long run. Some decisions have to be made on the basis of what will happen in the next two hours; others on what will happen in a week, a month, a season, a decade, when the children have grown up, or their children's children. An important part of wisdom is the ability to distinguish the time-conception that properly belongs to the thing in hand. The person who uses the wrong time-conception ranges from the dreamer who ignores the present to the philistine who can see nothing else. A true scale of values has a very acute sense of relative time.

Distant time, past and future, has somehow to be conceived. But as James says, "of the longer duration we have no direct 'realizing' sense."[4] The longest duration which we immediately feel is what is called the "specious present." It endures, according to Titchener, for about six seconds.[5] "All impressions within this period of time are present to us *at once*. This makes it possible for us to perceive changes and events as well as stationary objects. The perceptual present is supplemented by the ideational present. Through the combination of perceptions with memory images, entire days, months, and even years of the past are brought together into the present."

In this ideational present, vividness, as James said, is proportionate to the number of discriminations we perceive within it. Thus a vacation in which we were bored with nothing to do passes slowly while we are in it, but seems very short in memory. Great activity kills time rapidly, but in memory its duration is long. On the relation between the amount we discriminate and our time perspective James has an interesting passage:[6]

"We have every reason to think that creatures may possibly differ enormously in the amounts of duration which they intuitively feel, and in the fineness of the events that may fill it. Von Baer has indulged in some interesting computations of the effect of such differences in changing the aspect of Nature. Suppose we were able, within the length of a second, to note 10,000 events distinctly, instead of barely 10 as now;[7] if our life were then destined to hold the same number of impressions, it might be 1000 times as short. We should live less than a

---

[4] *Principles of Psychology*, Vol. I, p. 638.
[5] Cited by Warren, *Human Psychology*, p. 255.
[6] *Op. cit.*, Vol. I, p. 639.
[7] In the moving picture this effect is admirably produced by the ultra-rapid camera.

month, and personally know nothing of the change of seasons. If born in winter, we should believe in summer as we now believe in the heats of the carboniferous era. The motions of organic beings would be so slow to our senses as to be inferred, not seen. The sun would stand still in the sky, the moon be almost free from change, and so on. But now reverse the hypothesis and suppose a being to get only one 1000th part of the sensations we get in a given time, and consequently to live 1000 times as long. Winters and summers will be to him like quarters of an hour. Mushrooms and the swifter growing plants will shoot into being so rapidly as to appear instantaneous creations; annual shrubs will rise and fall from the earth like restless boiling water springs; the motions of animals will be as invisible as are to us the movements of bullets and cannon-balls; the sun will scour through the sky like a meteor, leaving a fiery trail behind him, etc."

## 5

In his Outline of History Mr. Wells has made a gallant effort to visualize "the true proportions of historical to geological time"[8] On a scale which represents the time from Columbus to ourselves by three inches of space, the reader would have to walk 55 feet to see the date of the painters of the Altamara caves, 550 feet to see the earlier Neanderthalers, a mile or so to the last of the dinosaurs. More or less precise chronology does not begin until after 1000 B.C., and at that time "Sargon I of the Akkadian-Sumerian Empire was a remote memory, . . . more remote than is Constantine the Great from the world of the present day. . . . Hammurabi had been dead a thousand years. . . . Stonehedge in England was already a thousand years old."

Mr. Wells was writing with a purpose. "In the brief period of ten thousand years these units (into which men have combined) have grown from the small family tribe of the early neolithic culture to the vast united realms—vast yet still too small and partial—of the present time." Mr. Wells hoped by changing the time perspective on our present problems to change the moral perspective. Yet the astronomical measure of time, the geological, the biological, any telescopic measure which minimizes the present is not "more true" than a microscopic. Mr. Simeon Strunsky is right when he insists that "if Mr. Wells is thinking of his subtitle, The Probable Future of Mankind, he is entitled to ask for any number of centuries to work out his solution. If he is thinking of the salvaging of this western civilization, reeling under the

---

[8] Vol. II, p. 605. See also James Harvey Robinson, *The New History*, p. 239.

effects of the Great War, he must think in decades and scores of years."[9]
It all depends upon the practical purpose for which you adopt the measure. There are situations when the time perspective needs to be
lengthened, and others when it needs to be shortened.

The man who says that it does not matter if 15,000,000 Chinese die
of famine, because in two generations the birthrate will make up the
loss, has used a time perspective to excuse his inertia. A person who
pauperizes a healthy young man because he is sentimentally overim-
pressed with an immediate difficulty has lost sight of the duration of the
beggar's life. The people who for the sake of an immediate peace are
willing to buy off an aggressive empire by indulging its appetite have
allowed a specious present to interfere with the peace of their children.
The people who will not be patient with a troublesome neighbor, who
want to bring everything to a "showdown," are no less the victims of a
specious present.


6


Into almost every social problem the proper calculation of time
enters. Suppose, for example, it is a question of timber. Some trees
grow faster than others. Then a sound forest policy is one in which the
amount of each species and of each age cut in each season is made
good by replanting. In so far as that calculation is correct the truest
economy has been reached. To cut less is waste, and to cut more is
exploitation. But there may come an emergency, say the need for aero-
plane spruce in a war, when the year's allowance must be exceeded. An
alert government will recognize that and regard the restoration of the
balance as a charge upon the future.

Coal involves a different theory of time, because coal, unlike a tree,
is produced on the scale of geological time. The supply is limited.
Therefore a correct social policy involves intricate computation of
the available reserves of the world, the indicated possibilities, the present rate of use, the present economy of use, and the alternative fuels.
But when that computation has been reached it must finally be
squared with an ideal standard involving time. Suppose, for example,
that engineers conclude that the present fuels are being exhausted at
a certain rate; that barring new discoveries industry will have to enter
a phase of contraction at some definite time in the future. We have
then to determine how much thrift and self-denial we will use, after
all feasible economies have been exercised, in order not to rob pos-

---

[9] In a review of *The Salvaging of Civilization, The Literary Review of the N. Y. Evening
Post*, June 18, 1921, p. 5.

terity. But what shall we consider posterity? Our grandchildren? Our great-grandchildren? Perhaps we shall decide to calculate on a hundred years, believing that to be ample time for the discovery of alternative fuels if the necessity is made clear at once. The figures are, of course, hypothetical. But in calculating that way we shall be employing what reason we have. We shall be giving social time its place in public opinion. Let us now imagine a somewhat different case: a contract between a city and a trolley-car company. The company says that it will not invest its capital unless it is granted a monopoly of the main highway for ninety-nine years. In the minds of the men who make that demand ninety-nine years is so long as to mean "forever." But suppose there is reason to think that surface cars, run from a central power plant on tracks, are going out of fashion in twenty years. Then it is a most unwise contract to make, for you are virtually condemning a future generation to inferior transportation. In making such a contract the city officials lack a realizing sense of ninety-nine years. Far better to give the company a subsidy now in order to attract capital than to stimulate investment by indulging a fallacious sense of eternity. No city official and no company official has a sense of real time when he talks about ninety-nine years.

Popular history is a happy hunting ground of time confusions. To the average Englishman, for example, the behavior of Cromwell, the corruption of the Act of Union, the Famine of 1847 are wrongs suffered by people long dead and done by actors long dead with whom no living person, Irish or English, has any real connection. But in the mind of a patriotic Irishman these same events are almost contemporary. His memory is like one of those historical paintings, where Virgil and Dante sit side by side conversing. These perspectives and foreshortenings are a great barrier between peoples. It is ever so difficult for a person of one tradition to remember what is contemporary in the tradition of another.

Almost nothing that goes by the name of Historic Rights or Historic Wrongs can be called a truly objective view of the past. Take, for example, the Franco-German debate about Alsace-Lorraine. It all depends on the original date you select. If you start with the Rauraci and Sequani, the lands are historically part of Ancient Gaul. If you prefer Henry I, they are historically a German territory; if you take 1273 they belong to the House of Austria; if you take 1648 and the Peace of Westphalia, most of them are French; if you take Louis XIV and the year 1688 they are almost all French. If you are using the argument from history you are fairly certain to select those dates in the past which support your view of what should be done now.

Arguments about "races" and nationalities often betray the same arbitrary view of time. During the war, under the influence of powerful feeling, the difference between "Teutons" on the one hand, and

"Anglo-Saxons" and French on the other, was popularly believed to be an eternal difference. They had always been opposing races. Yet a generation ago, historians, like Freeman, were emphasizing the common Teutonic origin of the West European peoples, and ethnologists would certainly insist that the Germans, English, and the greater part of the French are branches of what was once a common stock. The general rule is: if you like a people to-day you come down the branches to the trunk; if you dislike them you insist that the separate branches are separate trunks. In one case you fix your attention on the period before they were distinguishable; in the other on the period after which they became distinct. And the view which fits the mood is taken as the "truth."

An amiable variation is the family tree. Usually one couple are appointed the original ancestors, if possible, a couple associated with an honorific event like the Norman Conquest. That couple have no ancestors. They are not descendants. Yet they were the descendants of ancestors, and the expression that So-and-So was the founder of his house means not that he is the Adam of his family, but that he is the particular ancestor from whom it is desirable to start, or perhaps the earliest ancestor of which there is a record. But genealogical tables exhibit a deeper prejudice. Unless the female line happens to be especially remarkable descent is traced down through the males. The tree is male. At various moments females accrue to it as itinerant bees light upon an ancient apple tree.

7

But the future is the most illusive time of all. Our temptation here is to jump over necessary steps in the sequence; and as we are governed by hope or doubt, to exaggerate or to minimize the time required to complete various parts of a process. The discussion of the role to be exercised by wage-earners in the management of industry is riddled with this difficulty. For management is a word that covers many functions.[10] Some of these require no training; some require a little training; others can be learned only in a lifetime. And the truly discriminating program of industrial democratization would be one based on the proper time sequence, so that the assumption of responsibility would run parallel to a complementary program of industrial training. The proposal for a

---

[10] *Cf.* Carter L. Goodrich, *The Frontier of Control.*

sudden dictatorship of the proletariat is an attempt to do away with the intervening time of preparation; the resistance to all sharing of responsibility an attempt to deny the alteration of human capacity in the course of time. Primitive notions of democracy, such as rotation in office, and contempt for the expert, are really nothing but the old myth that the Goddess of Wisdom sprang mature and fully armed from the brow of Jove. They assume that what it takes years to learn need not be learned at all.

Whenever the phrase "backward people" is used as the basis of a policy, the conception of time is a decisive element. The Covenant of the League of Nations says,[11] for example, that "the character of the mandate must differ according to the stage of the development of the people," as well as on other grounds. Certain communities, it asserts, "have reached a stage of development" where their independence can be provisionally recognized, subject to advice and assistance "until such time as they are able to stand alone." The way in which the mandatories and the mandated conceive that time will influence deeply their relations. Thus in the case of Cuba the judgment of the American government virtually coincided with that of the Cuban patriots, and though there has been trouble, there is no finer page in the history of how strong powers have dealt with the weak. Oftener in that history the estimates have not coincided. Where the imperial people, whatever its public expressions, has been deeply convinced that the backwardness of the backward was so hopeless as not to be worth remedying, or so profitable that it was not desirable to remedy it, the tie has festered and poisoned the peace of the world. There have been a few cases, very few, where backwardness has meant to the ruling power the need for a program of forwardness, a program with definite standards and definite estimates of time. Far more frequently, so frequently in fact as to seem the rule, backwardness has been conceived as an intrinsic and eternal mark of inferiority. And then every attempt to be less backward has been frowned upon as the sedition, which, under these conditions, it undoubtedly is. In our own race wars we can see some of the results of the failure to realize that time would gradually obliterate the slave morality of the Negro, and that social adjustment based on this morality would begin to break down.

It is hard not to picture the future as if it obeyed our present purposes, to annihilate whatever delays our desire, or immortalize whatever stands between us and our fears.

---

[11] Article XIX.

# 8

In putting together our public opinions, not only do we have to picture more space than we can see with our eyes, and more time than we can feel, but we have to describe and judge more people, more actions, more things than we can ever count, or vividly imagine. We have to summarize and generalize. We have to pick out samples, and treat them as typical.

To pick fairly a good sample of a large class is not easy. The problem belongs to the science of statistics, and it is a most difficult affair for anyone whose mathematics is primitive, and mine remain azoic in spite of the half dozen manuals which I once devoutly imagined that I understood. All they have done for me is to make me a little more conscious of how hard it is to classify and to sample, how readily we spread a little butter over the whole universe.

Some time ago a group of social workers in Sheffield, England, started out to substitute an accurate picture of the mental equipment of the workers of that city for the impressionistic one they had.[12] They wished to say, with some decent grounds for saying it, how the workers of Sheffield were equipped. They found, as we all find the moment we refuse to let our first notion prevail, that they were beset with complications. Of the test they employed nothing need be said here except that it was a large questionnaire. For the sake of the illustration, assume that the questions were a fair test of mental equipment for English city life. Theoretically, then, those questions should have been put to every member of the working class. But it is not so easy to know who are the working class. However, assume again that the census knows how to classify them. Then there were roughly 104,000 men and 107,000 women who ought to have been questioned. They possessed the answers which would justify or refute the casual phrase about the "ignorant workers" or the "intelligent workers." But nobody could think of questioning the whole two hundred thousand.

So the social workers consulted an eminent statistician, Professor Bowley. He advised them that not less than 408 men and 408 women would prove to be a fair sample. According to mathematical calculation this number would not show a greater deviation from the average than 1 in 22.[13] They had, therefore, to question at least 816 people before they could pretend to talk about the average workingman. But which 816 people should they approach? "We might have gathered particulars concerning workers to whom one or another of us had a pre-

---

[12] *The Equipment of the Worker.*
[13] *Op. cit.*, footnote, p. 65.

inquiry access; we might have worked through philanthropic gentlemen and ladies who were in contact with certain sections of workers at
a club, a mission, an infirmary, a place of worship, a settlement. But
such a method of selection would produce entirely worthless results.
The workers thus selected would not be in any sense representative of
what is popularly called 'the average run of workers;' they would represent nothing but the little coteries to which they belonged.

"The right way of securing 'victims,' to which at immense cost of time
and labour we rigidly adhered, is to get hold of your workers by some
'neutral' or 'accidental' or 'random' method of approach." This they did.
And after all these precautions they came to no more definite conclusion
than that on their classification and according to their questionnaire,
among 200,000 Sheffield workers "about one quarter" were "well
equipped," "approaching three-quarters" were "inadequately equipped"
and that "about one-fifteenth" were "mal-equipped."

Compare this conscientious and almost pedantic method of arriving
at an opinion, with our usual judgments about masses of people, about
the volatile Irish, and the logical French, and the disciplined Germans,
and the ignorant Slavs, and the honest Chinese, and the untrustworthy
Japanese, and so on and so on. All these are generalizations drawn
from samples, but the samples are selected by a method that statisti-
cally is wholly unsound. Thus the employer will judge labor by the
most troublesome employee or the most docile that he knows, and
many a radical group has imagined that it was a fair sample of the working class. How many women's views on the "servant question" are little
more than the reflection of their own treatment of their servants? The
tendency of the casual mind is to pick out or stumble upon a sample
which supports or defies its prejudices, and then to make it the representative of a whole class.

A great deal of confusion arises when people decline to classify
themselves as we have classified them. Prophecy would be so much
easier if only they would stay where we put them. But, as a matter of
fact, a phrase like the working class will cover only some of the truth
for a part of the time. When you take all the people, below a certain
level of income, and call them the working class, you cannot help
assuming that the people so classified will behave in accordance with
your stereotype. Just who those people are you are not quite certain.
Factory hands and mine workers fit in more or less, but farm hands,
small farmers, peddlers, little shop keepers, clerks, servants, soldiers,
policemen, firemen slip out of the net. The tendency, when you are
appealing to the "working class," is to fix your attention on two or three
million more or less confirmed trade unionists, and treat them as
Labor; the other seventeen or eighteen million, who might qualify sta-
tistically, are tacitly endowed with the point of view ascribed to the
organized nucleus. How very misleading it was to impute to the British

working class in 1918–1921 the point of view expressed in the resolutions of the Trades Union Congress or in the pamphlets written by intellectuals.

The stereotype of Labor as Emancipator selects the evidence which supports itself and rejects the other. And so parallel with the real movements of working men there exists a fiction of the Labor Movement, in which an idealized mass moves towards an ideal goal. The fiction deals with the future. In the future possibilities are almost indistinguishable from probabilities and probabilities from certainties. If the future is long enough, the human will might turn what is just conceivable into what is very likely, and what is likely into what is sure to happen. James called this the faith ladder, and said that "it is a slope of goodwill on which in the larger questions of life men habitually live."[14]

> "1. There is nothing absurd in a certain view of the world being true, nothing contradictory;
>    2. It *might* have been true under certain conditions;
>    3. It *may* be true even now;
>    4. It is *fit* to be true;
>    5. It *ought* to be true;
>    6. It *must* be true;
>    7. It *shall* be true, at any rate true for me."

And, as he added in another place,[15] "your acting thus may in certain special cases be a means of making it securely true in the end." Yet no one would have insisted more than he, that, so far as we know how, we must avoid substituting the goal for the starting point, must avoid reading back into the present what courage, effort, and skill might create in the future. Yet this truism is inordinately difficult to live by, because every one of us is so little trained in the selection of our samples.

If we believe that a certain thing ought to be true, we can almost always find either an instance where it is true, or someone who believes it ought to be true. It is ever so hard when a concrete fact illustrates a hope to weigh that fact properly. When the first six people we meet agree with us, it is not easy to remember that they may all have read the same newspaper at breakfast. And yet we cannot send out a questionnaire to 816 random samples every time we wish to estimate a probability. In dealing with any large mass of facts, the presumption is against our having picked true samples, if we are acting on a casual impression.

---

[14] William James, *Some Problems of Philosophy*, p. 224.
[15] *A Pluralistic Universe*, p. 329.

9

And when we try to go one step further in order to seek the causes
and effects of unseen and complicated affairs, haphazard opinion is
very tricky. There are few big issues in public life where cause and
effect are obvious at once. They are not obvious to scholars who have
devoted years, let us say, to studying business cycles, or price and wage
movements, or the migration and the assimilation of peoples, or the
diplomatic purposes of foreign powers. Yet somehow we are all supposed to have opinions on these matters, and it is not surprising that the
commonest form of reasoning is the intuitive, post hoc ergo propter
hoc.

The more untrained a mind, the more readily it works out a theory
that two things which catch its attention at the same time are causally
connected. We have already dwelt at some length on the way things
reach our attention. We have seen that our access to information is
obstructed and uncertain, and that our apprehension is deeply controlled by our stereotypes; that the evidence available to our reason is
subject to illusions of defense, prestige, morality, space, time, and sampling. We must note now that with this initial taint, public opinions are
still further beset, because in a series of events seen mostly through
stereotypes, we readily accept sequence or parallelism as equivalent to
cause and effect.

This is most likely to happen when two ideas that come together
arouse the same feeling. If they come together they are likely to arouse
the same feeling; and even when they do not arrive together a powerful feeling attached to one is likely to suck out of all the corners of
memory any idea that feels about the same. Thus everything painful
tends to collect into one system of cause and effect, and likewise everything pleasant.

> "IId IIm (1675) This day I hear that G[od] has shot an arrow into the
> midst of this Town. The small pox is in an ordinary $y^e$ sign of the Swan,
> the ordinary Keepers name is Windsor. His daughter is sick of the dis-
> ease. It is observable that this disease begins at an alehouse, to testify
> God's displeasure $ag^t$ the sin of drunkenness & $y^t$ of multiplying ale-
> houses!"[16]

Thus Increase Mather, and thus in the year 1919 a distinguished
Professor of Celestial Mechanics discussing the Einstein theory:

---

[16] *The Heart of the Puritan*, p. 177, edited by Elizabeth Deering Hanscom.

"It may well be that. . . . Bolshevist uprisings are in reality the visible objects of some underlying, deep, mental disturbance, world-wide in character. . . . This same spirit of unrest has invaded science."[17]

In hating one thing violently, we readily associate with it as cause or effect most of the other things we hate or fear violently. They may have no more connection than smallpox and alehouses, or Relativity and Bolshevism, but they are bound together in the same emotion. In a superstitious mind, like that of the Professor of Celestial Mechanics, emotion is a stream of molten lava which catches and imbeds whatever it touches. When you excavate in it you find, as in a buried city, all sorts of objects ludicrously entangled in each other. Anything can be related to anything else, provided it feels like it. Nor has a mind in such a state any way of knowing how preposterous it is. Ancient fears, reinforced by more recent fears, coagulate into a snarl of fears where anything that is dreaded is the cause of anything else that is dreaded.

## 10

Generally it all culminates in the fabrication of a system of all evil, and of another which is the system of all good. Then our love of the absolute shows itself. For we do not like qualifying adverbs.[18] They clutter up sentences, and interfere with irresistible feeling. We prefer most to more, least to less, we dislike the words rather, perhaps, if, or, but, toward, not quite, almost, temporarily, partly. Yet nearly every opinion about public affairs needs to be deflated by some word of this sort. But in our free moments everything tends to behave absolutely, — one hundred percent, everywhere, forever.

It is not enough to say that our side is more right than the enemy's, that our victory will help democracy more than his. One must insist that our victory will end war forever, and make the world safe for democracy. And when the war is over, though we have thwarted a greater evil than those which still afflict us, the relativity of the result fades out, the absoluteness of the present evil overcomes our spirit, and we feel that we are helpless because we have not been irresistible. Between omnipotence and impotence the pendulum swings.

Real space, real time, real numbers, real connections, real weights are lost. The perspective and the background and the dimensions of action are clipped and frozen in the stereotype.

---

[17] Cited in *The New Republic*, Dec. 24, 1919, p. 120.
[18] *Cf.* Freud's discussion of absolutism in dreams, *Interpretation of Dreams*, Chapter VI, especially pp. 288, *et seq.*

# PART IV. INTERESTS

# XI. The Enlisting of Interest

## 1

B UT the human mind is not a film which registers once and for all each impression that comes through its shutters and lenses. The human mind is endlessly and persistently creative. The pictures fade or combine, are sharpened here, condensed there, as we make them more completely our own. They do not lie inert upon the surface of the mind, but are reworked by the poetic faculty into a personal expression of ourselves. We distribute the emphasis and participate in the action.

In order to do this we tend to personalize quantities, and to dramatize relations. As some sort of allegory, except in acutely sophisticated minds, the affairs of the world are represented. Social Movements, Economic Forces, National Interests, Public Opinion are treated as persons, or persons like the Pope, the President, Lenin, Morgan or the King become ideas and institutions. The deepest of all the stereotypes is the human stereotype which imputes human nature to inanimate or collective things.

The bewildering variety of our impressions, even after they have been censored in all kinds of ways, tends to force us to adopt the greater economy of the allegory. So great is the multitude of things that we cannot keep them vividly in mind. Usually, then, we name them, and let the name stand for the whole impression. But a name is porous. Old meanings slip out and new ones slip in, and the attempt to retain the full meaning of the name is almost as fatiguing as trying to recall the original impressions. Yet names are a poor currency for thought. They are too empty, too abstract, too inhuman. And so we begin to see the name through some personal stereotype, to read into it, finally to see in it the incarnation of some human quality.

Yet human qualities are themselves vague and fluctuating. They are best remembered by a physical sign. And therefore, the human qualities we tend to ascribe to the names of our impressions, themselves tend to be visualized in physical metaphors. The people of England, the history of England, condense into England, and England becomes John Bull, who is jovial and fat, not too clever, but well able to take care of himself. The migration of a people may appear to some as the meandering of a river, and to others like a devastating flood. The courage people display may be objectified as a rock; their purpose as a road, their doubts as forks of the road, their difficulties as ruts and rocks, their progress as a fertile valley. If they mobilize their dread-naughts they unsheath a sword. If their army surrenders they are thrown to earth. If they are oppressed they are on the rack or under the harrow.

When public affairs are popularized in speeches, headlines, plays, moving pictures, cartoons, novels, statues or paintings, their transformation into a human interest requires first abstraction from the original, and then animation of what has been abstracted. We cannot be much interested in, or much moved by, the things we do not see. Of public affairs each of us sees very little, and therefore, they remain dull and unappetizing, until somebody, with the makings of an artist, has translated them into a moving picture. Thus the abstraction, imposed upon our knowledge of reality by all the limitations of our access and of our prejudices, is compensated. Not being omnipresent and omniscient we cannot see much of what we have to think and talk about. Being flesh and blood we will not feed on words and names and grey theory. Being artists of a sort we paint pictures, stage dramas and draw cartoons out of the abstractions.

Or, if possible, we find gifted men who can visualize for us. For people are not all endowed to the same degree with the pictorial faculty. Yet one may, I imagine, assert with Bergson that the practical intelligence is most closely adapted to spatial qualities.[1] A "clear" thinker is almost always a good visualizer. But for that same reason, because he is "cinematographic," he is often by that much external and insensitive. For the people who have intuition, which is probably another name for musical or muscular perception, often appreciate the quality of an event and the inwardness of an act far better than the visualizer. They have more understanding when the crucial element is a desire that is never crudely overt, and appears on the surface only in a veiled gesture, or in a rhythm of speech. Visualization may catch the stimulus and the result. But the intermediate and internal is often as badly caricatured by a visualizer, as is the intention of the composer by an enormous soprano in the sweet maiden's part.

Nevertheless, though they have often a peculiar justice, intuitions remain highly private and largely incommunicable. But social intercourse depends on communication, and while a person can often steer

---

[1] *Creative Evolution*, Chs. III, IV.

his own life with the utmost grace by virtue of his intuitions, he usually has great difficulty in making them real to others. When he talks about them they sound like a sheaf of mist. For while intuition does give a fairer perception of human feeling, the reason with its spatial and tactile prejudice can do little with that perception. Therefore, where action depends on whether a number of people are of one mind, it is probably true that in the first instance no idea is lucid for practical decision until it has visual or tactile value. But it is also true, that no visual idea is significant to us until it has enveloped some stress of our own personality. Until it releases or resists, depresses or enhances, some craving of our own, it remains one of the objects which do not matter.

## 2

Pictures have always been the surest way of conveying an idea, and next in order, words that call up pictures in memory. But the idea conveyed is not fully our own until we have identified ourselves with some aspect of the picture. The identification, or what Vernon Lee has called empathy,[2] may be almost infinitely subtle and symbolic. The mimicry may be performed without our being aware of it, and sometimes in a way that would horrify those sections of our personality which support our self-respect. In sophisticated people the participation may not be in the fate of the hero, but in the fate of the whole idea to which both hero and villain are essential. But these are refinements.

In popular representation the handles for identification are almost always marked. You know who the hero is at once. And no work promises to be easily popular where the marking is not definite and the choice clear.[3] But that is not enough. The audience must have something to do, and the contemplation of the true, the good, and the beautiful is not something to do. In order not to sit inertly in the presence of the picture, and this applies as much to newspaper stories as to fiction and the cinema, the audience must be exercised by the image. Now there are two forms of exercise which far transcend all others, both as to ease with which they are aroused, and eagerness with which stimuli for them are sought. They are sexual passion and fighting, and the two have so many associations with each other, blend into each other so intimately, that a fight about sex outranks every other theme in the breadth of its appeal. There is none so engrossing or so careless of all distinctions of culture and frontiers.

The sexual motif figures hardly at all in American political imagery.

---

[2] *Beauty and Ugliness.*
[3] A fact which bears heavily on the character of news. *Cf.* Part VII.

Except in certain minor ecstasies of war, in an occasional scandal, or in phases of the racial conflict with Negroes or Asiatics, to speak of it at all would seem far-fetched. Only in moving pictures, novels, and some magazine fiction are industrial relations, business competition, politics, and diplomacy tangled up with the girl and the other woman. But the fighting motif appears at every turn. Politics is interesting when there is a fight, or as we say, an issue. And in order to make politics popular, issues have to be found, even when in truth and justice, there are none,—none, in the sense that the differences of judgment, or principle, or fact, do not call for the enlistment of pugnacity.[4]

But where pugnacity is not enlisted, those of us who are not directly involved find it hard to keep up our interest. For those who are involved the absorption may be real enough to hold them even when no issue is involved. They may be exercised by sheer joy in activity, or by subtle rivalry or invention. But for those to whom the whole problem is external and distant, these other faculties do not easily come into play. In order that the faint image of the affair shall mean something to them, they must be allowed to exercise the love of struggle, suspense, and victory.

Miss Patterson[5] insists that "suspense . . . constitutes the difference between the masterpieces in the Metropolitan Museum of Art and the pictures at the Rivoli or the Rialto Theatres." Had she made it clear that the masterpieces lack either an easy mode of identification or a theme popular for this generation, she would be wholly right in saying that this "explains why the people straggle into the Metropolitan by twos and threes and struggle into the Rialto and Rivoli by hundreds. The twos and threes look at a picture in the Art Museum for less than ten minutes—unless they chance to be art students, critics, or connoisseurs. The hundreds in the Rivoli or the Rialto look at the picture for more than an hour. As far as beauty is concerned there can be no comparison of the merits of the two pictures. Yet the motion picture draws more people and holds them at attention longer than do the masterpieces, not through any intrinsic merit of its own, but because it depicts unfolding events, the outcome of which the audience is breathlessly waiting. It possesses the element of struggle, which never fails to arouse suspense."

In order then that the distant situation shall not be a gray flicker on the edge of attention, it should be capable of translation into pictures in which the opportunity for identification is recognizable. Unless that

---

[4] *Cf.* Frances Taylor Patterson, *Cinema Craftsmanship*, pp. 31–32. "III. If the plot lacks suspense: 1. Add an antagonist, 2. Add an obstacle, 3. Add a problem, 4. Emphasize one of the questions in the minds of the spectator. . . ."

[5] *Op. cit.*, pp. 6–7.

happens it will interest only a few for a little while. It will belong to the sights seen but not felt, to the sensations that beat on our sense organs, and are not acknowledged. We have to take sides. We have to be able to take sides. In the recesses of our being we must step out of the audience on to the stage, and wrestle as the hero for the victory of good over evil. We must breathe into the allegory the breath of our life.

### 3

And so, in spite of the critics, a verdict is rendered in the old controversy about realism and romanticism. Our popular taste is to have the drama originate in a setting realistic enough to make identification plausible and to have it terminate in a setting romantic enough to be desirable, but not so romantic as to be inconceivable. In between the beginning and the end the canons are liberal, but the true beginning and the happy ending are landmarks. The moving picture audience rejects fantasy logically developed, because in pure fantasy there is no familiar foothold in the age of machines. It rejects realism relentlessly pursued because it does not enjoy defeat in a struggle that has become its own.

What will be accepted as true, as realistic, as good, as evil, as desirable, is not eternally fixed. These are fixed by stereotypes, acquired from earlier experiences and carried over into judgment of later ones. And, therefore, if the financial investment in each film and in popular magazines were not so exorbitant as to require instant and widespread popularity, men of spirit and imagination would be able to use the screen and the periodical, as one might dream of their being used, to enlarge and to refine, to verify and criticize the repertory of images with which our imaginations work. But, given the present costs, the men who make moving pictures, like the church and the court painters of other ages, must adhere to the stereotypes that they find, or pay the price of frustrating expectation. The stereotypes can be altered, but not in time to guarantee success when the film is released six months from now.

The men who do alter the stereotypes, the pioneering artists and critics, are naturally depressed and angered at managers and editors who protect their investments. They are risking everything, then why not the others? That is not quite fair, for in their righteous fury they have forgotten their own rewards, which are beyond any that their employers can hope to feel. They could not, and would not if they could, change places. And they have forgotten another thing in the unceasing war with Philistia. They have forgotten that they are measuring their own success by standards that artists and wise men of the past would never have dreamed of invoking. They are asking for circulations and audiences that were never considered by any artist until the last few generations. And when they do not get them, they are disappointed.

Those who catch on, like Sinclair Lewis in "Main Street," are men who have succeeded in projecting definitely what great numbers of other people were obscurely trying to say inside their heads. "You have said it for me." They establish a new form which is then endlessly copied until it, too, becomes a stereotype of perception. The next pioneer finds it difficult to make the public see Main Street any other way. And he, like the forerunners of Sinclair Lewis, has a quarrel with the public.

This quarrel is due not only to the conflict of stereotypes, but to the pioneering artist's reverence for his material. Whatever the plane he chooses, on that plane he remains. If he is dealing with the inwardness of an event he follows it to its conclusion regardless of the pain it causes. He will not tag his fantasy to help anyone, or cry peace where there is no peace. There is his America. But big audiences have no stomach for such severity. They are more interested in themselves than in anything else in the world. The selves in which they are interested are the selves that have been revealed by schools and by tradition. They insist that a work of art shall be a vehicle with a step where they can climb aboard, and that they shall ride, not according to the contours of the country, but to a land where for an hour there are no clocks to punch and no dishes to wash. To satisfy these demands there exists an intermediate class of artists who are able and willing to confuse the planes, to piece together a realistic-romantic compound out of the inventions of greater men, and, as Miss Patterson advises, give "what real life so rarely does—the triumphant resolution of a set of difficulties; the anguish of virtue and the triumph of sin . . . changed to the glorifications of virtue and the eternal punishment of its enemy."[6]

### 4

The ideologies of politics obey these rules. The foothold of realism is always there. The picture of some real evil, such as the German threat or class conflict, is recognizable in the argument. There is a description of some aspect of the world which is convincing because it agrees with familiar ideas. But as the ideology deals with an unseen future, as well as with a tangible present, it soon crosses imperceptibly the frontier of verification. In describing the present you are more or less tied down to common experience. In describing what nobody has

---

[6] *Op. cit.*, p. 46. "The hero and heroine must in general possess youth, beauty, goodness, exalted self-sacrifice, and unalterable constancy."

experienced you are bound to let go. You stand at Armageddon, more or less, but you battle for the Lord, perhaps. . . . A true beginning, true according to the standards prevailing, and a happy ending. Every Marxist is hard as nails about the brutalities of the present, and mostly sunshine about the day after the dictatorship. So were the war propagandists: there was not a bestial quality in human nature they did not find everywhere east of the Rhine, or west of it if they were Germans. The bestiality was there all right. But after the victory, eternal peace. Plenty of this is quite cynically deliberate. For the skilful propagandist knows that while you must start with a plausible analysis, you must not keep on analyzing, because the tedium of real political accomplishment will soon destroy interest. So the propagandist exhausts the interest in reality by a tolerably plausible beginning, and then stokes up energy for a long voyage by brandishing a passport to heaven.

The formula works when the public fiction enmeshes itself with a private urgency. But once enmeshed, in the heat of battle, the original self and the original stereotype which effected the junction may be wholly lost to sight.

# XII. Self-Interest Reconsidered

## 1

THEREFORE, the identical story is not the same story to all who hear it. Each will enter it at a slightly different point, since no two experiences are exactly alike; he will reënact it in his own way, and transfuse it with his own feelings. Sometimes an artist of compelling skill will force us to enter into lives altogether unlike our own, lives that seem at first glance dull, repulsive, or eccentric. But that is rare. In almost every story that catches our attention we become a character and act out the role with a pantomime of our own. The pantomime may be subtle or gross, may be sympathetic to the story, or only crudely analogous; but it will consist of those feelings which are aroused by our conception of the role. And so, the original theme as it circulates, is stressed, twisted, and embroidered by all the minds through which it goes. It is as if a play of Shakespeare's were rewritten each time it is performed with all the changes of emphasis and meaning that the actors and audience inspired.

Something very like that seems to have happened to the stories in the sagas before they were definitively written down. In our time the printed record, such as it is, checks the exuberance of each individual's fancy. But against rumor there is little or no check, and the original story, true or invented, grows wings and horns, hoofs and beaks, as the artist in each gossip works upon it. The first narrator's account does not keep its shape and proportions. It is edited and revised by all who played with it as they heard it, used it for day dreams, and passed it on.[1]

Consequently the more mixed the audience, the greater will be the variation in the response. For as the audience grows larger, the number of common words diminishes. Thus the common factors in the story become more abstract. This story, lacking precise character of its own, is heard by people of highly varied character. They give it their own character.

## 2

The character they give it varies not only with sex and age, race and religion and social position, but within these cruder classifications, according to the inherited and acquired constitution of the individual, his faculties, his career, the progress of his career, an emphasized aspect of his career, his moods and tenses, or his place on the board in any of the games of life that he is playing. What reaches him of public affairs, a few lines of print, some photographs, anecdotes, and some casual experience of his own, he conceives through his set patterns and recreates with his own emotions. He does not take his personal problems as partial samples of the greater environment. He takes his stories of the greater environment as a mimic enlargement of his private life.

But not necessarily of that private life as he would describe it to himself. For in his private life the choices are narrow, and much of himself is squeezed down and out of sight where it cannot directly govern his outward behavior. And thus, beside the more average people who project the happiness of their own lives into a general good will, or their unhappiness into suspicion and hate, there are the outwardly happy people who are brutal everywhere but in their own circle, as well as the people who, the more they detest their families, their friends, their jobs, the more they overflow with love for mankind.

As you descend from generalities to detail, it becomes more apparent that the character in which men deal with their affairs is not fixed. Possibly their different selves have a common stem and common qualities, but the branches and the twigs have many forms. Nobody confronts every situation with the same character. His character varies in some degree through the sheer influence of time and accumulating

---

[1] For an interesting example, see the case described by C. J. Jung, *Zentralblatt für Psychoanalyse*, 1911, Vol. I, p. 81. Translated by Constance Long, in *Analytical Psychology*, Ch. IV.

memory, since he is not an automaton. His character varies, not only in time, but according to circumstance. The legend of the solitary Englishman in the South Seas, who invariably shaves and puts on a black tie for dinner, bears witness to his own intuitive and civilized fear of losing the character which he has acquired. So do diaries, and albums, and souvenirs, old letters, and old clothes, and the love of unchanging routine testify to our sense of how hard it is to step twice in the Heraclitan river.

There is no one self always at work. And therefore it is of great importance in the formation of any public opinion, what self is engaged. The Japanese ask the right to settle in California. Clearly it makes a whole lot of difference whether you conceive the demand as a desire to grow fruit or to marry the white man's daughter. If two nations are disputing a piece of territory, it matters greatly whether the people regard the negotiations as a real estate deal, an attempt to humiliate them, or, in the excited and provocative language which usually enclouds these arguments, as a rape. For the self which takes charge of the instincts when we are thinking about lemons or distant acres is very different from the self which appears when we are thinking even potentially as the outraged head of a family. In one case the private feeling which enters into the opinion is tepid, in the other, red hot. And so while it is so true as to be mere tautology that "self-interest" determines opinion, the statement is not illuminating, until we know which self out of many selects and directs the interest so conceived.

Religious teaching and popular wisdom have always distinguished several personalities in each human being. They have been called the Higher and Lower, the Spiritual and the Material, the Divine and the Carnal; and although we may not wholly accept this classification, we cannot fail to observe that distinctions exist. Instead of two antithetic selves, a modern man would probably note a good many not so sharply separated. He would say that the distinction drawn by theologians was arbitrary and external, because many different selves were grouped together as higher provided they fitted into the theologian's categories, but he would recognize nevertheless that here was an authentic clue to the variety of human nature.

We have learned to note many selves, and to be a little less ready to issue judgment upon them. We understand that we see the same body, but often a different man, depending on whether he is dealing with a social equal, a social inferior, or a social superior; on whether he is making love to a woman he is eligible to marry, or to one whom he is not; on whether he is courting a woman, or whether he considers himself her proprietor; on whether he is dealing with his children, his partners, his most trusted subordinates, the boss who can make him or break him; on whether he is struggling for the necessities of life, or successful; on whether he is dealing with a friendly alien, or a despised one; on whether he is in great danger, or in perfect security; on whether he is alone in Paris or among his family in Peoria.

People differ widely, of course, in the consistency of their characters, so widely that they may cover the whole gamut of differences between a split soul like Dr. Jekyll's and an utterly singleminded Brand, Parsifal, or Don Quixote. If the selves are too unrelated, we distrust the man; if they are too inflexibly on one track we find him arid, stubborn, or eccentric. In the repertory of characters, meager for the isolated and the self-sufficient, highly varied for the adaptable, there is a whole range of selves, from that one at the top which we should wish God to see, to those at the bottom that we ourselves do not dare to see. There may be octaves for the family,—father, Jehovah, tyrant,—husband, proprietor, male,—lover, lecher,—for the occupation,—employer, master, exploiter,—competitor, intriguer, enemy,—subordinate, courtier, snob. Some never come out into public view. Others are called out only by exceptional circumstances. But the characters take their form from a man's conception of the situation in which he finds himself. If the environment to which he is sensitive happens to be the smart set, he will imitate the character he conceives to be appropriate. That character will tend to act as modulator of his bearing, his speech, his choice of subjects, his preferences. Much of the comedy of life lies here, in the way people imagine their characters for situations that are strange to them: the professor among promoters, the deacon at a poker game, the cockney in the country, the paste diamond among real diamonds.

### 3

Into the making of a man's characters there enters a variety of influences not easily separated.[2] The analysis in its fundamentals is perhaps still as doubtful as it was in the fifth century B.C. when Hippocrates formulated the doctrine of the humors, distinguished the sanguine, the melancholic, the choleric, and the phlegmatic dispositions, and ascribed them to the blood, the black bile, the yellow bile, and the phlegm. The latest theories, such as one finds them in Cannon,[3] Adler,[4] Kempf,[5] appear to follow much the same scent, from the outward behavior and the inner con-

---

[2] For an interesting sketch of the more noteworthy early attempts to explain character, see the chapter called "The Antecedents of the Study of Character and Temperament," in Joseph Jastrow's *The Psychology of Conviction.*

[3] *Bodily Changes in Pleasure Pain and Anger.*

[4] *The Neurotic Constitution.*

[5] *The Autonomic Functions and the Personality; Psychopathology. Cf.* also Louis Berman: *The Glands Regulating Personality.*

sciousness to the physiology of the body. But in spite of an immensely improved technique, no one would be likely to claim that there are settled conclusions which enable us to set apart nature from nurture, and abstract the native character from the acquired. It is only in what Joseph Jastrow has called the slums of psychology that the explanation of character is regarded as a fixed system to be applied by phrenologists, palmists, fortune-tellers, mind-readers, and a few political professors. There you will still find it asserted that "the Chinese are fond of colors, and have their eyebrows much vaulted" while "the heads of the Calmucks are depressed from above, but very large laterally, about the organ which gives the inclination to acquire; and this nation's propensity to steal, etc., is admitted."[6]

The modern psychologists are disposed to regard the outward behavior of an adult as an equation between a number of variables, such as the resistance of the environment, repressed cravings of several maturities, and the manifest personality.[7] They permit us to suppose, though I have not seen the notion formulated, that the repression or control of cravings is fixed not in relation to the whole person all the time, but more or less in respect to his various selves. There are things he will not do as a patriot that he will do when he is not thinking of himself as a patriot. No doubt there are impulses, more or less incipient in childhood, that are never exercised again in the whole of a man's life, except as they enter obscurely and indirectly into combination with other impulses. But even that is not certain, since repression is not irretrievable. For just as psychoanalysis can bring to the surface a buried impulse, so can social situations.[8] It is only when our surroundings remain normal and placid, when what is expected of us by those we meet is consistent, that we live without knowledge of many of our dispositions. When the unexpected occurs, we learn much about ourselves that we did not know.

The selves, which we construct with the help of all who influence us, prescribe which impulses, how emphasized, how directed, are appropriate to certain typical situations for which we have learned prepared

---

[6] Jastrow, *op. cit.*, p. 156.
[7] Formulated by Kempf, *Psychopathology*, p. 74, as follows:

| Manifest wishes | |
| over | |
| Later Repressed Wishes | |
| over | opposed by the resistance of the |
| Adolescent Repressed Wishes | environment=Behavior |
| over | |
| Preadolescent Repressed Wishes | |

[8] *Cf.* the very interesting book of Everett Dean Martin, *The Behavior of Crowds.*
Also Hobbes, *Leviathan*, Part II, Ch. 25. "For the passions of men, which asunder are moderate, as the heat of one brand, in an assembly are like many brands, that inflame one another, especially when they blow one another with orations. . . ."
LeBon, *The Crowd*, elaborates this observation of Hobbes's.

attitudes. For a recognizable type of experience, there is a character which controls the outward manifestations of our whole being. Murderous hate is, for example, controlled in civil life. Though you choke with rage, you must not display it as a parent, child, employer, politician. You would not wish to display a personality that exudes murderous hate. You frown upon it, and the people around you also frown. But if a war breaks out, the chances are that everybody you admire will begin to feel the justification of killing and hating. At first the vent for these feelings is very narrow. The selves which come to the front are those which are attuned to a real love of country, the kind of feeling that you find in Rupert Brooke, and in Sir Edward Grey's speech on August 3,1914, and in President Wilson's address to Congress on April 2, 1917. The reality of war is still abhorred, and what war actually means is learned but gradually. For previous wars are only transfigured memories. In that honeymoon phase, the realists of war rightly insist that the nation is not yet awake, and reassure each other by saying: "Wait for the casualty lists." Gradually the impulse to kill becomes the main business, and all those characters which might modify it, disintegrate. The impulse becomes central, is sanctified, and gradually turns unmanageable. It seeks a vent not alone on the idea of the enemy, which is all the enemy most people actually see during the war, but upon all the persons and objects and ideas that have always been hateful. Hatred of the enemy is legitimate. These other hatreds have themselves legitimized by the crudest analogy, and by what, once having cooled off, we recognize as the most far-fetched analogy. It takes a long time to subdue so powerful an impulse once it goes loose. And therefore, when the war is over in fact, it takes time and struggle to regain self-control, and to deal with the problems of peace in civilian character.

Modern war, as Mr. Herbert Croly has said, is inherent in the political structure of modern society, but outlawed by its ideals. For the civilian population there exists no ideal code of conduct in war, such as the soldier still possesses and chivalry once prescribed. The civilians are without standards, except those that the best of them manage to improvise. The only standards they possess make war an accursed thing. Yet though the war may be a necessary one, no moral training has prepared them for it. Only their higher selves have a code and patterns, and when they have to act in what the higher regards as a lower character profound disturbance results.

The preparation of characters for all the situations in which men may find themselves is one function of a moral education. Clearly then, it depends for its success upon the sincerity and knowledge with which the environment has been explored. For in a world falsely conceived, our own characters are falsely conceived, and we misbehave. So the moralist must choose: either he must offer a pattern of conduct for every phase of life, however distasteful some of its phases may be, or he must guarantee that his pupils will never be confronted by the situations he disapproves. Either he must abolish war, or teach people how to wage it with the greatest psychic economy; either he must abolish the economic life of man and feed him with stardust and dew, or he must investigate all the perplexities of economic life and offer patterns of conduct which are applicable in a world where no man is self-supporting. But that is just what the prevailing moral culture so generally refuses to do. In its best aspects it is diffident at the awful complication of the modern world. In its worst, it is just cowardly. Now whether the moralists study economics and politics and psychology, or whether the social scientists educate the moralists is no great matter. Each generation will go unprepared into the modern world, unless it has been taught to conceive the kind of person- ality it will have to be among the issues it will most likely meet.


4


Most of this the naïve view of self-interest leaves out of account. It forgets that self and interest are both conceived somehow, and that for the most part they are conventionally conceived. The ordinary doctrine of self-interest usually omits altogether the cognitive function. So insis- tent is it on the fact that human beings finally refer all things to them- selves, that it does not stop to notice that men's ideas of all things and of themselves are not instinctive. They are acquired.

Thus it may be true enough, as James Madison wrote in the tenth paper of the Federalist, that "a landed interest, a manufacturing interest, a mercantile interest, a moneyed interest, with many lesser interests, grow up of necessity in civilized nations, and divide them into different classes, actuated by different sentiments and views." But if you exam- ine the context of Madison's paper, you discover something which I think throws light upon that view of instinctive fatalism, called some- times the economic interpretation of history. Madison was arguing for the federal constitution, and "among the numerous advantages of the union" he set forth "its tendency to break and control the violence of faction." Faction was what worried Madison. And the causes of faction he traced to "the nature of man," where latent dispositions are "brought into different degrees of activity, according to the different circum- stances of civil society. A zeal for different opinions concerning religion, concerning government and many other points, as well of speculation as of practice; an attachment to different leaders ambitiously contend- ing for preëminence and power, or to persons of other descriptions whose fortunes have been interesting to the human passions, have, in turn, divided mankind into parties, inflamed them with mutual ani- mosity, and rendered them much more disposed to vex and oppress each other, than to cooperate for their common good. So strong is this propensity of mankind to fall into mutual animosities, that where no substantial occasion presents itself, the most frivolous and fanciful distinctions have been sufficient to kindle their unfriendly passions and excite their most violent conflicts. But the *most common* and *durable* source of factions has been the various and unequal distribution of property."

Madison's theory, therefore, is that the propensity to faction may be kindled by religious or political opinions, by leaders, but most commonly by the distribution of property. Yet note that Madison claims only that men are divided by their relation to property. He does not say that their property and their opinions are cause and effect, but that differences of property are the causes of differences of opinion. The pivotal word in Madison's argument is "different." From the existence of differing economic situations you can tentatively infer a probable difference of opinions, but you cannot infer what those opinions will necessarily be.

This reservation cuts radically into the claims of the theory as that theory is usually held. That the reservation is necessary, the enormous contradiction between dogma and practice among orthodox socialists bears witness. They argue that the next stage in social evolution is the inevitable result of the present stage. But in order to produce that inevitable next stage they organize and agitate to produce "class consciousness." Why, one asks, does not the economic situation produce consciousness of class in everybody? It just doesn't, that is all. And therefore the proud claim will not stand that the socialist philosophy rests on prophetic insight into destiny. It rests on an hypothesis about human nature.[9]

The socialist practice is based on a belief that if men are economically situated in different ways, they can then be induced to hold certain views. Undoubtedly they often come to believe, or can be induced to believe different things, as they are, for example, landlords or tenants, employees or employers, skilled or unskilled laborers, wageworkers or salaried men, buyers or sellers, farmers or middlemen, exporters or importers, creditors or debtors. Differences of income make a profound difference in contact and opportunity. Men who work at machines will tend, as Mr. Thorstein Veblen has so brilliantly demonstrated,[10] to interpret experience differently from handicraftsmen or traders. If this were all that the materialistic conception of politics asserted, the theory would be an immensely valuable hypothesis that every interpreter of opinion would have to use. But he would often

[9] *Cf.* Thorstein Veblen, "The Socialist Economics of Karl Marx and His Followers," in *The Place of Science in Modern Civilization*, esp. pp. 413–418.
[10] *The Theory of Business Enterprise.*

have to abandon the theory, and he would always have to be on guard. For in trying to explain a certain public opinion, it is rarely obvious which of a man's many social relations is effecting a particular opinion. Does Smith's opinion arise from his problems as a landlord, an importer, an owner of railway shares, or an employer? Does Jones's opinion, Jones being a weaver in a textile mill, come from the attitude of his boss, the competition of new immigrants, his wife's grocery bills, or the ever present contract with the firm which is selling him a Ford car and a house and lot on the instalment plan? Without special inquiry you cannot tell. The economic determinist cannot tell.

A man's various economic contacts limit or enlarge the range of his opinions. But which of the contacts, in what guise, on what theory, the materialistic conception of politics cannot predict. It can predict, with a high degree of probability, that if a man owns a factory, his ownership will figure in those opinions which seem to have some bearing on that factory. But how the function of being an owner will figure, no economic determinist as such, can tell you. There is no fixed set of opinions on any question that go with being the owner of a factory, no views on labor, on property, on management, let alone views on less immediate matters. The determinist can predict that in ninety-nine cases out of a hundred the owner will resist attempts to deprive him of ownership, or that he will favor legislation which he thinks will increase his profits. But since there is no magic in ownership which enables a business man to know what laws will make him prosper, there is no chain of cause and effect described in economic materialism which enables anyone to prophesy whether the owner will take a long view or a short one, a competitive or a coöperative.

Did the theory have the validity which is so often claimed for it, it would enable us to prophesy. We could analyze the economic interests of a people, and deduce what the people was bound to do. Marx tried that, and after a good guess about the trusts, went wholly wrong. The first socialist experiment came, not as he predicted, out of the culmination of capitalist development in the West, but out of the collapse of a pre-capitalist system in the East. Why did he go wrong? Why did his greatest disciple, Lenin, go wrong? Because the Marxians thought that men's economic position would irresistibly produce a clear conception of their economic interests. They thought they themselves possessed that clear conception, and that what they knew the rest of mankind would learn. The event has shown, not only that a clear conception of interest does not arise automatically in everyone, but that it did not arise even in Marx and Lenin themselves. After all that Marx and Lenin have written, the social behavior of mankind is still obscure. It ought not to be, if economic position alone determined public opinion. Position ought, if their theory were correct, not only to divide mankind into classes, but to supply each class with a view of its interest and a coherent policy for obtaining it. Yet nothing is more certain than that all classes of men are in constant perplexity as to what their interests are.[11]

This dissolves the impact of economic determinism. For if our economic interests are made up of our variable concepts of those interests, then as the master key to social processes the theory fails. That theory assumes that men are capable of adopting only one version of their interest, and that having adopted it, they move fatally to realize it. It assumes the existence of a specific class interest. That assumption is false. A class interest can be conceived largely or narrowly, selfishly or unselfishly, in the light of no facts, some facts, many facts, truth and error. And so collapses the Marxian remedy for class conflicts. That remedy assumes that if all property could be held in common, class differences would disappear. The assumption is false. Property might well be held in common, and yet not be conceived as a whole. The moment any group of people failed to see communism in a communist manner, they would divide into classes on the basis of what they saw.

In respect to the existing social order Marxian socialism emphasizes property conflict as the maker of opinion, in respect to the loosely defined working class it ignores property conflict as the basis of agitation, in respect to the future it imagines a society without property conflict, and, therefore, without conflict of opinion. Now in the existing social order there may be more instances where one man must lose if another is to gain, than there would be under socialism, but for every case where one must lose for another to gain, there are endless cases where men simply imagine the conflict because they are uneducated. And under socialism, though you removed every instance of absolute conflict, the partial access of each man to the whole range of facts would nevertheless create conflict. A socialist state will not be able to

---

[11] As a matter of fact, when it came to the test, Lenin completely abandoned the materialistic interpretation of politics. Had he held sincerely to the Marxian formula when he seized power in 1917, he would have said to himself: according to the teachings of Marx, socialism will develop out of a mature capitalism . . . here am I, in control of a nation that is only entering upon a capitalist development . . . it is true that I am a socialist, but I am a scientific socialist . . . it follows that for the present all idea of a socialist republic is out of the question . . . we must advance capitalism in order that the evolution which Marx predicted may take place. But Lenin did nothing of the sort. Instead of waiting for evolution to evolve, he tried by will, force, and education, to defy the historical process which his philosophy assumed.

Since this was written Lenin has abandoned communism on the ground that Russia does not possess the necessary basis in a mature capitalism. He now says that Russia must create capitalism, which will create a proletariat, which will some day create communism. This is at least consistent with Marxist dogma. But it shows how little determinism there is in the opinions of a determinist.

dispense with education, morality, or liberal science, though on strict materialistic grounds the communal ownership of properties ought to make them superfluous. The communists in Russia would not propagate their faith with such unflagging zeal if economic determinism were alone determining the opinion of the Russian people.

5

The socialist theory of human nature is, like the hedonistic calculus, an example of false determinism. Both assume that the unlearned dispositions fatally but intelligently produce a certain type of behavior. The socialist believes that the dispositions pursue the economic interest of a class; the hedonist believes that they pursue pleasure and avoid pain. Both theories rest on a naïve view of instinct, a view, defined by James,[12] though radically qualified by him, as "the faculty of acting in such a way as to produce certain ends, without foresight of the ends and without previous education in the performance."

It is doubtful whether instinctive action of this sort figures at all in the social life of mankind. For as James pointed out:[13] "every instinctive act in an animal with memory must cease to be 'blind' after being once repeated." Whatever the equipment at birth, the innate dispositions are from earliest infancy immersed in experience which determines what shall excite them as stimulus. "They become capable," as Mr. McDougall says,[14] "of being initiated, not only by the perception of objects of the kind which directly excite the innate disposition, the natural or native excitants of the instinct, but also by ideas of such objects, and by perceptions and by ideas of objects of other kinds."[15]

It is only the "central part of the disposition"[16] says Mr. McDougall further, "that retains its specific character and remains common to all individuals and all situations in which the instinct is excited." The cognitive processes, and the actual bodily movements by which the instinct achieves its end may be indefinitely complicated. In other words, man has an instinct of fear, but what he will fear and how he will try to escape, is determined not from birth, but by experience.

If it were not for this variability, it would be difficult to conceive the

---

[12] *Principles of Psychology*, Vol. II, p. 383.

[13] *Op. cit.*, Vol. II, p. 390.

[14] Introduction to *Social Psychology*, Fourth Edition, pp. 31–32.

[15] "Most definitions of instincts and instinctive actions take account only of their conative aspects . . . and it is a common mistake to ignore the cognitive and affective aspects of the instinctive mental process." Footnote *op. cit.*, p. 29.

[16] P. 34.

inordinate variety of human nature. But when you consider that all the important tendencies of the creature, his appetites, his loves, his hates, his curiosity, his sexual cravings, his fears, and pugnacity, are freely attachable to all sorts of objects as stimulus, and to all kinds of objects as gratification, the complexity of human nature is not so inconceivable. And when you think that each new generation is the casual victim of the way a previous generation was conditioned, as well as the inheritor of the environment that resulted, the possible combinations and permutations are enormous.

There is no prima facie case then for supposing that because persons crave some particular thing, or behave in some particular way, human nature is fatally constituted to crave that and act thus. The craving and the action are both learned, and in another generation might be learned differently. Analytic psychology and social history unite in supporting this conclusion. Psychology indicates how essentially casual is the nexus between the particular stimulus and the particular response. Anthropology in the widest sense reinforces the view by demonstrating that the things which have excited men's passions, and the means which they have used to realize them, differ endlessly from age to age and from place to place.

Men pursue their interest. But how they shall pursue it is not fatally determined, and, therefore, within whatever limits of time this planet will continue to support human life, man can set no term upon the creative energies of men. He can issue no doom of automatism. He can say, if he must, that for his life there will be no changes which he can recognize as good. But in saying that he will be confining his life to what he can see with his eye, rejecting what he might see with his mind; he will be taking as the measure of good a measure which is only the one he happens to possess. He can find no ground for abandoning his highest hopes and relaxing his conscious effort unless he chooses to regard the unknown as the unknowable, unless he elects to believe that what no one knows no one will know, and that what someone has not yet learned no one will ever be able to teach.

# PART V. THE MAKING OF A COMMON WILL

# XIII. The Transfer of Interest

## 1

THIS goes to show that there are many variables in each man's impressions of the invisible world. The points of contact vary, the stereotyped expectations vary, the interest enlisted varies most subtly of all. The living impressions of a large number of people are to an immeasurable degree personal in each of them, and unmanageably complex in the mass. How, then, is any practical relationship established between what is in people's heads and what is out there beyond their ken in the environment? How in the language of democratic theory, do great numbers of people feeling each so privately about so abstract a picture, develop any common will? How does a simple and constant idea emerge from this complex of variables? How are those things known as the Will of the People, or the National Purpose, or Public Opinion crystalized out of such fleeting and casual imagery?

That there is a real difficulty here was shown by an angry tilt in the spring of 1921 between the American Ambassador to England and a very large number of other Americans. Mr. Harvey, speaking at a British dinner table, had assured the world without the least sign of hesitancy what were the motives of Americans in 1917.[1] As he described them, they were not the motives which President Wilson had insisted upon when *he* enunciated the American mind. Now, of course, neither Mr. Harvey nor Mr. Wilson, nor the critics and friends of either, nor any one else, can know quantitatively and qualitatively what went on in thirty or forty million adult minds. But what everybody knows is that a war was fought and won by a multitude of efforts, stimulated, no one knows in what proportion, by the motives of Wilson and the motives of Harvey and all kinds of hybrids of the two. People enlisted and fought, worked, paid taxes, sacrificed to a common end, and yet no one can begin to say exactly what moved each person to do each thing that he

---

[1] *New York Times*, May 20, 1921.

did. It is no use, then, Mr. Harvey telling a soldier who thought this was
a war to end war that the soldier did not think any such thing. The soldier who thought that *thought that*. And Mr. Harvey, who thought
something else, thought *something else*.

In the same speech Mr. Harvey formulated with equal clarity what
the voters of 1920 had in their minds. That is a rash thing to do, and, if
you simply assume that all who voted your ticket voted as you did, then
it is a disingenuous thing to do. The count shows that sixteen million
voted Republican, and nine millions Democratic. They voted, says Mr.
Harvey, for and against the League of Nations, and in support of this
claim, he can point to Mr. Wilson's request for a referendum, and to
the undeniable fact that the Democratic party and Mr. Cox insisted
that the League was the issue. But then, saying that the League was the
issue did not make the League the issue, and by counting the votes on
election day you do not know the real division of opinion about the
League. There were, for example, nine million Democrats. Are you
entitled to believe that all of them are staunch supporters of the
League? Certainly you are not. For your knowledge of American politics tells you that many of the millions voted, as they always do, to
maintain the existing social system in the South, and that whatever
their views on the League, they did not vote to express their views.
Those who wanted the League were no doubt pleased that the
Democratic party wanted it too. Those who disliked the League may
have held their noses as they voted. But both groups of Southerners
voted the same ticket.

Were the Republicans more unanimous? Anybody can pick
Republican voters enough out of his circle of friends to cover the whole
gamut of opinion from the irreconcilability of Senators Johnson and
Knox to the advocacy of Secretary Hoover and Chief Justice Taft. No
one can say definitely how many people felt in any particular way about
the League, nor how many people let their feelings on that subject
determine their vote. When there are only two ways of expressing a
hundred varieties of feeling, there is no certain way of knowing what
the decisive combination was. Senator Borah found in the Republican
ticket a reason for voting Republican, but so did President Lowell. The
Republican majority was composed of men and women who thought a
Republican victory would kill the League, plus those who thought it
the most practical way to secure the League, plus those who thought it
the surest way offered to obtain an amended League. All these voters
were inextricably entangled with their own desire, or the desire of other
voters to improve business, or put labor in its place, or to punish the
Democrats for going to war, or to punish them for not having gone
sooner, or to get rid of Mr. Burleson, or to improve the price of wheat,
or to lower taxes, or to stop Mr. Daniels from outbuilding the world, or
to help Mr. Harding do the same thing.

And yet a sort of decision emerged; Mr. Harding moved into the White House. For the least common denominator of all the votes was that the Democrats should go and the Republicans come in. That was the only factor remaining after all the contradictions had cancelled each other out. But that factor was enough to alter policy for four years. The precise reasons why change was desired on that November day in 1920 are not recorded, not even in the memories of the individual voters. The reasons are not fixed. They grow and change and melt into other reasons, so that the public opinions Mr. Harding has to deal with are not the opinions that elected him. That there is no inevitable connection between an assortment of opinions and a particular line of action everyone saw in 1916. Elected apparently on the cry that he kept us out of war, Mr. Wilson within five months led the country into war.

The working of the popular will, therefore, has always called for explanation. Those who have been most impressed by its erratic working have found a prophet in M. LeBon, and have welcomed generalizations about what Sir Robert Peel called "that great compound of folly, weakness, prejudice, wrong feeling, right feeling, obstinacy and newspaper paragraphs which is called public opinion." Others have concluded that since out of drift and incoherence, settled aims do appear, there must be a mysterious contrivance at work somewhere over and above the inhabitants of a nation. They invoke a collective soul, a national mind, a spirit of the age which imposes order upon random opinion. An oversoul seems to be needed, for the emotions and ideas in the members of a group do not disclose anything so simple and so crystalline as the formula which those same individuals will accept as a true statement of their Public Opinion.

2

But the facts can, I think, be explained more convincingly without the help of the oversoul in any of its disguises. After all, the art of inducing all sorts of people who think differently to vote alike is practiced in every political campaign. In 1916, for example, the Republican candidate had to produce Republican votes out of many different kinds of Republicans. Let us look at Mr. Hughes' first speech after accepting the nomination.[2] The context is still clear enough in our minds to obviate much explanation; yet the issues are no longer contentious. The candidate was a man of unusually plain speech, who had been out of politics for several years and was not personally committed on the issues of the recent past. He had, moreover, none of that wizardry

---

[2] Delivered at Carnegie Hall, New York City, July 31, 1916.

which popular leaders like Roosevelt, Wilson, or Lloyd George possess, none of that histrionic gift by which such men impersonate the feelings of their followers. From that aspect of politics he was by temperament and by training remote. But yet he knew by calculation what the politician's technic is. He was one of those people who know just how to do a thing, but who can not quite do it themselves. They are often better teachers than the virtuoso to whom the art is so much second nature that he himself does not know how he does it. The statement that those who can, do; those who cannot, teach, is not nearly so much of a reflection on the teacher as it sounds.

Mr. Hughes knew the occasion was momentous, and he had prepared his manuscript carefully. In a box sat Theodore Roosevelt just back from Missouri. All over the house sat the veterans of Armageddon in various stages of doubt and dismay. On the platform and in the other boxes the ex-whited sepulchres and ex-second-story men of 1912 were to be seen, obviously in the best of health and in a melting mood. Out beyond the hall there were powerful pro-Germans and powerful pro-Allies; a war party in the East and in the big cities; a peace party in the middle and far west. There was strong feeling about Mexico. Mr. Hughes had to form a majority against the Democrats out of people divided into all sorts of combinations on Taft vs. Roosevelt, pro-Germans vs. pro-Allies, war vs. neutrality, Mexican intervention vs. non-intervention.

About the morality or the wisdom of the affair we are, of course, not concerned here. Our only interest is in the method by which a leader of heterogeneous opinion goes about the business of securing a homogeneous vote.

> "This *representative* gathering is a happy augury. It means the strength of *reunion*. It means that the party of *Lincoln* is restored. . . ."

The italicized words are binders: *Lincoln* in such a speech has of course, no relation to Abraham Lincoln. It is merely a stereotype by which the piety which surrounds that name can be transferred to the Republican candidate who now stands in his shoes. Lincoln reminds the Republicans, Bull Moose and Old Guard, that before the schism they had a common history. About the schism no one can afford to speak. But it is there, as yet unhealed.

The speaker must heal it. Now the schism of 1912 had arisen over domestic questions; the reunion of 1916 was, as Mr. Roosevelt had declared, to be based on a common indignation against Mr. Wilson's conduct of international affairs. But international affairs were also a dangerous source of conflict. It was necessary to find an opening subject which would not only ignore 1912 but would avoid also the explosive conflicts of 1916. The speaker skilfully selected the spoils system in diplomatic appointments. "Deserving Democrats" was a discrediting phrase, and Mr. Hughes at once evokes it. The record being indefensible, there is no hesitation in the vigor of the attack. Logically it was an ideal introduction to a common mood.

Mr. Hughes then turns to Mexico, beginning with an historical review. He had to consider the general sentiment that affairs were going badly in Mexico; also, a no less general sentiment that war should be avoided; and two powerful currents of opinion, one of which said President Wilson was right in not recognizing Huerta, the other which preferred Huerta to Carranza, and intervention to both. Huerta was the first sore spot in the record . . .

> "He was certainly in fact the head of the Government in Mexico."

But the moralists who regarded Huerta as a drunken murderer had to be placated.

> "Whether or not he should be recognized was a question to be determined in the exercise of a sound discretion, but according to correct principles."

So instead of saying that Huerta should have been recognized, the candidate says that correct principles ought to be applied. Everybody believes in correct principles, and everybody, of course, believes he possesses them. To blur the issue still further President Wilson's policy is described as "intervention." It was that in law, perhaps, but not in the sense then currently meant by the word. By stretching the word to cover what Mr. Wilson had done, as well as what the real interventionists wanted, the issue between the two factions was to be repressed.

Having got by the two explosive points "Huerta" and "intervention" by letting the words mean all things to all men, the speech passes for a while to safer ground. The candidate tells the story of Tampico, Vera Cruz, Villa, Santa Ysabel, Columbus and Carrizal. Mr. Hughes is specific, either because the facts as known from the newspapers are irritating, or because the true explanation is, as for example in regard to Tampico, too complicated. No contrary passions could be aroused by such a record. But at the end the candidate had to take a position. His audience expected it. The indictment was Mr. Roosevelt's. Would Mr. Hughes adopt his remedy, intervention?

> "The nation has no policy of aggression toward Mexico. We have no desire for any part of her territory. We wish her to have peace, stability and prosperity. We should be ready to aid her in binding up her wounds, in relieving her from starvation and distress, in giving her in every practicable way the benefits of our disinterested friendship. The conduct of this administration has created difficulties which we shall have to surmount. . . . *We*

*shall have to adopt a new policy,* a policy of *firmness* and consistency through which alone we can promote an enduring *friendship*."

The theme friendship is for the non-interventionists, the theme "new policy" and "firmness" is for the interventionists. On the non-contentious record, the detail is overwhelming; on the issue everything is cloudy.

Concerning the European war Mr. Hughes employed an ingenious formula:

"I stand for the unflinching maintenance of *all* American rights on land and sea."

In order to understand the force of that statement at the time it was spoken, we must remember how each faction during the period of neutrality believed that the nations it opposed in Europe were alone violating American rights. Mr. Hughes seemed to say to the pro-Allies: I would have coerced Germany. But the pro-Germans had been insisting that British sea power was violating most of our rights. The formula covers two diametrically opposed purposes by the symbolic phrase "American rights."

But there was the Lusitania. Like the 1912 schism, it was an invincible obstacle to harmony.

". . . I am confident that there would have been no destruction of American lives by the sinking of the Lusitania."

Thus, what cannot be compromised must be obliterated, when there is a question on which we cannot all hope to get together, let us pretend that it does not exist. About the future of American relations with Europe Mr. Hughes was silent. Nothing he could say would possibly please the two irreconcilable factions for whose support he was bidding.

It is hardly necessary to say that Mr. Hughes did not invent this technic and did not employ it with the utmost success. But he illustrated how a public opinion constituted out of divergent opinions is clouded; how its meaning approaches the neutral tint formed out of the blending of many colors. Where superficial harmony is the aim and conflict the fact, obscurantism in a public appeal is the usual result. Almost always vagueness at a crucial point in public debate is a symptom of cross-purposes.

3

But how is it that a vague idea so often has the power to unite deeply felt opinions? These opinions, we recall, however deeply they may be felt, are not in continual and pungent contact with the facts they profess to treat. On the unseen environment, Mexico, the European war, our grip is slight though our feeling may be intense. The original pictures and words which aroused it have not anything like the force of the feeling itself. The account of what has happened out of sight and hearing in a place where we have never been, has not and never can have, except briefly as in a dream or fantasy, all the dimensions of reality. But it can arouse all, and sometimes even more emotion than the reality. For the trigger can be pulled by more than one stimulus.

The stimulus which originally pulled the trigger may have been a series of pictures in the mind aroused by printed or spoken words. These pictures fade and are hard to keep steady; their contours and their pulse fluctuate. Gradually the process sets in of knowing what you feel without being entirely certain why you feel it. The fading pictures are displaced by other pictures, and then by names or symbols. But the emotion goes on, capable now of being aroused by the substituted images and names. Even in severe thinking these substitutions take place, for if a man is trying to compare two complicated situations, he soon finds exhausting the attempt to hold both fully in mind in all their detail. He employs a shorthand of names and signs and samples. He has to do this if he is to advance at all, because he cannot carry the whole baggage in every phrase through every step he takes. But if he forgets that he has substituted and simplified, he soon lapses into verbalism, and begins to talk about names regardless of objects. And then he has no way of knowing when the name divorced from its first thing is carrying on a misalliance with some other thing. It is more difficult still to guard against changelings in casual politics.

For by what is known to psychologists as conditioned response, an emotion is not attached merely to one idea. There are no end of things which can arouse the emotion, and no end of things which can satisfy it. This is particularly true where the stimulus is only dimly and indirectly perceived, and where the objective is likewise indirect. For you can associate an emotion, say fear, first with something immediately dangerous, then with the idea of that thing, then with something similar to that idea, and so on and on. The whole structure of human culture is in one respect an elaboration of the stimuli and responses of which the original emotional capacities remain a fairly fixed center. No doubt the quality of emotion has changed in the course of history, but with nothing like the speed, or elaboration, that has characterized the conditioning of it.

People differ widely in their susceptibility to ideas. There are some in whom the idea of a starving child in Russia is practically as vivid as a starving child within sight. There are others who are almost incapable of being excited by a distant idea. There are many gradations between. And there are people who are insensitive to facts, and aroused only by ideas. But though the emotion is aroused by the idea, we are unable to satisfy the emotion by acting ourselves upon the scene itself. The idea of the starving Russian child evokes a desire to feed the child. But the person so aroused cannot feed it. He can only give money to an impersonal organization, or to a personification which he calls Mr. Hoover. His money does not reach that child. It goes to a general pool from which a mass of children are fed. And so just as the idea is second hand, so are the effects of the action second hand. The cognition is indirect, the conation is indirect, only the affect is immediate. Of the three parts of the process, the stimulus comes from somewhere out of sight, the response reaches somewhere out of sight, only the emotion exists entirely within the person. Of the child's hunger he has only an idea, of the child's relief he has only an idea, but of his own desire to help he has a real experience. It is the central fact of the business, the emotion within himself, which is first hand.

Within limits that vary, the emotion is transferable both as regards stimulus and response. Therefore, if among a number of people, possessing various tendencies to respond, you can find a stimulus which will arouse the same emotion in many of them, you can substitute it for the original stimuli. If, for example, one man dislikes the League, another hates Mr. Wilson, and a third fears labor, you may be able to unite them if you can find some symbol which is the antithesis of what they all hate. Suppose that symbol is Americanism. The first man may read it as meaning the preservation of American isolation, or as he may call it, independence; the second as the rejection of a politician who clashes with his idea of what an American president should be, the third as a call to resist revolution. The symbol in itself signifies literally no one thing in particular, but it can be associated with almost anything. And because of that it can become the common bond of common feelings, even though those feelings were originally attached to disparate ideas.

When political parties or newspapers declare for Americanism, Progressivism, Law and Order, Justice, Humanity, they hope to amalgamate the emotion of conflicting factions which would surely divide, if, instead of these symbols, they were invited to discuss a specific program. For when a coalition around the symbol has been effected, feeling flows toward conformity under the symbol rather than toward critical scrutiny of the measures. It is, I think, convenient and technically correct to call multiple phrases like these symbolic. They do not stand for specific ideas, but for a sort of truce or junction between ideas. They are like a strategic railroad center where many roads converge regardless of their ultimate origin or their ultimate destination. But he who captures the symbols by which public feeling is for the moment contained, controls by that much the approaches of public policy. And as long as a particular symbol has the power of coalition, ambitious factions will fight for possession. Think, for example, of Lincoln's name or of Roosevelt's. A leader or an interest that can make itself master of current symbols is master of the current situation. There are limits, of course. Too violent abuse of the actualities which groups of people think the symbol represents, or too great resistance in the name of that symbol to new purposes, will, so to speak, burst the symbol. In this manner, during the year 1917, the imposing symbol of Holy Russia and the Little Father burst under the impact of suffering and defeat.

## 4

The tremendous consequences of Russia's collapse were felt on all the fronts and among all the peoples. They led directly to a striking experiment in the crystallization of a common opinion out of the varieties of opinion churned up by the war. The Fourteen Points were addressed to all the governments, allied, enemy, neutral, and to all the peoples. They were an attempt to knit together the chief imponderables of a world war. Necessarily this was a new departure, because this was the first great war in which all the deciding elements of mankind could be brought to think about the same ideas, or at least about the same names for ideas, simultaneously. Without cable, radio, telegraph, and daily press, the experiment of the Fourteen Points would have been impossible. It was an attempt to exploit the modern machinery of communication to start the return to a "common consciousness" throughout the world.

But first we must examine some of the circumstances as they presented themselves at the end of 1917. For in the form which the document finally assumed, all these considerations are somehow represented. During the summer and autumn a series of events had occurred which profoundly affected the temper of the people and the course of the war. In July the Russians had made a last offensive, had been disastrously beaten, and the process of demoralization which led to the Bolshevik revolution of November had begun. Somewhat earlier the French had suffered a severe and almost disastrous defeat in Champagne which produced mutinies in the army and a defeatist agitation among the civilians. England was suffering from the effects of the submarine raids, from the terrible losses of the Flanders battles, and in November at Cambrai the British armies met a reverse that appalled the troops at the front and the leaders at home. Extreme war weariness pervaded the whole of western Europe.

In effect, the agony and disappointment had jarred loose men's concentration on the accepted version of the war. Their interests were no longer held by the ordinary official pronouncements, and their attention began to wander, fixing now upon their own suffering, now upon their party and class purposes, now upon general resentments against the governments. That more or less perfect organization of perception by official propaganda, of interest and attention by the stimuli of hope, fear, and hatred, which is called morale, was by way of breaking down. The minds of men everywhere began to search for new attachments that promised relief.

Suddenly they beheld a tremendous drama. On the Eastern front there was a Christmas truce, an end of slaughter, an end of noise, a promise of peace. At Brest-Litovsk the dream of all simple people had come to life: it was possible to negotiate, there was some other way to end the ordeal than by matching lives with the enemy. Timidly, but with rapt attention, people began to turn to the East. Why not, they asked? What is it all for? Do the politicians know what they are doing? Are we really fighting for what they say? Is it possible, perhaps, to secure it without fighting? Under the ban of the censorship, little of this was allowed to show itself in print, but, when Lord Lansdowne spoke, there was a response from the heart. The earlier symbols of the war had become hackneyed, and had lost their power to unify. Beneath the surface a wide schism was opening up in each Allied country.

Something similar was happening in Central Europe. There too the original impulse of the war was weakened; the union sacrée was broken. The vertical cleavages along the battle front were cut across by horizontal divisions running in all kinds of unforeseeable ways. The moral crisis of the war had arrived before the military decision was in sight. All this President Wilson and his advisers realized. They had not, of course, a perfect knowledge of the situation, but what I have sketched they knew.

They knew also that the Allied Governments were bound by a series of engagements that in letter and in spirit ran counter to the popular conception of what the war was about. The resolutions of the Paris Economic Conference were, of course, public property, and the network of secret treaties had been published by the Bolsheviks in November of 1917.[3] Their terms were only vaguely known to the peoples, but it was definitely believed that they did not comport with the idealistic slogan of self-determination, no annexations and no indemnities. Popular questioning took the form of asking how many thousand English lives Alsace-Lorraine or Dalmatia were worth, how many French lives Poland or Mesopotamia were worth. Nor was such ques-

---

[3] President Wilson stated at his conference with the Senators that he had never heard of these treaties until he reached Paris. That statement is perplexing. The Fourteen Points, as the text shows, could not have been formulated without a knowledge of the secret treaties. The substance of those treaties was before the President when he and Colonel House prepared the final published text of the Fourteen Points.

tioning entirely unknown in America. The whole Allied cause had been put on the defensive by the refusal to participate at Brest-Litovsk.

Here was a highly sensitive state of mind which no competent leader could fail to consider. The ideal response would have been joint action by the Allies. That was found to be impossible when it was considered at the Interallied Conference of October. But by December the pressure had become so great that Mr. George and Mr. Wilson were moved independently to make some response. The form selected by the President was a statement of peace terms under fourteen heads. The numbering of them was an artifice to secure precision, and to create at once the impression that here was a business-like document. The idea of stating "peace terms" instead of "war aims" arose from the necessity of establishing a genuine alternative to the Brest-Litovsk negotiations. They were intended to compete for attention by substituting for the spectacle of Russo-German parleys the much grander spectacle of a public world-wide debate.

Having enlisted the interest of the world, it was necessary to hold that interest unified and flexible for all the different possibilities which the situation contained. The terms had to be such that the majority among the Allies would regard them as worth while. They had to meet the national aspirations of each people, and yet to limit those aspirations so that no one nation would regard itself as a catspaw for another. The terms had to satisfy official interests so as not to provoke official disunion, and yet they had to meet popular conceptions so as to prevent the spread of demoralization. They had, in short, to preserve and confirm Allied unity in case the war was to go on.

But they had also to be the terms of a possible peace, so that in case the German center and left were ripe for agitation, they would have a text with which to smite the governing class. The terms had, therefore, to push the Allied governors nearer to their people, drive the German governors away from their people, and establish a line of common understanding between the Allies, the non-official Germans, and the subject peoples of Austria-Hungary. The Fourteen Points were a daring attempt to raise a standard to which almost everyone might repair. If a sufficient number of the enemy people were ready there would be peace; if not, then the Allies would be better prepared to sustain the shock of war.

All these considerations entered into the making of the Fourteen Points. No one man may have had them all in mind, but all the men concerned had some of them in mind. Against this background let us examine certain aspects of the document. The first five points and the fourteenth deal with "open diplomacy," "freedom of the seas," "equal trade opportunities," "reduction of armaments," no imperialist annexation of colonies, and the League of Nations. They might be described as a statement of the popular generalizations in which everyone at that time professed to believe. But number three is more specific. It was aimed consciously and directly at the resolutions of the Paris Economic Conference, and was meant to relieve the German people of their fear of suffocation.

Number six is the first point dealing with a particular nation. It was intended as a reply to Russian suspicion of the Allies, and the eloquence of its promises was attuned to the drama of Brest-Litovsk. Number seven deals with Belgium, and is as unqualified in form and purpose as was the conviction of practically the whole world, including very large sections of Central Europe. Over number eight we must pause. It begins with an absolute demand for evacuation and restoration of French territory, and then passes on to the question of Alsace-Lorraine. The phrasing of this clause most perfectly illustrates the character of a public statement which must condense a vast complex of interests in a few words. "And the wrong done to France by Prussia in 1871 in the matter of Alsace-Lorraine, which has unsettled the peace of the world for nearly fifty years, should be righted. . . ." Every word here was chosen with meticulous care. The wrong done should be righted; why not say that Alsace-Lorraine should be restored? It was not said, because it was not certain that all of the French *at that time* would fight on indefinitely for reannexation if they were offered a plebiscite; and because it was even less certain whether the English and Italians would fight on. The formula had, therefore, to cover both contingencies. The word "righted" guaranteed satisfaction to France, but did not read as a commitment to simple annexation. But why speak of the wrong done by *Prussia* in 1871? The word Prussia was, of course, intended to remind the South Germans that Alsace-Lorraine belonged not to them but to Prussia. Why speak of peace unsettled for "fifty years," and why the use of "1871"? In the first place, what the French and the rest of the world remembered was 1871. That was the nodal point of their grievance. But the formulators of the Fourteen Points knew that French officialdom planned for more than the Alsace-Lorraine of 1871. The secret memoranda that had passed between the Czar's ministers and French officials in 1916 covered the annexation of the Saar Valley and some sort of dismemberment of the Rhineland. It was planned to include the Saar Valley under the term "Alsace-Lorraine" because it had been part of Alsace-Lorraine in 1814, though it had been detached in 1815, and was no part of the territory at the close of the Franco-Prussian war. The official French formula for annexing the Saar was to subsume it under "Alsace-Lorraine" meaning the Alsace-Lorraine of 1814-1815. By insistence on "1871" the President was really defining the ultimate boundary between Germany and France, was adverting to the secret treaty, and was casting it aside.

Number nine, a little less subtly, does the same thing in respect to Italy. "Clearly recognizable lines of nationality" are exactly what the lines of the Treaty of London were not. Those lines were partly strategic, partly economic, partly imperialistic, partly ethnic. The only part of them that could possibly procure allied sympathy was that which would recover the genuine Italia Irredenta. All the rest, as everyone who was informed knew, merely delayed the impending Jugoslav revolt.

## 5

It would be a mistake to suppose that the apparently unanimous enthusiasm which greeted the Fourteen Points represented agreement on a program. Everyone seemed to find something that he liked and stressed this aspect and that detail. But no one risked a discussion. The phrases, so pregnant with the underlying conflicts of the civilized world, were accepted. They stood for opposing ideas, but they evoked a common emotion. And to that extent they played a part in rallying the western peoples for the desperate ten months of war which they had still to endure.

As long as the Fourteen Points dealt with that hazy and happy future when the agony was to be over, the real conflicts of interpretation were not made manifest. They were plans for the settlement of a wholly invisible environment, and because these plans inspired all groups each with its own private hope, all hopes ran together as a public hope. For harmonization, as we saw in Mr. Hughes's speech, is a hierarchy of symbols. As you ascend the hierarchy in order to include more and more factions you may for a time preserve the emotional connection though you lose the intellectual. But even the emotion becomes thinner. As you go further away from experience, you go higher into generalization or subtlety. As you go up in the balloon you throw more and more concrete objects overboard, and when you have reached the top with some phrase like the Rights of Humanity or the World Made Safe for Democracy, you see far and wide, but you see very little. Yet the people whose emotions are entrained do not remain passive. As the public appeal becomes more and more all things to all men, as the emotion is stirred while the meaning is dispersed, their very private meanings are given a universal application. Whatever you want badly is the Rights of Humanity. For the phrase, ever more vacant, capable of meaning almost anything, soon comes to mean pretty nearly everything. Mr. Wilson's phrases were understood in endlessly different ways in every corner of the earth. No document negotiated and made of public record existed to correct the confusion.[4] And so, when the day of settlement came, everybody expected everything. The European

---

[4] The American interpretation of the fourteen points was explained to the allied statesmen just before the armistice.

authors of the treaty had a large choice, and they chose to realize those expectations which were held by those of their countrymen who wielded the most power at home.

They came down the hierarchy from the Rights of Humanity to the Rights of France, Britain, and Italy. They did not abandon the use of symbols. They abandoned only those which after the war had no permanent roots in the imagination of their constituents. They preserved the unity of France by the use of symbolism, but they would not risk anything for the unity of Europe. The symbol France was deeply attached, the symbol Europe had only a recent history. Nevertheless the distinction between an omnibus like Europe and a symbol like France is not sharp. The history of states and empires reveals times when the scope of the unifying idea increases and also times when it shrinks. One cannot say that men have moved consistently from smaller loyalties to larger ones, because the facts will not bear out the claim. The Roman Empire and the Holy Roman Empire bellied out further than those national unifications in the Nineteenth Century from which believers in a World State argue by analogy. Nevertheless, it is probably true that the real integration has increased regardless of the temporary inflation and deflation of empires.

## 6

Such a real integration has undoubtedly occurred in American history. In the decade before 1789 most men, it seems, felt that their state and their community were real, but that the confederation of states was unreal. The idea of their state, its flag, its most conspicuous leaders, or whatever it was that represented Massachusetts, or Virginia, were genuine symbols. That is to say, they were fed by actual experiences from childhood, occupation, residence, and the like. The span of men's experience had rarely traversed the imaginary boundaries of their states. The word Virginian was related to pretty nearly everything that most Virginians had ever known or felt. It was the most extensive political idea which had genuine contact with their experience.

Their experience, not their needs. For their needs arose out of their real environment, which in those days was at least as large as the thirteen colonies. They needed a common defense. They needed a financial and economic regime as extensive as the Confederation. But as long as the pseudo-environment of the state encompassed them, the state symbols exhausted their political interest. An interstate idea, like the Confederation, represented a powerless abstraction. It was an omnibus, rather than a symbol, and the harmony among divergent groups, which the omnibus creates, is transient.

I have said that the idea of confederation was a powerless abstraction.

Yet the need of unity existed in the decade before the Constitution was adopted. The need existed, in the sense that affairs were askew unless the need of unity was taken into account. Gradually certain classes in each colony began to break through the state experience. Their personal interests led across the state lines to interstate experiences, and gradually there was constructed in their minds a picture of the American environment which was truly national in scope. For them the idea of federation became a true symbol, and ceased to be an omnibus. The most imaginative of these men was Alexander Hamilton. It happened that he had no primitive attachment to any one state, for he was born in the West Indies, and had, from the very beginning of his active life, been associated with the common interests of all the states. Thus to most men of the time the question of whether the capital should be in Virginia or in Philadelphia was of enormous importance, because they were locally minded. To Hamilton this question was of no emotional consequence; what he wanted was the assumption of the state debts because they would further nationalize the proposed union. So he gladly traded the site of the capitol for two necessary votes from men who represented the Potomac district. To Hamilton the Union was a symbol that represented all his interests and his whole experience; to White and Lee from the Potomac, the symbol of their province was the highest political entity they served, and they served it though they hated to pay the price. They agreed, says Jefferson, to change their votes, "White with a revulsion of stomach almost convulsive."[5]

In the crystallizing of a common will, there is always an Alexander Hamilton at work.


# XIV. Yes or No

## 1

SYMBOLS are often so useful and so mysteriously powerful that the word itself exhales a magical glamor. In thinking about symbols it is tempting to treat them as if they possessed independent energy. Yet no end of symbols which once provoked ecstasy have quite ceased to affect anybody. The museums and the books of folklore are full of dead emblems and incantations, since there is no power in the symbol, except that which it acquires by association in the human mind. The symbols that have lost their power, and the symbols incessantly suggested

---

[5] *Works*, Vol. IX, p. 87. Cited by Beard, *Economic Origins of Jeffersonian Democracy*, p. 172.

which fail to take root, remind us that if we were patient enough to study in detail the circulation of a symbol, we should behold an entirely secular history.

In the Hughes campaign speech, in the Fourteen Points, in Hamilton's project, symbols are employed. But they are employed by somebody at a particular moment. The words themselves do not crystallize random feeling. The words must be spoken by people who are strategically placed, and they must be spoken at the opportune moment. Otherwise they are mere wind. The symbols must be earmarked. For in themselves they mean nothing, and the choice of possible symbols is always so great that we should, like the donkey who stood equidistant between two bales of hay, perish from sheer indecision among the symbols that compete for our attention.

Here, for example, are the reasons for their vote as stated by certain private citizens to a newspaper just before the election of 1920.

For Harding:

"The patriotic men and women of to-day, who cast their ballots for Harding and Coolidge will be held by posterity to have signed our Second Declaration of Independence."

Mr. Wilmot——, inventor.

"He will see to it that the United States does not enter into 'entangling alliances.' Washington as a city will benefit by changing the control of the government from the Democrats to the Republicans."

Mr. Clarence——, salesman.

For Cox:

"The people of the United States realize that it is our duty pledged on the fields of France, to join the League of Nations. We must shoulder our share of the burden of enforcing peace throughout the world."

Miss Marie——, stenographer.

"We should lose our own respect and the respect of other nations were we to refuse to enter the League of Nations in obtaining international peace."

Mr. Spencer——, statistician.

The two sets of phrases are equally noble, equally true, and almost reversible. Would Clarence and Wilmot have admitted for an instant that they intended to default in our duty pledged on the fields of France; or that they did not desire international peace? Certainly not. Would Marie and Spencer have admitted that they were in favor of entangling alliances or the surrender of American independence? They would have argued with you that the League was, as President

Wilson called it, a disentangling alliance, as well as a Declaration of Independence for all the world, plus a Monroe Doctrine for the planet.

## 2

Since the offering of symbols is so generous, and the meaning that can be imputed is so elastic, how does any particular symbol take root in any particular person's mind? It is planted there by another human being whom we recognize as authoritative. If it is planted deeply enough, it may be that later we shall call the person authoritative who waves that symbol at us. But in the first instance symbols are made congenial and important because they are introduced to us by congenial and important people.

For we are not born out of an egg at the age of eighteen with a realistic imagination; we are still, as Mr. Shaw recalls, in the era of Burge and Lubin, where in infancy we are dependent upon older beings for our contacts. And so we make our connections with the outer world through certain beloved and authoritative persons. They are the first bridge to the invisible world. And though we may gradually master for ourselves many phases of that larger environment, there always remains a vaster one that is unknown. To that we still relate ourselves through authorities. Where all the facts are out of sight a true report and a plausible error read alike, sound alike, feel alike. Except on a few subjects where our own knowledge is great, we cannot choose between true and false accounts. So we choose between trustworthy and untrustworthy reporters.[1]

Theoretically we ought to choose the most expert on each subject. But the choice of the expert, though a good deal easier than the choice of truth, is still too difficult and often impracticable. The experts themselves are not in the least certain who among them is the most expert. And at that, the expert, even when we can identify him, is, likely as not, too busy to be consulted, or impossible to get at. But there are people whom we can identify easily enough because they are the people who are at the head of affairs. Parents, teachers, and masterful friends are the first people of this sort we encounter. Into the difficult question of why children trust one parent rather than another, the history teacher rather than the Sunday school teacher, we need not try to enter. Nor how trust gradually spreads through a newspaper or an acquaintance who is interested in public affairs to public personages. The literature of psychoanalysis is rich in suggestive hypothesis.

---

[1] See an interesting, rather quaint old book: George Cornewall Lewis, *An Essay on the Influence of Authority in Matters of Opinion.*

At any rate we do find ourselves trusting certain people, who constitute our means of junction with pretty nearly the whole realm of
unknown things. Strangely enough, this fact is sometimes regarded as
inherently undignified, as evidence of our sheep-like, ape-like nature.
But complete independence in the universe is simply unthinkable. If
we could not take practically everything for granted, we should spend
our lives in utter triviality. The nearest thing to a wholly independent
adult is a hermit, and the range of a hermit's action is very short. Acting
entirely for himself, he can act only within a tiny radius and for simple
ends. If he has time to think great thoughts we can be certain that he
has accepted without question, before he went in for being a hermit, a
whole repertory of painfully acquired information about how to keep
warm and how to keep from being hungry, and also about what the
great questions are.

On all but a very few matters for short stretches in our lives, the
utmost independence that we can exercise is to multiply the authorities
to whom we give a friendly hearing. As congenital amateurs our quest
for truth consists in stirring up the experts, and forcing them to answer
any heresy that has the accent of conviction. In such a debate we can
often judge who has won the dialectical victory, but we are virtually
defenseless against a false premise that none of the debaters has chal-
lenged, or a neglected aspect that none of them has brought into the
argument. We shall see later how the democratic theory proceeds on
the opposite assumption and assumes for the purposes of government
an unlimited supply of self-sufficient individuals.

The people on whom we depend for contact with the outer world are
those who seem to be running it.[2] They may be running only a very
small part of the world. The nurse feeds the child, bathes it, and puts it
to bed. That does not constitute the nurse an authority on physics, zoölogy, and the Higher Criticism. Mr. Smith runs, or at least hires, the man
who runs the factory. That does not make him an authority on
the Constitution of the United States, nor on the effects of the Fordney
tariff. Mr. Smoot runs the Republican party in the State of Utah. That
in itself does not prove he is the best man to consult about taxation. But
the nurse may nevertheless determine for a while what zoölogy the child
shall learn, Mr. Smith will have much to say on what the Constitution
shall mean to his wife, his secretary, and perhaps even to his parson, and
who shall define the limits of Senator Smoot's authority?

The priest, the lord of the manor, the captains and the kings, the party
leaders, the merchant, the boss, however these men are chosen, whether
by birth, inheritance, conquest or election, they and their organized

---

[2] *Cf.* Bryce, *Modern Democracies*, Vol. II, pp. 544–545.

following administer human affairs. They are the officers, and although the same man may be field marshal at home, second lieutenant at the office, and scrub private in politics, although in many institutions the hierarchy of rank is vague or concealed, yet in every institution that requires the coöperation of many persons, some such hierarchy exists.[3] In American politics we call it a machine, or "the organization."

## 3

There are a number of important distinctions between the members of the machine and the rank and file. The leaders, the steering committee and the inner circle, are in direct contact with their environment. They may, to be sure, have a very limited notion of what they ought to define as the environment, but they are not dealing almost wholly with abstractions. There are particular men they hope to see elected, particular balance sheets they wish to see improved, concrete objectives that must be attained. I do not mean that they escape the human propensity to stereotyped vision. Their stereotypes often make them absurd routineers. But whatever their limitations, the chiefs are in actual contact with some crucial part of that larger environment. They decide. They give orders. They bargain. And something definite, perhaps not at all what they imagined, actually happens.

Their subordinates are not tied to them by a common conviction. That is to say the lesser members of a machine do not dispose their loyalty according to independent judgment about the wisdom of the leaders. In the hierarchy each is dependent upon a superior and is in turn superior to some class of his dependents. What holds the machine together is a system of privileges. These may vary according to the opportunities and the tastes of those who seek them, from nepotism and patronage in all their aspects to clannishness, hero-worship or a fixed idea. They vary from military rank in armies, through land and services in a feudal system, to jobs and publicity in a modern democracy. That is why you can break up a particular machine by abolishing its privileges. But the machine in every coherent group is, I believe, certain to reappear. For privilege is entirely relative, and uniformity is impossible. Imagine the most absolute communism of which your mind is capable, where no one possessed any object that everyone else did not possess, and still, if the communist group had to take any action whatever, the mere pleasure of being the friend of the man who was

---

[3] *Cf.* M. Ostrogorski, *Democracy and the Organization of Political Parties, passim;* R. Michels, *Political Parties, passim;* and Bryce, *Modern Democracies,* particularly Chap. LXXV; also Ross, *Principles of Sociology,* Chaps. XXII–XXIV.

going to make the speech that secured the most votes, would, I am convinced, be enough to crystallize an organization of insiders around him.

It is not necessary, then, to invent a collective intelligence in order to explain why the judgments of a group are usually more coherent, and often more true to form than the remarks of the man in the street. One mind, or a few can pursue a train of thought, but a group trying to think in concert can as a group do little more than assent or dissent. The members of a hierarchy can have a corporate tradition. As apprentices they learn the trade from the masters, who in turn learned it when they were apprentices, and in any enduring society, the change of personnel within the governing hierarchies is slow enough to permit the transmission of certain great stereotypes and patterns of behavior. From father to son, from prelate to novice, from veteran to cadet, certain ways of seeing and doing are taught. These ways become familiar, and are recognized as such by the mass of outsiders.

## 4

Distance alone lends enchantment to the view that masses of human beings ever coöperate in any complex affair without a central machine managed by a very few people. "No one," says Bryce,[4] "can have had some years' experience of the conduct of affairs in a legislature or an administration without observing how extremely small is the number of persons by whom the world is governed." He is referring, of course, to affairs of state. To be sure if you consider all the affairs of mankind the number of people who govern is considerable, but if you take any particular institution, be it a legislature, a party, a trade union, a nationalist movement, a factory, or a club, the number of those who govern is a very small percentage of those who are theoretically supposed to govern.

Landslides can turn one machine out and put another in; revolutions sometimes abolish a particular machine altogether. The democratic revolution set up two alternating machines, each of which in the course of a few years reaps the advantage from the mistakes of the other. But nowhere does the machine disappear. Nowhere is the idyllic theory of democracy realized. Certainly not in trades unions, nor in socialist parties, nor in communist governments. There is an inner circle, surrounded by concentric circles which fade out gradually into the disinterested or uninterested rank and file.

Democrats have never come to terms with this commonplace of group life. They have invariably regarded it as perverse. For there are two visions of democracy: one presupposes the self-sufficient individual; the

---

[4] *Op. cit.*, Vol. II, p. 542.

other an Oversoul regulating everything. Of the two the Oversoul has some advantage because it does at least recognize that the mass makes decisions that are not spontaneously born in the breast of every member. But the Oversoul as presiding genius in corporate behavior is a superfluous mystery if we fix our attention upon the machine. The machine is a quite prosaic reality. It consists of human beings who wear clothes and live in houses, who can be named and described. They perform all the duties usually assigned to the Oversoul.

## 5

The reason for the machine is not the perversity of human nature. It is that out of the private notions of any group no common idea emerges by itself. For the number of ways is limited in which a multitude of people can act directly upon a situation beyond their reach. Some of them can migrate, in one form or another, they can strike or boycott, they can applaud or hiss. They can by these means occasionally resist what they do not like, or coerce those who obstruct what they desire. But by mass action nothing can be constructed, devised, negotiated, or administered. A public as such, without an organized hierarchy around which it can gather, may refuse to buy if the prices are too high, or refuse to work if wages are too low. A trade union can by mass action in a strike break an opposition so that the union officials can negotiate an agreement. It may win, for example, the *right* to joint control. But it cannot exercise the right except through an organization. A nation can clamor for war, but when it goes to war it must put itself under orders from a general staff.

The limit of direct action is for all practical purposes the power to say Yes or No on an issue presented to the mass.[5] For only in the very simplest cases does an issue present itself in the same form spontaneously and approximately at the same time to all the members of a public. There are unorganized strikes and boycotts, not merely industrial ones, where the grievance is so plain that virtually without leadership the same reaction takes place in many people. But even in these rudimentary cases there are persons who know what they want to do more quickly than the rest, and who become impromptu ringleaders. Where they do not appear a crowd will mill about aimlessly beset by all its private aims, or stand by fatalistically, as did a crowd of fifty persons the other day, and watch a man commit suicide.

For what we make out of most of the impressions that come to us from

---

[5] Cf. James, *Some Problems of Philosophy*, p. 227. "But for most of our emergencies, fractional solutions are impossible. Seldom can we *act* fractionally."
Cf. Lowell, *Public Opinion and Popular Government*, pp. 91, 92.

the invisible world is a kind of pantomime played out in revery. The number of times is small that we consciously decide anything about events
beyond our sight, and each man's opinion of what he could accomplish
if he tried, is slight. There is rarely a practical issue, and therefore no great
habit of decision. This would be more evident were it not that most information when it reaches us carries with it an aura of suggestion as to how
we ought to feel about the news. That suggestion we need, and if we do
not find it in the news we turn to the editorials or to a trusted adviser. The
revery, if we feel ourselves implicated, is uncomfortable until we know
where we stand, that is, until the facts have been formulated so that we
can feel Yes or No in regard to them.

When a number of people all say Yes they may have all kinds of reasons for saying it. They generally do. For the pictures in their minds are,
as we have already noted, varied in subtle and intimate ways. But this
subtlety remains within their minds; it becomes represented publicly
by a number of symbolic phrases which carry the individual emotion
after evacuating most of the intention. The hierarchy, or, if it is a contest, then the two hierarchies, associate the symbols with a definite
action, a vote of Yes or No, an attitude pro or con. Then Smith who was
against the League and Jones who was against Article X, and Brown
who was against Mr. Wilson and all his works, each for his own reason,
all in the name of more or less the same symbolic phrase, register a vote
*against* the Democrats by voting for the Republicans. A common will
has been expressed.

A concrete choice had to be presented, the choice had to be connected, by the transfer of interest through the symbols, with individual
opinion. The professional politicians learned this long before the
democratic philosophers. And so they organized the caucus, the nom-
inating convention, and the steering committee, as the means of formulating a definite choice. Everyone who wishes to accomplish anything that requires the coöperation of a large number of people follows
their example. Sometimes it is done rather brutally as when the Peace
Conference reduced itself to the Council of Ten, and the Council of
Ten to the Big Three or Four; and wrote a treaty which the minor allies,
their own constituents, and the enemy were permitted to take or leave.
More consultation than that is generally possible and desirable. But the
essential fact remains that a small number of heads present a choice to
a large group.

6

The abuses of the steering committee have led to various proposals
such as the initiative, referendum and direct primary. But these merely
postponed or obscured the need for a machine by complicating the

elections, or as H. G. Wells once said with scrupulous accuracy, the selections. For no amount of balloting can obviate the need of creating an issue, be it a measure or a candidate, on which the voters can say Yes, or No. There is, in fact, no such thing as "direct legislation." For what happens where it is supposed to exist? The citizen goes to the polls, receives a ballot on which a number of measures are printed, almost always in abbreviated form, and, if he says anything at all, he says Yes or No. The most brilliant amendment in the world may occur to him. He votes Yes or No on that bill and no other. You have to commit violence against the English language to call that legislation. I do not argue, of course, that there are no benefits, whatever you call the process. I think that for certain kinds of issues there are distinct benefits. But the necessary simplicity of any mass decision is a very important fact in view of the inevitable complexity of the world in which those decisions operate. The most complicated form of voting that anyone proposes is, I suppose, the preferential ballot. Among a number of candidates presented the voter under that system, instead of saying yes to one candidate and no to all the others, states the order of his choice. But even here, immensely more flexible though it is, the action of the mass depends upon the quality of the choices presented.[6] And those choices are presented by the energetic coteries who hustle about with petitions and round up the delegates. The Many can elect after the Few have nominated.

# XV.   Leaders and the Rank and File

## 1

BECAUSE of their transcendent practical importance, no successful leader has ever been too busy to cultivate the symbols which organize his following. What privileges do within the hierarchy, symbols do for the rank and file. They conserve unity. From the totem pole to the

---

[6] Cf. H. J. Laski, *Foundations of Sovereignty*, p. 224. ". . . proportional representation . . . by leading, as it seems to lead, to the group system . . . may deprive the electors of their choice of leaders." The group system undoubtedly tends, as Mr. Laski says, to make the selection of the executive more indirect, but there is no doubt also that it tends to produce legislative assemblies in which currents of opinion are more fully represented. Whether that is good or bad cannot be determined a priori. But one can say that successful cooperation and responsibility in a more accurately representative assembly require a higher organization of political intelligence and political habit, than in a rigid two-party house. It is a more complex political form and may therefore work less well.

national flag, from the wooden idol to God the Invisible King, from the magic word to some diluted version of Adam Smith or Bentham, symbols have been cherished by leaders, many of whom were themselves unbelievers, because they were focal points where differences merged. The detached observer may scorn the "star-spangled" ritual which hedges the symbol, perhaps as much as the king who told himself that Paris was worth a few masses. But the leader knows by experience that only when symbols have done their work is there a handle he can use to move a crowd. In the symbol emotion is discharged at a common target, and the idiosyncrasy of real ideas blotted out. No wonder he hates what he calls destructive criticism, sometimes called by free spirits the elimination of buncombe. "Above all things," says Bagehot, "our royalty is to be reverenced, and if you begin to poke about it you cannot reverence it."[1] For poking about with clear definitions and candid statements serves all high purposes known to man, except the easy conservation of a common will. Poking about, as every responsible leader suspects, tends to break the transference of emotion from the individual mind to the institutional symbol. And the first result of that is, as he rightly says, a chaos of individualism and warring sects. The disintegration of a symbol, like Holy Russia, or the Iron Diaz, is always the beginning of a long upheaval.

These great symbols possess by transference all the minute and detailed loyalties of an ancient and stereotyped society. They evoke the feeling that each individual has for the landscape, the furniture, the faces, the memories that are his first, and in a static society, his only reality. That core of images and devotions without which he is unthinkable to himself, is nationality. The great symbols take up these devotions, and can arouse them without calling forth the primitive images. The lesser symbols of public debate, the more casual chatter of politics, are always referred back to these proto-symbols, and if possible associated with them. The question of a proper fare on a municipal subway is symbolized as an issue between the People and the Interests, and then the People is inserted in the symbol American, so that finally in the heat of a campaign, an eight cent fare becomes unAmerican. The Revolutionary fathers died to prevent it. Lincoln suffered that it might not come to pass, resistance to it was implied in the death of those who sleep in France.

Because of its power to siphon emotion out of distinct ideas, the symbol is both a mechanism of solidarity, and a mechanism of exploitation. It enables people to work for a common end, but just because the few who are strategically placed must choose the concrete objectives, the

---

[1] *The English Constitution*, p. 127. D. Appleton & Company, 1914.

symbol is also an instrument by which a few can fatten on many, deflect criticism, and seduce men into facing agony for objects they do not understand.

Many aspects of our subjection to symbols are not flattering if we choose to think of ourselves as realistic, self-sufficient, and self-governing personalities. Yet it is impossible to conclude that symbols are altogether instruments of the devil. In the realm of science and contemplation they are undoubtedly the tempter himself. But in the world of action they may be beneficent, and are sometimes a necessity. The necessity is often imagined, the peril manufactured. But when quick results are imperative, the manipulation of masses through symbols may be the only quick way of having a critical thing done. It is often more important to act than to understand. It is sometimes true that the action would fail if everyone understood it. There are many affairs which cannot wait for a referendum or endure publicity, and there are times, during war for example, when a nation, an army, and even its commanders must trust strategy to a very few minds; when two conflicting opinions, though one happens to be right, are more perilous than one opinion which is wrong. The wrong opinion may have bad results, but the two opinions may entail disaster by dissolving unity.[2]

Thus Foch and Sir Henry Wilson, who foresaw the impending disaster to Gough's army, as a consequence of the divided and scattered reserves, nevertheless kept their opinions well within a small circle, knowing that even the risk of a smashing defeat was less certainly destructive, than would have been an excited debate in the newspapers. For what matters most under the kind of tension which prevailed in March, 1918, is less the rightness of a particular move than the unbroken expectation as to the source of command. Had Foch "gone to the people" he might have won the debate, but long before he could have won it, the armies which he was to command would have dissolved. For the spectacle of a row on Olympus is diverting and destructive.

But so also is a conspiracy of silence. Says Captain Wright: "It is in the High Command and not in the line, that the art of camouflage is most practiced, and reaches to highest flights. All chiefs everywhere are now kept painted, by the busy work of numberless publicists, so as to be mistaken for Napoleons—at a distance. . . . It becomes almost impossible to displace these Napoleons, whatever their incompetence, because of the enormous public support created by hiding or glossing failure, and exaggerating or inventing success. . . . But the most insidious and worst effect of this so highly organized falsity is on the generals

---

[2] Captain Peter S. Wright, Assistant Secretary of the Supreme War Council, *At the Supreme War Council*, is well worth careful reading on secrecy and unity of command, even though in respect to the allied leaders he wages a passionate polemic.

themselves: modest and patriotic as they mostly are, and as most men must be to take up and follow the noble profession of arms, they themselves are ultimately affected by these universal illusions, and reading it every morning in the paper, they also grow persuaded they are thunderbolts of war and infallible, however much they fail, and that their maintenance in command is an end so sacred that it justifies the use of any means. . . . These various conditions, of which this great deceit is the greatest, at last emancipate all General Staffs from all control. They no longer live for the nation: the nation lives, or rather dies, for them. Victory or defeat ceases to be the prime interest. What matters to these semi-sovereign corporations is whether dear old Willie or poor old Harry is going to be at their head, or the Chantilly party prevail over the Boulevard des Invalides party."[3]

Yet Captain Wright who can be so eloquent and so discerning about the dangers of silence is forced nevertheless to approve the silence of Foch in not publicly destroying the illusions. There is here a complicated paradox, arising as we shall see more fully later on, because the traditional democratic view of life is conceived, not for emergencies and dangers, but for tranquility and harmony. And so where masses of people must coöperate in an uncertain and eruptive environment, it is usually necessary to secure unity and flexibility without real consent. The symbol does that. It obscures personal intention, neutralizes discrimination, and obfuscates individual purpose. It immobilizes personality, yet at the same time it enormously sharpens the intention of the group and welds that group, as nothing else in a crisis can weld it, to purposeful action. It renders the mass mobile though it immobilizes personality. The symbol is the instrument by which in the short run the mass escapes from its own inertia, the inertia of indecision, or the inertia of headlong movement, and is rendered capable of being led along the zigzag of a complex situation.

2

But in the longer run, the give and take increases between the leaders and the led. The word most often used to describe the state of mind in the rank and file about its leaders is morale. That is said to be good when the individuals do the part allotted to them with all their energy; when each man's whole strength is evoked by the command from above. It follows that every leader must plan his policy with this in mind. He must consider his decision not only on "the merits," but also

---

in its effect on any part of his following whose continued support he requires. If he is a general planning an attack, he knows that his organized military units will scatter into mobs if the percentage of casualties rises too high.

In the Great War previous calculations were upset to an extraordinary degree, for "out of every nine men who went to France five became casualties."[4] The limit of endurance was far greater than anyone had supposed. But there was a limit somewhere. And so, partly because of its effect on the enemy, but also in great measure because of its effect on the troops and their families, no command in this war dared to publish a candid statement of its losses. In France the casualty lists were never published. In England, America, and Germany publication of the losses of a big battle were spread out over long periods so as to destroy a unified impression of the total. Only the insiders knew until long afterwards what the Somme had cost, or the Flanders battles;[5] and Ludendorff undoubtedly had a very much more accurate idea of these casualties than any private person in London, Paris or Chicago. All the leaders in every camp did their best to limit the amount of actual war which any one soldier or civilian could vividly conceive. But, of course, among old veterans like the French troops of 1917, a great deal more is known about war than ever reaches the public. Such an army begins to judge its commanders in terms of its own suffering. And then, when another extravagant promise of victory turns out to be the customary bloody defeat, you may find that a mutiny breaks out over some comparatively minor blunder,[6] like Nivelle's offensive of 1917, because it is a cumulative blunder. Revolutions and mutinies generally follow a small sample of a big series of evils.[7]

The incidence of policy determines the relation between leader and following. If those whom he needs in his plan are remote from the place where the action takes place, if the results are hidden or postponed, if the individual obligations are indirect or not yet due, above all if assent is an exercise of some pleasurable emotion, the leader is likely to have a free hand. Those programs are immediately most popular, like prohibition among teetotalers, which do not at once impinge upon the private habits of the followers. That is one

---

[4] *Op cit.*, p. 37. Figures taken by Captain Wright from the statistical abstract of the war in the Archives of the War Office. The figures refer apparently to the English losses alone, possibly to the English and French.

[5] *Op cit.*, p. 34, the Somme cost nearly 500,000 casualties; the Arras and Flanders offensives of 1917 cost 650,000 British casualties.

[6] The Allies suffered many bloodier defeats than that on the Chemin des Dames.

[7] *Cf.* Pierrefeu's account, *op. cit.*, on the causes of the Soissons mutinies, and the method adopted by Pétain to deal with them. Vol. I, Part III, *et seq.*

great reason why governments have such a free hand in foreign affairs. Most of the frictions between two states involve a series of obscure and long-winded contentions, occasionally on the frontier, but far more often in regions about which school geographies have supplied no precise ideas. In Czechoslovakia America is regarded as the Liberator; in American newspaper paragraphs and musical comedy, in American conversation by and large, it has never been finally settled whether the country we liberated is Czechoslavia or Jugoslovakia.

In foreign affairs the incidence of policy is for a very long time confined to an unseen environment. Nothing that happens out there is felt to be wholly real. And so, because in the ante-bellum period, nobody has to fight and nobody has to pay, governments go along according to their lights without much reference to their people. In local affairs the cost of a policy is more easily visible. And therefore, all but the most exceptional leaders prefer policies in which the costs are as far as possible indirect. They do not like direct taxation. They do not like to pay as they go. They like long term debts. They like to have the voters believe that the foreigner will pay. They have always been compelled to calculate prosperity in terms of the producer rather than in terms of the consumer, because the incidence on the consumer is distributed over so many trivial items. Labor leaders have always preferred an increase of money wages to a decrease in prices. There has always been more popular interest in the profits of millionaires, which are visible but comparatively unimportant, than in the wastes of the industrial system, which are huge but elusive. A legislature dealing with a shortage of houses, such as exists when this is written, illustrates this rule, first by doing nothing to increase the number of houses, second by smiting the greedy landlord on the hip, third by investigating the profiteering builders and working men. For a constructive policy deals with remote and uninteresting factors, while a greedy landlord, or a profiteering plumber is visible and immediate.

But while people will readily believe that in an unimagined future and in unseen places a certain policy will benefit them, the actual working out of policy follows a different logic from their opinions. A nation may be induced to believe that jacking up the freight rates will make the railroads prosperous. But that belief will not make the roads prosperous, if the impact of those rates on farmers and shippers is such as to produce a commodity price beyond what the consumer can pay. Whether the consumer will pay the price depends not upon whether he nodded his head nine months previously at the proposal to raise rates and save business, but on whether he now wants a new hat or a new automobile enough to pay for them.

### 3

Leaders often pretend that they have merely uncovered a program which existed in the minds of their public. When they believe it, they are usually deceiving themselves. Programs do not invent themselves synchronously in a multitude of minds. That is not because a multitude of minds is necessarily inferior to that of the leaders, but because thought is the function of an organism, and a mass is not an organism.

This fact is obscured because the mass is constantly exposed to suggestion. It reads not the news, but the news with an aura of suggestion about it, indicating the line of action to be taken. It hears reports, not objective as the facts are, but already stereotyped to a certain pattern of behavior. Thus the ostensible leader often finds that the real leader is a powerful newspaper proprietor. But if, as in a laboratory, one could remove all suggestion and leading from the experience of a multitude, one would, I think, find something like this: A mass exposed to the same stimuli would develop responses that could theoretically be charted in a polygon of error. There would be a certain group that felt sufficiently alike to be classified together. There would be variants of feeling at both ends. These classifications would tend to harden as individuals in each of the classifications made their reactions vocal. That is to say, when the vague feelings of those who felt vaguely had been put into words, they would know more definitely what they felt, and would then feel it more definitely.

Leaders in touch with popular feeling are quickly conscious of these reactions. They know that high prices are pressing upon the mass, or that certain classes of individuals are becoming unpopular, or that feeling towards another nation is friendly or hostile. But, always barring the effect of suggestion which is merely the assumption of leadership by the reporter, there would be nothing in the feeling of the mass that fatally determined the choice of any particular policy. All that the feeling of the mass demands is that policy as it is developed and exposed shall be, if not logically, then by analogy and association, connected with the original feeling.

So when a new policy is to be launched, there is a preliminary bid for community of feeling, as in Mark Antony's speech to the followers of Brutus.[8] In the first phase, the leader vocalizes the prevalent opinion of the mass. He identifies himself with the familiar attitudes of his audience, sometimes by telling a good story, sometimes by brandishing his patriotism, often by pinching a grievance. Finding that he is trustwor-

---

[8] Excellently analyzed in Martin, *The Behavior of Crowds*, pp. 130-132.

thy, the multitude milling hither and thither may turn in towards him. He will then be expected to set forth a plan of campaign. But he will not find that plan in the slogans which convey the feelings of the mass. It will not even always be indicated by them. Where the incidence of policy is remote, all that is essential is that the program shall be verbally and emotionally connected at the start with what has become vocal in the multitude. Trusted men in a familiar role subscribing to the accepted symbols can go a very long way on their own initiative without explaining the substance of their programs.

But wise leaders are not content to do that. Provided they think publicity will not strengthen opposition too much, and that debate will not delay action too long, they seek a certain measure of consent. They take, if not the whole mass, then the subordinates of the hierarchy sufficiently into their confidence to prepare them for what might happen, and to make them feel that they have freely willed the result. But however sincere the leader may be, there is always, when the facts are very complicated, a certain amount of illusion in these consultations. For it is impossible that all the contingencies shall be as vivid to the whole public as they are to the more experienced and the more imaginative. A fairly large percentage are bound to agree without having taken the time, or without possessing the background, for appreciating the choices which the leader presents to them. No one, however, can ask for more. And only theorists do. If we have had our day in court, if what we had to say was heard, and then if what is done comes out well, most of us do not stop to consider how much our opinion effected the business in hand.

And therefore, if the established powers are sensitive and well-informed, if they are visibly trying to meet popular feeling, and actually removing some of the causes of dissatisfaction, no matter how slowly they proceed, provided they are seen to be proceeding, they have little to fear. It takes stupendous and persistent blundering, plus almost infinite tactlessness, to start a revolution from below. Palace revolutions, interdepartmental revolutions, are a different matter. So, too, is demagogy. That stops at relieving the tension by expressing the feeling. But the statesman knows that such relief is temporary, and if indulged too often, unsanitary. He, therefore, sees to it that he arouses no feeling which he cannot sluice into a program that deals with the facts to which the feelings refer.

But all leaders are not statesmen, all leaders hate to resign, and most leaders find it hard to believe that bad as things are, the other fellow would not make them worse. They do not passively wait for the public to feel the incidence of policy, because the incidence of that discovery is generally upon their own heads. They are, therefore, intermittently engaged in mending their fences and consolidating their position.

The mending of fences consists in offering an occasional scapegoat, in redressing a minor grievance affecting a powerful individual or faction, rearranging certain jobs, placating a group of people who want an arsenal in their home town, or a law to stop somebody's vices. Study the daily activity of any public official who depends on election and you can enlarge this list. There are Congressmen elected year after year who never think of dissipating their energy on public affairs. They prefer to do a little service for a lot of people on a lot of little subjects, rather than to engage in trying to do a big service out there in the void. But the number of people to whom any organization can be a successful valet is limited, and shrewd politicians take care to attend either the influential, or somebody so blatantly uninfluential that to pay any attention to him is a mark of sensational magnanimity. The far greater number who cannot be held by favors, the anonymous multitude, receive propaganda.

The established leaders of any organization have great natural advantages. They are believed to have better sources of information. The books and papers are in their offices. They took part in the important conferences. They met the important people. They have responsibility. It is, therefore, easier for them to secure attention and to speak in a convincing tone. But also they have a very great deal of control over the access to the facts. Every official is in some degree a censor. And since no one can suppress information, either by concealing it or forgetting to mention it, without some notion of what he wishes the public to know, every leader is in some degree a propagandist. Strategically placed, and compelled often to choose even at the best between the equally cogent though conflicting ideals of safety for the institution, and candor to his public, the official finds himself deciding more and more consciously what facts, in what setting, in what guise he shall permit the public to know.

## 4

That the manufacture of consent is capable of great refinements no one, I think, denies. The process by which public opinions arise is certainly no less intricate than it has appeared in these pages, and the opportunities for manipulation open to anyone who understands the process are plain enough.

The creation of consent is not a new art. It is a very old one which was supposed to have died out with the appearance of democracy. But it has not died out. It has, in fact, improved enormously in technic, because it is now based on analysis rather than on rule of thumb. And so, as a result of psychological research, coupled with the modern means of communication, the practice of democracy has turned a corner. A revolution is taking place, infinitely more significant than any shifting of economic power.

Within the life of the generation now in control of affairs, persuasion has become a self-conscious art and a regular organ of popular government. None of us begins to understand the consequences, but it is no daring prophecy to say that the knowledge of how to create consent will alter every political calculation and modify every political premise. Under the impact of propaganda, not necessarily in the sinister meaning of the word alone, the old constants of our thinking have become variables. It is no longer possible, for example, to believe in the original dogma of democracy; that the knowledge needed for the management of human affairs comes up spontaneously from the human heart. Where we act on that theory we expose ourselves to self-deception, and to forms of persuasion that we cannot verify. It has been demonstrated that we cannot rely upon intuition, conscience, or the accidents of casual opinion if we are to deal with the world beyond our reach.

# PART VI.   THE IMAGE OF DEMOCRACY

"I confess that in America I saw more than America;
I sought the image of democracy itself."
                              Alexis de Tocqueville.

# XVI. The Self-Centered Man

## 1

SINCE Public Opinion is supposed to be the prime mover in democracies, one might reasonably expect to find a vast literature. One does not find it. There are excellent books on government and parties, that is, on the machinery which in theory registers public opinions after they are formed. But on the sources from which these public opinions arise, on the processes by which they are derived, there is relatively little. The existence of a force called Public Opinion is in the main taken for granted, and American political writers have been most interested either in finding out how to make government express the common will, or in how to prevent the common will from subverting the purposes for which they believe the government exists. According to their traditions they have wished either to tame opinion or to obey it. Thus the editor of a notable series of text-books writes that "the most difficult and the most momentous question of government [is] how to transmit the force of individual opinion into public action."[1]

But surely there is a still more momentous question, the question of how to validate our private versions of the political scene. There is, as I shall try to indicate further on, the prospect of radical improvement by the development of principles already in operation. But this development will depend on how well we learn to use knowledge of the way opinions are put together to watch over our own opinions when they are being put

---

[1] Albert Bushnell Hart in the Introductory note to A. Lawrence Lowell's *Public Opinion and Popular Government*.

together. For casual opinion, being the product of partial contact, of tradition, and personal interests, cannot in the nature of things take kindly to a method of political thought which is based on exact record, measurement, analysis and comparison. Just those qualities of the mind which determine what shall seem interesting, important, familiar, personal, and dramatic, are the qualities which in the first instance realistic opinion frustrates. Therefore, unless there is in the community at large a growing conviction that prejudice and intuition are not enough, the working out of realistic opinion, which takes time, money, labor, conscious effort, patience, and equanimity, will not find enough support. That conviction grows as self-criticism increases, and makes us conscious of buncombe, contemptuous of ourselves when we employ it, and on guard to detect it. Without an ingrained habit of analyzing opinion when we read, talk, and decide, most of us would hardly suspect the need of better ideas, nor be interested in them when they appear, nor be able to prevent the new technic of political intelligence from being manipulated.

Yet democracies, if we are to judge by the oldest and most powerful of them, have made a mystery out of public opinion. There have been skilled organizers of opinion who understood the mystery well enough to create majorities on election day. But these organizers have been regarded by political science as low fellows or as "problems," not as possessors of the most effective knowledge there was on how to create and operate public opinion. The tendency of the people who have voiced the ideas of democracy, even when they have not managed its action, the tendency of students, orators, editors, has been to look upon Public Opinion as men in other societies looked upon the uncanny forces to which they ascribed the last word in the direction of events.

For in almost every political theory there is an inscrutable element which in the heyday of that theory goes unexamined. Behind the appearances there is a Fate, there are Guardian Spirits, or Mandates to a Chosen People, a Divine Monarchy, a Vice-Regent of Heaven, or a Class of the Better Born. The more obvious angels, demons, and kings are gone out of democratic thinking, but the need for believing that there are reserve powers of guidance persists. It persisted for those thinkers of the Eighteenth Century who designed the matrix of democracy. They had a pale god, but warm hearts, and in the doctrine of popular sovereignty they found the answer to their need of an infallible origin for the new social order. There was the mystery, and only enemies of the people touched it with profane and curious hands.

## 2

They did not remove the veil because they were practical politicians in a bitter and uncertain struggle. They had themselves felt the aspiration of democracy, which is ever so much deeper, more intimate and more important than any theory of government. They were engaged, as against the prejudice of ages, in the assertion of human dignity. What possessed them was not whether John Smith had sound views on any public question, but that John Smith, scion of a stock that had always been considered inferior, would now bend his knee to no other man. It was this spectacle that made it bliss "in that dawn to be alive." But every analyst seems to degrade that dignity, to deny that all men are reasonable all the time, or educated, or informed, to note that people are fooled, that they do not always know their own interests, and that all men are not equally fitted to govern.

The critics were about as welcome as a small boy with a drum. Every one of these observations on the fallibility of man was being exploited ad nauseam. Had democrats admitted there was truth in any of the aristocratic arguments they would have opened a breach in the defenses. And so just as Aristotle had to insist that the slave was a slave by nature, the democrats had to insist that the free man was a legislator and administrator by nature. They could not stop to explain that a human soul might not yet have, or indeed might never have, this technical equipment, and that nevertheless it had an inalienable right not to be used as the unwilling instrument of other men. The superior people were still too strong and too unscrupulous to have refrained from capitalizing so candid a statement.

So the early democrats insisted that a reasoned righteousness welled up spontaneously out of the mass of men. All of them hoped that it would, many of them believed that it did, although the cleverest, like Thomas Jefferson, had all sorts of private reservations. But one thing was certain: if public opinion did not come forth spontaneously, nobody in that age believed it would come forth at all. For in one fundamental respect the political science on which democracy was based was the same science that Aristotle formulated. It was the same science for democrat and aristocrat, royalist and republican, in that its major premise assumed the art of government to be a natural endowment. Men differed radically when they tried to name the men so endowed; but they agreed in thinking that the greatest question of all was to find those in whom political wisdom was innate. Royalists were sure that kings were born to govern. Alexander Hamilton thought that while "there are strong minds in every walk of life . . . the representative body, with too few exceptions to have any influence on the spirit of the government, will be composed of landholders, merchants, and men of the learned professions."[2] Jefferson thought the political faculties were

---

[2] *The Federalist*, Nos. 35, 36. *Cf.* comment by Henry Jones Ford in his *Rise and Growth of American Politics.* Ch. V.

deposited by God in farmers and planters, and sometimes spoke as if they were found in all the people.[3] The main premise was the same: to govern was an instinct that appeared, according to your social preferences, in one man or a chosen few, in all males, or only in males who were white and twenty-one, perhaps even in all men and all women.

In deciding who was most fit to govern, knowledge of the world was taken for granted. The aristocrat believed that those who dealt with large affairs possessed the instinct, the democrats asserted that all men possessed the instinct and could therefore deal with large affairs. It was no part of political science in either case to think out how knowledge of the world could be brought to the ruler. If you were for the people you did not try to work out the question of how to keep the voter informed. By the age of twenty-one he had his political faculties. What counted was a good heart, a reasoning mind, a balanced judgment. These would ripen with age, but it was not necessary to consider how to inform the heart and feed the reason. Men took in their facts as they took in their breath.

### 3

But the facts men could come to possess in this effortless way were limited. They could know the customs and more obvious character of the place where they lived and worked. But the outer world they had to conceive, and they did not conceive it instinctively, nor absorb trustworthy knowledge of it just by living. Therefore, the only environment in which spontaneous politics were possible was one confined within the range of the ruler's direct and certain knowledge. There is no escaping this conclusion, wherever you found government on the natural range of men's faculties. "If," as Aristotle said,[4] "the citizens of a state are to judge and distribute offices according to merit, then they must know each other's characters; where they do not possess this knowledge, both the election to offices and the decision of law suits will go wrong."

Obviously this maxim was binding upon every school of political thought. But it presented peculiar difficulties to the democrats. Those who believed in class government could fairly claim that in the court of the king, or in the country houses of the gentry, men did know each other's characters, and as long as the rest of mankind was passive, the only characters one needed to know were the characters of men in the ruling class. But the democrats, who wanted to raise the dignity of all men, were immediately involved by the immense size and confusion of

---

[3] See below p. 145.
[4] *Politics*, Bk. VII, Ch. 4.

their ruling class—the male electorate. Their science told them that politics was an instinct, and that the instinct worked in a limited environment. Their hopes bade them insist that all men in a very large environment could govern. In this deadly conflict between their ideals and their science, the only way out was to assume without much discussion that the voice of the people was the voice of God.

The paradox was too great, the stakes too big, their ideal too precious for critical examination. They could not show how a citizen of Boston was to stay in Boston and conceive the views of a Virginian, how a Virginian in Virginia could have real opinions about the government at Washington, how Congressmen in Washington could have opinions about China or Mexico. For in that day it was not possible for many men to have an unseen environment brought into the field of their judgment. There had been some advances, to be sure, since Aristotle. There were a few newspapers, and there were books, better roads perhaps, and better ships. But there was no great advance, and the political assumptions of the Eighteenth Century had essentially to be those that had prevailed in political science for two thousand years. The pioneer democrats did not possess the material for resolving the conflict between the known range of man's attention and their illimitable faith in his dignity.

Their assumptions antedated not only the modern newspaper, the world-wide press services, photography and moving pictures, but, what is really more significant, they antedated measurement and record, quantitative and comparative analysis, the canons of evidence, and the ability of psychological analysis to correct and discount the prejudices of the witness. I do not mean to say that our records are satisfactory, our analysis unbiased, our measurements sound. I do mean to say that the key inventions have been made for bringing the unseen world into the field of judgment. They had not been made in the time of Aristotle, and they were not yet important enough to be visible for political theory in the age of Rousseau, Montesquieu, or Thomas Jefferson. In a later chapter I think we shall see that even in the latest theory of human reconstruction, that of the English Guild Socialists, all the deeper premises have been taken over from this older system of political thought.

That system, whenever it was competent and honest, had to assume that no man could have more than a very partial experience of public affairs. In the sense that he can give only a little time to them, that assumption is still true, and of the utmost consequence. But ancient theory was compelled to assume, not only that men could give little attention to public questions, but that the attention available would have to be confined to matters close at hand. It would have been visionary to suppose that a time would come when distant and complicated events could conceivably be reported, analyzed, and presented in such a form that a really valuable choice could be made by an amateur. That time is now in sight. There is no longer any doubt that the continuous reporting of an unseen environment is feasible. It is often done badly, but the fact that it is done at all shows that it can be done, and the fact that we begin to know how badly it is often done, shows that it can be done better. With varying degrees of skill and honesty distant complexities are reported every day by engineers and accountants for business men, by secretaries and civil servants for officials, by intelligence officers for the General Staff, by some journalists for some readers. These are crude beginnings but radical, far more radical in the literal meaning of that word than the repetition of wars, revolutions, abdications, and restorations; as radical as the change in the scale of human life which has made it possible for Mr. Lloyd George to discuss Welsh coal mining after breakfast in London, and the fate of the Arabs before dinner in Paris.

For the possibility of bringing any aspect of human affairs within the range of judgment breaks the spell which has lain upon political ideas. There have, of course, been plenty of men who did not realize that the range of attention was the main premise of political science. They have built on sand. They have demonstrated in their own persons the effects of a very limited and self-centered knowledge of the world. But for the political thinkers who have counted, from Plato and Aristotle through Machiavelli and Hobbes to the democratic theorists, speculation has revolved around the self-centered man who had to see the whole world by means of a few pictures in his head.

# XVII. The Self-Contained Community

## 1

THAT groups of self-centered people would engage in a struggle for existence if they rubbed against each other has always been evident. This much truth there is at any rate in that famous passage in the Leviathan where Hobbes says that "though there had never been any time wherein particular men were in a condition of war one against another, yet at all times kings and *persons of sovereign authority because* of their *independency,* are in continual jealousies and in the state and posture of gladiators, having their weapons pointing, and their eyes fixed on one another . . ."[1]

---

[1] *Leviathan,* Ch. XIII. Of the Natural Condition of Mankind as concerning their Felicity and Misery.

## 2

To circumvent this conclusion one great branch of human thought, which had and has many schools, proceeded in this fashion: it conceived an ideally just pattern of human relations in which each person had well defined functions and rights. If he conscientiously filled the role allotted to him, it did not matter whether his opinions were right or wrong. He did his duty, the next man did his, and all the dutiful people together made a harmonious world. Every caste system illustrates this principle; you find it in Plato's Republic and in Aristotle, in the feudal ideal, in the circles of Dante's Paradise, in the bureaucratic type of socialism, and in laissez-faire, to an amazing degree in syndicalism, guild socialism, anarchism, and in the system of international law idealized by Mr. Robert Lansing. All of them assume a preestablished harmony, inspired, imposed, or innate, by which the self-opinionated person, class, or community is orchestrated with the rest of mankind. The more authoritarian imagine a conductor for the symphony who sees to it that each man plays his part; the anarchistic are inclined to think that a more divine concord would be heard if each player improvised as he went along.

But there have also been philosophers who were bored by these schemes of rights and duties, took conflict for granted, and tried to see how their side might come out on top. They have always seemed more realistic, even when they seemed alarming, because all they had to do was to generalize the experience that nobody could escape. Machiavelli is the classic of this school, a man most mercilessly maligned, because he happened to be the first naturalist who used plain language in a field hitherto preëmpted by supernaturalists.[2] He has a worse name and more disciples than any political thinker who ever lived. He truly described the technic of existence for the self-contained state. That is why he has the disciples. He has the bad name chiefly because he cocked his eye at the Medici family, dreamed in his study at night where he wore his "noble court dress" that Machiavelli was himself the Prince, and turned a pungent description of the way things are done into an eulogy on that way of doing them.

In his most infamous chapter[3] he wrote that "a prince ought to take care that he never lets anything slip from his lips that is not replete with the above-named five qualities, that he may appear to him who hears and sees him altogether merciful, faithful, humane, upright, and religious.

---

[2] F. S. Oliver in his *Alexander Hamilton*, says of Machiavelli (p. 174): "Assuming the conditions which exist—the nature of man and of things—to be unchangeable, he proceeds in a calm, unmoral way, like a lecturer on frogs, to show how a valiant and sagacious ruler can best turn events to his own advantage and the security of his dynasty."

[3] *The Prince*, Ch. XVIII. "Concerning the way in which Princes should keep faith." Translation by W. K. Marriott.

There is nothing more necessary to appear to have than this last quality, inasmuch as men judge generally more by the eye than by the hand, because it belongs to everybody to see you, to few to come in touch with you. Everyone sees what you appear to be, few really know what you are, and those few dare not oppose themselves to the opinion of the many, who have the majesty of the state to defend them; and in the actions of all men, and especially of princes, which it is not prudent to challenge, one judges by the result. . . . One prince of the present time, whom it is not well to name, never preaches anything else but peace and good faith, and to both he is most hostile, and either, if he had kept it, would have deprived him of reputation and kingdom many a time."

That is cynical. But it is the cynicism of a man who saw truly without knowing quite why he saw what he saw. Machiavelli is thinking of the run of men and princes "who judge generally more by the eye than by the hand," which is his way of saying that their judgments are subjective. He was too close to earth to pretend that the Italians of his day saw the world steadily and saw it whole. He would not indulge in fantasies, and he had not the materials for imagining a race of men that had learned how to correct their vision.

The world, as he found it, was composed of people whose vision could rarely be corrected, and Machiavelli knew that such people, since they see all public relations in a private way, are involved in perpetual strife. What they see is their own personal, class, dynastic, or municipal version of affairs that in reality extend far beyond the boundaries of their vision. They see their aspect. They see it as right. But they cross other people who are similarly self-centered. Then their very existence is endangered, or at least what they, for unsuspected private reasons, regard as their existence and take to be a danger. The end, which is impregnably based on a real though private experience justifies the means. They will sacrifice any one of these ideals to save all of them, . . . "one judges by the result . . ."

### 3

These elemental truths confronted the democratic philosophers. Consciously or otherwise, they knew that the range of political knowledge was limited, that the area of self-government would have to be limited, and that self-contained states when they rubbed against each other were in the posture of gladiators. But they knew just as certainly, that there was in men a will to decide their own fate, and to find a peace that was not imposed by force. How could they reconcile the wish and the fact?

They looked about them. In the city states of Greece and Italy they found a chronicle of corruption, intrigue and war.[4] In their own cities they saw faction, artificiality, fever. This was no environment in which the democratic ideal could prosper, no place where a group of independent and equally competent people managed their own affairs spontaneously. They looked further, guided somewhat perhaps by Jean Jacques Rousseau, to remote, unspoiled country villages. They saw enough to convince themselves that there the ideal was at home. Jefferson in particular felt this, and Jefferson more than any other man formulated the American image of democracy. From the townships had come the power that had carried the American Revolution to victory. From the townships were to come the votes that carried Jefferson's party to power. Out there in the farming communities of Massachusetts and Virginia, if you wore glasses that obliterated the slaves, you could see with your mind's eye the image of what democracy was to be.

"The American Revolution broke out," says de Tocqueville,[5] "and the doctrine of the sovereignty of the people, which had been nurtured in the townships, took possession of the state." It certainly took possession of the minds of those men who formulated and popularized the stereotypes of democracy. "The cherishment of the people was our principle," wrote Jefferson.[6] But the people he cherished almost exclusively were the small landowning farmers: "Those who labor in the earth are the chosen people of God, if ever He had a chosen people, whose breasts He has made his peculiar deposit for substantial and genuine virtue. It is the focus in which He keeps alive that sacred fire, which otherwise might escape from the face of the earth. Corruption of morals in the mass of cultivators is a phenomenon of which no age nor nation has furnished an example."

However much of the romantic return to nature may have entered into this exclamation, there was also an element of solid sense. Jefferson was right in thinking that a group of independent farmers comes nearer to fulfilling the requirements of spontaneous democracy than any other human society. But if you are to preserve the ideal, you must fence off these ideal communities from the abominations of the world. If the farmers are to manage their own affairs, they must confine affairs to those they are accustomed to managing. Jefferson drew all these logical conclusions. He disapproved of manufacture, of foreign

---

[4] Democracies have ever been spectacles of turbulence and contention . . . and have in general been as short in their lives as they have been violent in their deaths." Madison, *Federalist*, No. 10.

[5] *Democracy in America*, Vol. I, p. 51. Third Edition.

[6] Cited in Charles Beard, *Economic Origins of Jeffersonian Democracy*. Ch. XIV.

commerce, and a navy, of intangible forms of property, and in theory of any form of government that was not centered in the small self-governing group. He had critics in his day: one of them remarked that "wrapt up in the fullness of self-consequence and strong enough, in reality, to defend ourselves against every invader, we might enjoy an eternal rusticity and live, forever, thus apathized and vulgar under the shelter of a selfish, satisfied indifference."[7]

4

The democratic ideal, as Jefferson moulded it, consisting of an ideal environment and a selected class, did not conflict with the political science of his time. It did conflict with the realities. And when the ideal was stated in absolute terms, partly through exuberance and partly for campaign purposes, it was soon forgotten that the theory was originally devised for very special conditions. It became the political gospel, and supplied the stereotypes through which Americans of all parties have looked at politics.

That gospel was fixed by the necessity that in Jefferson's time no one could have conceived public opinions that were not spontaneous and subjective. The democratic tradition is therefore always trying to see a world where people are exclusively concerned with affairs of which the causes and effects all operate within the region they inhabit. Never has democratic theory been able to conceive itself in the context of a wide and unpredictable environment. The mirror is concave. And although democrats recognize that they are in contact with external affairs, they see quite surely that every contact outside that self-contained group is a threat to democracy as originally conceived. That is a wise fear. If democracy is to be spontaneous, the interests of democracy must remain simple, intelligible, and easily managed. Conditions must approximate those of the isolated rural township if the supply of information is to be left to casual experience. The environment must be confined within the range of every man's direct and certain knowledge.

The democrat has understood what an analysis of public opinion seems to demonstrate: that in dealing with an unseen environment decisions "are manifestly settled at haphazard, which clearly they ought not to be."[8] So he has always tried in one way or another to minimize the importance of that unseen environment. He feared foreign trade because trade involves foreign connections; he distrusted manufactures because they produced big cities and collected crowds; if he had

---

[7] *Op. cit.*, p. 426.
[8] Aristotle, *Politics*, Bk. VII, Ch. IV.

nevertheless to have manufactures, he wanted protection in the interest of self-sufficiency. When he could not find these conditions in the real world, he went passionately into the wilderness, and founded Utopian communities far from foreign contacts. His slogans reveal his prejudice. He is for Self-Government, Self-Determination, Independence. Not one of these ideas carries with it any notion of consent or community beyond the frontiers of the self-governing groups. The field of democratic action is a circumscribed area. Within protected boundaries the aim has been to achieve self-sufficiency and avoid entanglement. This rule is not confined to foreign policy, but it is plainly evident there, because life outside the national boundaries is more distinctly alien than any life within. And as history shows, democracies in their foreign policy have had generally to choose between splendid isolation and a diplomacy that violated their ideals. The most successful democracies, in fact, Switzerland, Denmark, Australia, New Zealand, and America until recently, have had no foreign policy in the European sense of that phrase. Even a rule like the Monroe Doctrine arose from the desire to supplement the two oceans by a glacis of states that were sufficiently republican to have no foreign policy.

Whereas danger is a great, perhaps an indispensable condition of autocracy,[9] security was seen to be a necessity if democracy was to work. There must be as little disturbance as possible of the premise of a self-contained community. Insecurity involves surprises. It means that there are people acting upon your life, over whom you have no control, with whom you cannot consult. It means that forces are at large which disturb the familiar routine, and present novel problems about which quick and unusual decisions are required. Every democrat feels in his bones that dangerous crises are incompatible with democracy, because he knows that the inertia of masses is such that to act quickly a very few must decide and the rest follow rather blindly. This has not made non-resistants out of democrats, but it has resulted in all democratic wars being fought for pacifist aims. Even when the wars are in fact wars of conquest, they are sincerely believed to be wars in defense of civilization.

These various attempts to enclose a part of the earth's surface were not inspired by cowardice, apathy, or, what one of Jefferson's critics called a willingness to live under monkish discipline. The democrats had caught sight of a dazzling possibility, that every human being

---

[9] Fisher Ames, frightened by the democratic revolution of 1800, wrote to Rufus King in 1802: "We need, as all nations do, the compression on the outside of our circle of a formidable neighbor, whose presence shall at all times excite stronger fears than demagogues can inspire the people with towards their government." Cited by Ford, *Rise and Growth of American Politics*, p. 69.

should rise to his full stature, freed from man-made limitations. With what they knew of the art of government, they could, no more than Aristotle before them, conceive a society of autonomous individuals, except an enclosed and simple one. They could, then, select no other premise if they were to reach the conclusion that all the people could spontaneously manage their public affairs.

5

Having adopted the premise because it was necessary to their keenest hope, they drew other conclusions as well. Since in order to have spontaneous self-government, you had to have a simple self-contained community, they took it for granted that one man was as competent as the next to manage these simple and self-contained affairs. Where the wish is father to the thought such logic is convincing. Moreover, the doctrine of the omnicompetent citizen is for most practical purposes true in the rural township. Everybody in a village sooner or later tries his hand at everything the village does. There is rotation in office by men who are jacks of all trades. There was no serious trouble with the doctrine of the omnicompetent citizen until the democratic stereotype was universally applied, so that men looked at a complicated civilization and saw an enclosed village.

Not only was the individual citizen fitted to deal with all public affairs, but he was consistently public-spirited and endowed with unflagging interest. He was public-spirited enough in the township, where he knew everybody and was interested in everybody's business. The idea of enough for the township turned easily into the idea of enough for any purpose, for as we have noted, quantitative thinking does not suit a stereotype. But there was another turn to the circle. Since everybody was assumed to be interested enough in important affairs, only those affairs came to seem important in which everybody was interested.

This meant that men formed their picture of the world outside from the unchallenged pictures in their heads. These pictures came to them well stereotyped by their parents and teachers, and were little corrected by their own experience. Only a few men had affairs that took them across state lines. Even fewer had reason to go abroad. Most voters lived their whole lives in one environment, and with nothing but a few feeble newspapers, some pamphlets, political speeches, their religious training, and rumor to go on, they had to conceive that larger environment of commerce and finance, of war and peace. The number of public opinions based on any objective report was very small in proportion to those based on casual fancy.

And so for many different reasons, self-sufficiency was a spiritual ideal in the formative period. The physical isolation of the township, the loneliness of the pioneer, the theory of democracy, the Protestant tradition, and the limitations of political science all converged to make men believe that out of their own consciences they must extricate political wisdom. It is not strange that the deduction of laws from absolute principles should have usurped so much of their free energy. The American political mind had to live on its capital. In legalism it found a tested body of rules from which new rules could be spun without the labor of earning new truths from experience. The formulae became so curiously sacred that every good foreign observer has been amazed at the contrast between the dynamic practical energy of the American people and the static theorism of their public life. That steadfast love of fixed principles was simply the only way known of achieving self-sufficiency. But it meant that the public opinions of any one community about the outer world consisted chiefly of a few stereotyped images arranged in a pattern deduced from their legal and their moral codes, and animated by the feeling aroused by local experiences.

Thus democratic theory, starting from its fine vision of ultimate human dignity, was forced by lack of the instruments of knowledge for reporting its environment, to fall back upon the wisdom and experience which happened to have accumulated in the voter. God had, in the words of Jefferson, made men's breasts "His peculiar deposit for substantial and genuine virtue." These chosen people in their self-contained environment had all the facts before them. The environment was so familiar that one could take it for granted that men were talking about substantially the same things. The only real disagreements, therefore, would be in judgments about the same facts. There was no need to guarantee the sources of information. They were obvious, and equally accessible to all men. Nor was there need to trouble about the ultimate criteria. In the self-contained community one could assume, or at least did assume, a homogeneous code of morals. The only place, therefore, for differences of opinion was in the logical application of accepted standards to accepted facts. And since the reasoning faculty was also well standardized, an error in reasoning would be quickly exposed in a free discussion. It followed that truth could be obtained by liberty within these limits. The community could take its supply of information for granted; its codes it passed on through school, church, and family, and the power to draw deductions from a premise, rather than the ability to find the premise, was regarded as the chief end of intellectual training.

# XVIII. The Role of Force, Patronage and Privilege

## 1

"IT has happened as was to have been foreseen," wrote Hamilton,[1] "the measures of the Union have not been executed; the delinquencies of the States have, step by step, matured themselves to an extreme which has at length arrested all the wheels of the national government and brought them to an awful stand." . . . For "in our case the concurrence of thirteen distinct sovereign wills is requisite, under the confederation, to the complete execution of every important measure that proceeds from the Union." How could it be otherwise, he asked: "The rulers of the respective members . . . will undertake to judge of the propriety of the measures themselves. They will consider the conformity of the thing proposed or required to their immediate interests or aims; the momentary conveniences or inconveniences that would attend its adoption. All this will be done, and in a spirit of interested and suspicious scrutiny, without that knowledge of national circumstances and reasons of state which is essential to right judgment, and with that strong predilection in favor of local objects which can hardly fail to mislead the decision. The same process must be repeated in every member of which the body is constituted; and the execution of the plans framed by the councils of the whole, will always fluctuate on the discretion of the ill-informed and prejudiced opinion of every part. Those who have been conversant in the proceedings of popular assemblies, who have seen how difficult it often is, when there is no exterior pressure of circumstances, to bring them to harmonious resolutions on important points, will readily conceive how impossible it must be to induce a number of such assemblies, deliberating at a distance from each other, at different times, and under different impressions, long to cooperate in the same views and pursuits."

Over ten years of storm and stress with a congress that was, as John Adams said,[2] "only a diplomatic assembly," had furnished the leaders of the revolution "with an instructive but afflicting lesson"[3] in what happens when a number of self-centered communities are entangled in the same environment. And so, when they went to Philadelphia in May of 1787, ostensibly to revise the Articles of Confederation, they were really in full reaction against the fundamental premise of Eighteenth Century democracy. Not only were the leaders consciously opposed to

---

[1] *Federalist*, No. 15.
[2] Ford, *op. cit.*, p. 36.
[3] *Federalist*, No. 15.

the democratic spirit of the time, feeling, as Madison said, that "democracies have ever been spectacles of turbulence and contention," but within the national frontiers they were determined to offset as far as they could the ideal of self-governing communities in self-contained environments. The collisions and failures of concave democracy, where men spontaneously managed all their own affairs, were before their eyes. The problem as they saw it, was to restore government as against democracy. They understood government to be the power to make national decisions and enforce them throughout the nation; democracy they believed was the insistence of localities and classes upon self-determination in accordance with their immediate interests and aims.

They could not consider in their calculations the possibility of such an organization of knowledge that separate communities would act simultaneously on the same version of the facts. We just begin to conceive this possibility for certain parts of the world where there is free circulation of news and a common language, and then only for certain aspects of life. The whole idea of a voluntary federalism in industry and world politics is still so rudimentary, that, as we see in our own experience, it enters only a little, and only very modestly, into practical politics. What we, more than a century later, can only conceive as an incentive to generations of intellectual effort, the authors of the Constitution had no reason to conceive at all. In order to set up national government, Hamilton and his colleagues had to make plans, not on the theory that men would cooperate because they had a sense of common interest, but on the theory that men could be governed, if special interests were kept in equilibrium by a balance of power. "Ambition," Madison said,[4] "must be made to counteract ambition."

They did not, as some writers have supposed, intend to balance every interest so that the government would be in a perpetual deadlock. They intended to deadlock local and class interest to prevent these from obstructing government. "In framing a government which is to be administered by men over men," wrote Madison,[5] "the great difficulty lies in this: *you must first enable the government to control the governed*, and in the next place, oblige it to control itself." In one very important sense, then, the doctrine of checks and balances was the remedy of the federalist leaders for the problem of public opinion. They saw no other way to substitute "the mild influence of the magistracy" for the "sanguinary agency of the sword"[6] except by devising an ingenious machine to neutralize local opinion. They did not understand how to

---

[4] *Federalist*, No. 51, cited by Ford, *op. cit.*, p. 60.
[5] *Id.*
[6] *Federalist*, No. 15.

manipulate a large electorate, any more than they saw the possibility of common consent upon the basis of common information. It is true that Aaron Burr taught Hamilton a lesson which impressed him a good deal when he seized control of New York City in 1800 by the aid of Tammany Hall. But Hamilton was killed before he was able to take account of this new discovery, and, as Mr. Ford says,[7] Burr's pistol blew the brains out of the Federal party.

## 2

When the constitution was written, "politics could still be managed by conference and agreement among gentlemen"[8] and it was to the gentry that Hamilton turned for a government. It was intended that they should manage national affairs when local prejudice had been brought into equilibrium by the constitutional checks and balances. No doubt Hamilton, who belonged to this class by adoption, had a human prejudice in their favor. But that by itself is a thin explanation of his statecraft. Certainly there can be no question of his consuming passion for union, and it is, I think, an inversion of the truth to argue that he made the Union to protect class privileges, instead of saying that he used class privileges to make the Union. "We must take man as we find him," Hamilton said, "and if we expect him to serve the public we must interest his passions in doing so."[9] He needed men to govern, whose passions could be most quickly attached to a national interest. These were the gentry, the public creditors, manufacturers, shippers, and traders,[10] and there is probably no better instance in history of the adaptation of shrewd means to clear ends, than in the series of fiscal measures, by which Hamilton attached the provincial notables to the new government.

Although the constitutional convention worked behind closed doors, and although ratification was engineered by "a vote of probably not more than one-sixth of the adult males,"[11] there was little or no pretence. The Federalists argued for union, not for democracy, and even the word republic had an unpleasant sound to George Washington when he had been for more than two years a republican president. The constitution was a candid attempt to limit the sphere of popular rule; the only democratic organ it was intended the government should possess was the House, based on a suffrage highly limited by property

---

[7] Ford, *op. cit.*, p. 119.
[8] *Op. cit.*, p. 144.
[9] *Op. cit.*, p. 47.
[10] Beard, *Economic Interpretation of the Constitution, passim.*
[11] Beard, *op. cit.*, p. 325.

qualifications. And even at that, the House, it was believed, would be so licentious a part of the government, that it was carefully checked and balanced by the Senate, the electoral college, the Presidential veto, and by judicial interpretation.

Thus at the moment when the French Revolution was kindling popular feeling the world over, the American revolutionists of 1776 came under a constitution which went back, as far as it was expedient, to the British Monarchy for a model. This conservative reaction could not endure. The men who had made it were a minority, their motives were under suspicion, and when Washington went into retirement, the position of the gentry was not strong enough to survive the inevitable struggle for the succession. The anomaly between the original plan of the Fathers and the moral feeling of the age was too wide not to be capitalized by a good politician.

### 3

Jefferson referred to his election as "the great revolution of 1800," but more than anything else it was a revolution in the mind. No great policy was altered, but a new tradition was established. For it was Jefferson who first taught the American people to regard the Constitution as an instrument of democracy, and he stereotyped the images, the ideas, and even many of the phrases, in which Americans ever since have described politics to each other. So complete was the mental victory, that twenty-five years later de Tocqueville, who was received in Federalist homes, noted that even those who were "galled by its continuance"—were not uncommonly heard to "laud the delights of a republican government, and the advantages of democratic institutions when they are in public."[12]

The Constitutional Fathers with all their sagacity had failed to see that a frankly undemocratic constitution would not long be tolerated. The bold denial of popular rule was bound to offer an easy point of attack to a man, like Jefferson, who so far as his constitutional opinions ran, was not a bit more ready than Hamilton to turn over government to the "unrefined" will of the people.[13] The Federalist leaders had been men of definite convictions who stated them bluntly. There was little real discrepancy between their public and their private views. But Jefferson's mind was a mass of ambiguities, not solely because of its

---

[12] *Democracy in America*, Vol. I, Ch. X (Third Edition, 1838), p. 216.

[13] *Cf.* his plan for the Constitution of Virginia, his ideas for a senate of property holders, and his views on the judicial veto. Beard, *Economic Origins of Jeffersonian Democracy*, pp. 450 *et seq.*

defects, as Hamilton and his biographers have thought, but because he believed in a union and he believed in spontaneous democracies, and in the political science of his age there was no satisfactory way to reconcile the two. Jefferson was confused in thought and action because he had a vision of a new and tremendous idea that no one had thought out in all its bearings. But though popular sovereignty was not clearly understood by anybody, it seemed to imply so great an enhancement of human life, that no constitution could stand which frankly denied it. The frank denials were therefore expunged from consciousness, and the document, which is on its face an honest example of limited constitutional democracy, was talked and thought about as an instrument for direct popular rule. Jefferson actually reached the point of believing that the Federalists had perverted the Constitution, of which in his fancy they were no longer the authors. And so the Constitution was, in spirit, rewritten. Partly by actual amendment, partly by practice, as in the case of the electoral college, but chiefly by looking at it through another set of stereotypes, the façade was no longer permitted to look oligarchic.

The American people came to believe that their Constitution was a democratic instrument, and treated it as such. They owe that fiction to the victory of Thomas Jefferson, and a great conservative fiction it has been. It is a fair guess that if everyone had always regarded the Constitution as did the authors of it, the Constitution would have been violently overthrown, because loyalty to the Constitution and loyalty to democracy would have seemed incompatible. Jefferson resolved that paradox by teaching the American people to read the Constitution as an expression of democracy. He himself stopped there. But in the course of twenty-five years or so social conditions had changed so radically, that Andrew Jackson carried out the political revolution for which Jefferson had prepared the tradition.[14]

### 4

The political center of that revolution was the question of patronage. By the men who founded the government public office was regarded as a species of property, not lightly to be disturbed, and it was undoubtedly their hope that the offices would remain in the hands of their social class. But the democratic theory had as one of its main principles the doctrine of the omnicompetent citizen. Therefore, when people

---

[14] The reader who has any doubts as to the extent of the revolution that separated Hamilton's opinions from Jackson's practice should turn to Mr. Henry Jones Ford's *Rise and Growth of American Politics*.

began to look at the Constitution as a democratic instrument, it was certain that permanence in office would seem undemocratic. The natural ambitions of men coincided here with the great moral impulse of their age. Jefferson had popularized the idea without carrying it ruthlessly into practice, and removals on party grounds were comparatively few under the Virginian Presidents. It was Jackson who founded the practice of turning public office into patronage.

Curious as it sounds to us, the principle of rotation in office with short terms was regarded as a great reform. Not only did it acknowledge the new dignity of the average man by treating him as fit for any office, not only did it destroy the monopoly of a small social class and appear to open careers to talent, but "it had been advocated for centuries as a sovereign remedy for political corruption," and as the one way to prevent the creation of a bureaucracy.[15] The practice of rapid change in public office was the application to a great territory of the image of democracy derived from the self-contained village.

Naturally it did not have the same results in the nation that it had in the ideal community on which the democratic theory was based. It produced quite unexpected results, for it founded a new governing class to take the place of the submerged federalists. Unintentionally, patronage did for a large electorate what Hamilton's fiscal measures had done for the upper classes. We often fail to realize how much of the stability of our government we owe to patronage. For it was patronage that weaned natural leaders from too much attachment to the self-centered community, it was patronage that weakened the local spirit and brought together in some kind of peaceful cooperation, the very men who, as provincial celebrities, would, in the absence of a sense of common interest, have torn the union apart.

But of course, the democratic theory was not supposed to produce a new governing class, and it has never accommodated itself to the fact. When the democrat wanted to abolish monopoly of offices, to have rotation and short terms, he was thinking of the township where anyone could do a public service, and return humbly to his own farm. The idea of a special class of politicians was just what the democrat did not like. But he could not have what he did like, because his theory was derived from an ideal environment, and he was living in a real one. The more deeply he felt the moral impulse of democracy, the less ready he was to see the profound truth of Hamilton's statement that communities deliberating at a distance and under different impressions could not long coöperate in the same views and pursuits. For that truth postpones anything like the full realization of democracy in public

---

[15] Ford, *op. cit.*, p. 169.

affairs until the art of obtaining common consent has been radically improved. And so while the revolution under Jefferson and Jackson produced the patronage which made the two party system, which created a substitute for the rule of the gentry, and a discipline for governing the deadlock of the checks and balances, all that happened, as it were, invisibly.

Thus, rotation in office might be the ostensible theory, in practice the offices oscillated between the henchmen. Tenure might not be a permanent monopoly, but the professional politician was permanent. Government might be, as President Harding once said, a simple thing, but winning elections was a sophisticated performance. The salaries in office might be as ostentatiously frugal as Jefferson's home-spun, but the expenses of party organization and the fruits of victory were in the grand manner. The stereotype of democracy controlled the visible government; the corrections, the exceptions and adaptations of the American people to the real facts of their environment have had to be invisible, even when everybody knew all about them. It was only the words of the law, the speeches of politicians, the platforms, and the formal machinery of administration that have had to conform to the pristine image of democracy.

## 5

If one had asked a philosophical democrat how these self-contained communities were to coöperate, when their public opinions were so self-centered, he would have pointed to representative government embodied in the Congress. And nothing would surprise him more than the discovery of how steadily the prestige of representative government has declined, while the power of the Presidency has grown.

Some critics have traced this to the custom of sending only local celebrities to Washington. They have thought that if Congress could consist of the nationally eminent men, the life of the capital would be more brilliant. It would be, of course, and it would be a very good thing if retiring Presidents and Cabinet officers followed the example of John Quincy Adams. But the absence of these men does not explain the plight of Congress, for its decline began when it was relatively the most eminent branch of the government. Indeed it is more probable that the reverse is true, and that Congress ceased to attract the eminent as it lost direct influence on the shaping of national policy.

The main reason for the discredit, which is world wide, is, I think, to be found in the fact that a congress of representatives is essentially a group of blind men in a vast, unknown world. With some exceptions, the only method recognized in the Constitution or in the theory of representative government, by which Congress can inform itself, is to exchange opinions from the districts. There is no systematic, adequate, and authorized way for Congress to know what is going on in the world. The theory is that the best man of each district brings the best wisdom of his constituents to a central place, and that all these wisdoms combined are all the wisdom that Congress needs. Now there is no need to question the value of expressing local opinions and exchanging them. Congress has great value as the market-place of a continental nation. In the coatrooms, the hotel lobbies, the boarding houses of Capitol Hill, at the tea-parties of the Congressional matrons, and from occasional entries into the drawing rooms of cosmopolitan Washington, new vistas are opened, and wider horizons. But even if the theory were applied, and the districts always sent their wisest men, the sum or a combination of local impressions is not a wide enough base for national policy, and no base at all for the control of foreign policy. Since the real effects of most laws are subtle and hidden, they cannot be understood by filtering local experiences through local states of mind. They can be known only by controlled reporting and objective analysis. And just as the head of a large factory cannot know how efficient it is by talking to the foreman, but must examine cost sheets and data that only an accountant can dig out for him, so the lawmaker does not arrive at a true picture of the state of the union by putting together a mosaic of local pictures. He needs to know the local pictures, but unless he possesses instruments for calibrating them, one picture is as good as the next, and a great deal better.

The President does come to the assistance of Congress by delivering messages on the state of the Union. He is in a position to do that because he presides over a vast collection of bureaus and their agents, which report as well as act. But he tells Congress what he chooses to tell it. He cannot be heckled, and the censorship as to what is compatible with the public interest is in his hands. It is a wholly one-sided and tricky relationship, which sometimes reaches such heights of absurdity, that Congress, in order to secure an important document has to thank the enterprise of a Chicago newspaper, or the calculated indiscretion of a subordinate official. So bad is the contact of legislators with necessary facts that they are forced to rely either on private tips or on that legalized atrocity, the Congressional investigation, where Congressmen, starved of their legitimate food for thought, go on a wild and feverish man-hunt, and do not stop at cannibalism.

Except for the little that these investigations yield, the occasional communications from the executive departments, interested and disinterested data collected by private persons, such newspapers, periodicals, and books as Congressmen read, and a new and excellent practice of calling for help from expert bodies like the Interstate Commerce

Commission, the Federal Trade Commission, and the Tariff Commission, the creation of Congressional opinion is incestuous. From this it follows either that legislation of a national character is prepared by a few informed insiders, and put through by partisan force; or that the legislation is broken up into a collection of local items, each of which is enacted for a local reason. Tariff schedules, navy yards, army posts, rivers and harbors, post offices and federal buildings, pensions and patronage: these are fed out to concave communities as tangible evidence of the benefits of national life. Being concave, they can see the white marble building which rises out of federal funds to raise local realty values and employ local contractors more readily than they can judge the cumulative cost of the pork barrel. It is fair to say that in a large assembly of men, each of whom has practical knowledge only of his own district, laws dealing with translocal affairs are rejected or accepted by the mass of Congressmen without creative participation of any kind. They participate only in making those laws that can be treated as a bundle of local issues. For a legislature without effective means of information and analysis must oscillate between blind regularity, tempered by occasional insurgency, and logrolling. And it is the logrolling which makes the regularity palatable, because it is by logrolling that a Congressman proves to his more active constituents that he is watching their interests as they conceive them.

This is no fault of the individual Congressman's, except when he is complacent about it. The cleverest and most industrious representative cannot hope to understand a fraction of the bills on which he votes. The best he can do is to specialize on a few bills, and take somebody's word about the rest. I have known Congressmen, when they were boning up on a subject, to study as they had not studied since they passed their final examinations, many large cups of black coffee, wet towels and all. They had to dig for information, sweat over arranging and verifying facts, which, in any consciously organized government, should have been easily available in a form suitable for decision. And even when they really knew a subject, their anxieties had only begun. For back home the editors, the board of trade, the central federated union, and the women's clubs had spared themselves these labors, and were prepared to view the Congressman's performance through local spectacles.

6

What patronage did to attach political chieftains to the national government, the infinite variety of local subsidies and privileges do for self-centered communities. Patronage and pork amalgamate and stabilize thousands of special opinions, local discontents, private ambitions.

There are but two other alternatives. One is government by terror and obedience, the other is government based on such a highly developed system of information, analysis, and self-consciousness that "the knowledge of national circumstances and reasons of state" is evident to all men. The autocratic system is in decay, the voluntary system is in its very earliest development; and so, in calculating the prospects of association among large groups of people, a League of Nations, industrial government, or a federal union of states, the degree to which the material for a common consciousness exists, determines how far cooperation will depend upon force, or upon the milder alternative to force, which is patronage and privilege. The secret of great state-builders, like Alexander Hamilton, is that they know how to calculate these principles.

# XIX. The Old Image in a New Form: Guild Socialism

## 1

WHENEVER the quarrels of self-centered groups become unbearable, reformers in the past found themselves forced to choose between two great alternatives. They could take the path to Rome and impose a Roman peace upon the warring tribes. They could take the path to isolation, to autonomy and self-sufficiency. Almost always they chose that path which they had least recently travelled. If they had tried out the deadening monotony of empire, they cherished above all other things the simple freedom of their own community. But if they had seen this simple freedom squandered in parochial jealousies they longed for the spacious order of a great and powerful state.

Whichever choice they made, the essential difficulty was the same. If decisions were decentralized they soon floundered in a chaos of local opinions. If they were centralized, the policy of the state was based on the opinions of a small social set at the capital. In any case force was necessary to defend one local right against another, or to impose law and order on the localities, or to resist class government at the center, or to defend the whole society, centralized or decentralized, against the outer barbarian.

Modern democracy and the industrial system were both born in a time of reaction against kings, crown government, and a regime of detailed economic regulation. In the industrial sphere this reaction took the form of extreme devolution, known as laissez-faire individualism. Each economic decision was to be made by the man who had title to the property involved. Since almost everything was owned by somebody, there would be somebody to manage everything. This was plural sovereignty with a vengeance.

It was economic government by anybody's economic philosophy, though it was supposed to be controlled by immutable laws of political economy that must in the end produce harmony. It produced many splendid things, but enough sordid and terrible ones to start countercurrents. One of these was the trust, which established a kind of Roman peace within industry, and a Roman predatory imperialism outside. People turned to the legislature for relief. They invoked representative government, founded on the image of the township farmer, to regulate the semi-sovereign corporations. The working class turned to labor organization. There followed a period of increasing centralization and a sort of race of armaments. The trusts interlocked, the craft unions federated and combined into a labor movement, the political system grew stronger at Washington and weaker in the states, as the reformers tried to match its strength against big business.

In this period practically all the schools of socialist thought from the Marxian left to the New Nationalists around Theodore Roosevelt, looked upon centralization as the first stage of an evolution which would end in the absorption of all the semi-sovereign powers of business by the political state. The evolution never took place, except for a few months during the war. That was enough, and there was a turn of the wheel against the omnivorous state in favor of several new forms of pluralism. But this time society was to swing back not to the atomic individualism of Adam Smith's economic man and Thomas Jefferson's farmer, but to a sort of molecular individualism of voluntary groups.

One of the interesting things about all these oscillations of theory is that each in turn promises a world in which no one will have to follow Machiavelli in order to survive. They are all established by some form of coercion, they all exercise coercion in order to maintain themselves, and they are all discarded as a result of coercion. Yet they do not accept coercion, either physical power or special position, patronage, or privilege, as part of their ideal. The individualist said that self-enlightened self-interest would bring internal and external peace. The socialist is sure that the motives to aggression will disappear. The new pluralist hopes they will.[1] Coercion is the surd in almost all social theory, except the Machiavellian. The temptation to ignore it, because it is absurd, inexpressible, and unmanageable, becomes overwhelming in any man who is trying to rationalize human life.

---

[1] See G. D. H. Cole, *Social Theory*, p. 142.

## 2

The lengths to which a clever man will sometimes go in order to escape a full recognition of the role of force is shown by Mr. G. D. H. Cole's book on Guild Socialism. The present state, he says, "is primarily an instrument of coercion;"[2] in a guild socialist society there will be no sovereign power, though there will be a coördinating body. He calls this body the Commune.

He then begins to enumerate the powers of the Commune, which, we recall, is to be primarily not an instrument of coercion.[3] It settles price disputes. Sometimes it fixes prices, allocates the surplus or distributes the loss. It allocates natural resources, and controls the issue of credit. It also "allocates communal labor-power." It ratifies the budgets of the guilds and the civil services. It levies taxes. "All questions of income" fall within its jurisdiction. It "allocates" income to the non-productive members of the community. It is the final arbiter in all questions of policy and jurisdiction between the guilds. It passes constitutional laws fixing the functions of the functional bodies. It appoints the judges. It confers coercive powers upon the guilds, and ratifies their by-laws wherever these involve coercion. It declares war and makes peace. It controls the armed forces. It is the supreme representative of the nation abroad. It settles boundary questions within the national state. It calls into existence new functional bodies, or distributes new functions to old ones. It runs the police. It makes whatever laws are necessary to regulate personal conduct and personal property.

These powers are exercised not by one commune, but by a federal structure of local and provincial communes with a National commune at the top. Mr. Cole is, of course, welcome to insist that this is not a sovereign state, but if there is a coercive power now enjoyed by any modern government for which he has forgotten to make room, I cannot think of it.

He tells us, however, that Guild society will be non-coercive: "we want to build a new society which will be conceived in the spirit, not of coercion, but of free service."[4] Everyone who shares that hope, as most men and women do, will therefore look closely to see what there is in the Guild Socialist plan which promises to reduce coercion to its lowest limits, even though the Guildsmen of to-day have already reserved for their communes the widest kind of coercive power. It is acknowledged at once that the new society cannot be brought into existence by universal consent. Mr. Cole is too honest to shirk the element of force required to make the transition.[5] And while obviously he can-

---

[2] Cole, *Guild Socialism*, p. 107.
[3] *Op. cit.* Ch. VIII.
[4] *Op. cit.*, p. 141.
[5] *Cf. op. cit.*, Ch. X.

not predict how much civil war there might be, he is quite clear that there would have to be a period of direct action by the trade unions.


3


But leaving aside the problems of transition, and any consideration of what the effect is on their future action, when men have hacked their way through to the promised land, let us imagine the Guild Society in being. What keeps it running as a non-coercive society?

Mr. Cole has two answers to this question. One is the orthodox Marxian answer that the abolition of capitalist property will remove the motive to aggression. Yet he does not really believe that, because if he did, he would care as little as does the average Marxian how the working class is to run the government, once it is in control. If his diagnosis were correct, the Marxian would be quite right: if the disease were the capitalist class and only the capitalist class, salvation would automatically follow its extinction. But Mr. Cole is enormously concerned about whether the society which follows the revolution is to be run by state collectivism, by guilds or coöperative societies, by a democratic parliament or by functional representation. In fact, it is as a new theory of representative government that guild socialism challenges attention.

The guildsmen do not expect a miracle to result from the disappearance of capitalist property rights. They do expect, and of course quite rightly, that if equality of income were the rule, social relations would be profoundly altered. But they differ, as far as I can make out, from the orthodox Russian communist in this respect: The communist proposes to establish equality by force of the dictatorship of the proletariat, believing that if once people were equalized both in income and in service, they would then lose the incentives to aggression. The guildsmen also propose to establish equality by force, but are shrewd enough to see that if an equilibrium is to be maintained they have to provide institutions for maintaining it. Guildsmen, therefore, put their faith in what they believe to be a new theory of democracy.

Their object, says Mr. Cole, is "to get the mechanism right, and to adjust it as far as possible to the expression of men's social wills."[6] These wills need to be given opportunity for self-expression in self-government "in any and every form of social action." Behind these words is the true democratic impulse, the desire to enhance human dignity, as well as the traditional assumption that this human dignity is impugned, unless each person's will enters into the management of everything that

---

[6] *Op. cit.*, p. 16.

affects him. The guildsman, like the earlier democrat therefore, looks about him for an environment in which this ideal of self-government can be realized. A hundred years and more have passed since Rousseau and Jefferson, and the center of interest has shifted from the country to the city. The new democrat can no longer turn to the idealized rural township for the image of democracy. He turns now to the workshop. "The spirit of association must be given free play in the sphere in which it is best able to find expression. This is manifestly the factory, in which men have the habit and tradition of working together. The factory is the natural and fundamental unit of industrial democracy. This involves, not only that the factory must be free, as far as possible, to manage its own affairs, but also that the democratic unit of the factory must be made the basis of the larger democracy of the Guild, and that the larger organs of Guild administration and government must be based largely on the principle of factory representation."[7]

Factory is, of course, a very loose word, and Mr. Cole asks us to take it as meaning mines, shipyards, docks, stations, and every place which is "a natural center of production."[8] But a factory in this sense is quite a different thing from an industry. The factory, as Mr. Cole conceives it, is a work place where men are really in personal contact, an environment small enough to be known directly to all the workers. "This democracy if it is to be real, must come home to, and be exercisable directly by, every individual member of the Guild."[9] This is important, because Mr. Cole, like Jefferson, is seeking a natural unit of government. The only natural unit is a perfectly familiar environment. Now a large plant, a railway system, a great coal field, is not a natural unit in this sense. Unless it is a very small factory indeed, what Mr. Cole is really thinking about is the shop. That is where men can be supposed to have "the habit and tradition of working together." The rest of the plant, the rest of the industry, is an inferred environment.

4

Anybody can see, and almost everybody will admit, that self-government in the purely internal affairs of the shop is government of affairs that "can be taken in at a single view."[10] But dispute would arise as to what constitute the internal affairs of a shop. Obviously the biggest interests, like wages, standards of production, the pur-

---

[7] *Op. cit.*, p. 40.
[8] *Op. cit.*, p. 41.
[9] *Op. cit.*, p. 40.
[10] Aristotle, *Politics*, Bk. VII, Ch. IV.

chase of supplies, the marketing of the product, the larger planning of work, are by no means purely internal. The shop democracy has freedom, subject to enormous limiting conditions from the outside. It can deal to a certain extent with the arrangement of work laid out for the shop, it can deal with the temper and temperament of individuals, it can administer petty industrial justice, and act as a court of first instance in somewhat larger individual disputes. Above all it can act as a unit in dealing with other shops, and perhaps with the plant as a whole. But isolation is impossible. The unit of industrial democracy is thoroughly entangled in foreign affairs. And it is the management of these external relations that constitutes the test of the guild socialist theory.

They have to be managed by representative government arranged in a federal order from the shop to the plant, the plant to the industry, the industry to the nation, with intervening regional grouping of representatives. But all this structure derives from the shop, and all its peculiar virtues are ascribed to this source. The representatives who choose the representatives who choose the representatives who finally "coördinate" and "regulate" the shops are elected, Mr. Cole asserts, by a true democracy. Because they come originally from a self-governing unit, the whole federal organism will be inspired by the spirit and the reality of self-government. Representatives will aim to carry out the workers' "actual will as understood by themselves,"[11] that is, as understood by the individual in the shops.

A government run literally on this principle would, if history is any guide, be either a perpetual logroll, or a chaos of warring shops. For while the worker in the shop can have a real opinion about matters entirely within the shop, his "will" about the relation of that shop to the plant, the industry, and the nation is subject to all the limitations of access, stereotype, and self-interest that surround any other self-centered opinion. His experience in the shop at best brings only aspects of the whole to his attention. His opinion of what is right within the shop he can reach by direct knowledge of the essential facts. His opinion of what is right in the great complicated environment out of sight is more likely to be wrong than right if it is a generalization from the experience of the individual shop. As a matter of experience, the representatives of a guild society would find, just as the higher trade union officials find today, that on a great number of questions which they have to decide there is no "actual will as understood" by the shops.

---

[11] *Op. cit.*, p. 42.

5

The guildsmen insist, however, that such criticism is blind because it ignores a great political discovery. You may be quite right, they would say, in thinking that the representatives of the shops would have to make up their own minds on many questions about which the shops have no opinion. But you are simply entangled in an ancient fallacy: you are looking for somebody to represent a group of people. He cannot be found. The only representative possible is one who acts for "some particular function,"[12] and therefore each person must help choose as many representatives "as there are distinct essential groups of functions to be performed."

Assume then that the representatives speak, not for the men in the shops, but for certain functions in which the men are interested. They are, mind you, disloyal if they do not carry out the will of the group about the function, as understood by the group.[13] These functional representatives meet. Their business is to coordinate and regulate. By what standard does each judge the proposals of the other, assuming, as we must, that there is conflict of opinion between the shops, since if there were not, there would be no need to coördinate and regulate?

Now the peculiar virtue of functional democracy is supposed to be that men vote candidly according to their own interests, which it is assumed they know by daily experience. They can do that within the self-contained group. But in its external relations the group as a whole, or its representative, is dealing with matters that transcend immediate experience. The shop does not arrive spontaneously at a view of the whole situation. Therefore, the public opinions of a shop about its rights and duties in the industry and in society, are matters of education or propaganda, not the automatic product of shop-consciousness. Whether the guildsmen elect a delegate, or a representative, they do not escape the problem of the orthodox democrat. Either the group as a whole, or the elected spokesman, must stretch his mind beyond the limits of direct experience. He must vote on questions coming up from other shops, and on matters coming from beyond the frontiers of the whole industry. The primary interest of the shop does not even cover the function of a whole industrial vocation. The function of a vocation, a great industry, a district, a nation is a concept, not an experience, and has to be imagined, invented, taught and believed. And even though you define function as carefully as possible, once you admit that the view of each shop on that function will not necessarily coincide with

---

[12] *Op. cit.*, pp. 23–24.
[13] *Cf.* Part V, "The Making of a Common Will."

the view of other shops, you are saying that the representative of one interest is concerned in the proposals made by other interests. You are saying that he must conceive a common interest. And in voting for him you are choosing a man who will not simply represent your view of your function, which is all that you know at first hand, but a man who will represent your views about other people's views of that function. You are voting as indefinitely as the orthodox democrat.

6

The guildsmen in their own minds have solved the question of how to conceive a common interest by playing with the word function. They imagine a society in which all the main work of the world has been analysed into functions, and these functions in turn synthesized harmoniously.[14] They suppose essential agreement about the purposes of society as a whole, and essential agreement about the role of every organized group in carrying out those purposes. It was a nice sentiment, therefore, which led them to take the name of their theory from an institution that arose in a Catholic feudal society. But they should remember that the scheme of function which the wise men of that age assumed was not worked out by mortal man. It is unclear how the guildsmen think the scheme is going to be worked out and made acceptable in the modern world. Sometimes they seem to argue that the scheme will develop from trade union organization, at other times that the communes will define the constitutional function of the groups. But it makes a considerable practical difference whether they believe that the groups define their own functions or not.

In either case, Mr. Cole assumes that society can be carried on by a social contract based on an accepted idea of "distinct essential groups of functions." How does one recognize these distinct essential groups? So far as I can make out, Mr. Cole thinks that a function is what a group of people are interested in. "The essence of functional democracy is that a man should count as many times over as there are functions in which he is interested."[15] Now there are at least two meanings to the word interested. You can use it to mean that a man is involved, or that his mind is occupied. John Smith, for example, may have been tremendously interested in the Stillman divorce case. He may have read every word of the news in every lobster edition. On the other hand, young Guy Stillman, whose legitimacy was at stake, probably did not trouble himself at all. John Smith was interested in a suit that did

---

[14] *Cf. op. cit.*, Ch. XIX.
[15] *Social Theory*, p. 102 *et seq.*

not affect his "interests," and Guy was uninterested in one that would determine the whole course of his life. Mr. Cole, I am afraid, leans towards John Smith. He is answering the "very foolish objection" that to vote by functions is to be voting very often: "If a man is not interested enough to vote, and cannot be aroused to interest enough to make him vote, on, say, a dozen distinct subjects, he waives his right to vote and the result is no less democratic than if he voted blindly and without interest."

Mr. Cole thinks that the uninstructed voter "waives his right to vote." From this it follows that the votes of the instructed reveal their interest, and their interest defines the function.[16] "Brown, Jones, and Robinson must therefore have, not one vote each, but as many different functional votes as there are different questions calling for associative action in which they are interested."[17] I am considerably in doubt whether Mr. Cole thinks that Brown, Jones and Robinson should qualify in any election where they assert that they are interested, or that somebody else, not named, picks the functions in which they are entitled to be interested. If I were asked to say what I believe Mr. Cole thinks, it would be that he has smoothed over the difficulty by the enormously strange assumption that it is the uninstructed voter who waives his right to vote; and has concluded that whether functional voting is arranged by a higher power, or "from below" on the principle that a man may vote when it interests him to vote, only the instructed will be voting anyway, and therefore the institution will work.

But there are two kinds of uninstructed voter. There is the man who does not know and knows that he does not know. He is generally an enlightened person. He is the man who waives his right to vote. But there is also the man who is uninstructed and does not know that he is, or care. He can always be gotten to the polls, if the party machinery is working. His vote is the basis of the machine. And since the communes of the guild society have large powers over taxation, wages, prices, credit, and natural resources, it would be preposterous to assume that elections will not be fought at least as passionately as our own.

The way people exhibit their interest will not then delimit the functions of a functional society. There are two other ways that function might be defined. One would be by the trade unions which fought the battle that brought guild socialism into being. Such a struggle would harden groups of men together in some sort of functional relation, and these groups would then become the vested interests of the guild

---

[16] *Cf.* Ch. XVIII of this book. "Since everybody was assumed to be interested enough in important affairs, only those affairs came to seem important in which everybody was interested."

[17] *Guild Socialism,* p. 24.

socialist society. Some of them, like the miners and railroad men, would be very strong, and probably deeply attached to the view of their function which they learned from the battle with capitalism. It is not at all unlikely that certain favorably placed trade unions would under a socialist state become the center of coherence and government. But a guild society would inevitably find them a tough problem to deal with, for direct action would have revealed their strategic power, and some of their leaders at least would not offer up this power readily on the altar of freedom. In order to "coördinate" them, guild society would have to gather together its strength, and fairly soon one would find, I think, that the radicals under guild socialism would be asking for communes strong enough to define the functions of the guilds.

But if you are going to have the government (commune) define functions, the premise of the theory disappears. It had to suppose that a scheme of functions was obvious in order that the concave shops would voluntarily relate themselves to society. If there is no settled scheme of functions in every voter's head, he has no better way under guild socialism than under orthodox democracy of turning a self-centered opinion into a social judgment. And, of course, there can be no such settled scheme, because, even if Mr. Cole and his friends devised a good one, the shop democracies from which all power derives, would judge the scheme in operation by what they learn of it and by what they can imagine. The guilds would see the same scheme differently. And so instead of the scheme being the skeleton that keeps guild society together, the attempt to define what the scheme ought to be, would be under guild socialism as elsewhere, the main business of politics. If we could allow Mr. Cole his scheme of functions we could allow him almost everything. Unfortunately he has inserted in his premise what he wishes a guild society to deduce.[18]

---

[18] I have dealt with Mr. Cole's theory rather than with the experience of Soviet Russia because, while the testimony is fragmentary, all competent observers seem to agree that Russia in 1921 does not illustrate a communist state in working order. Russia is in revolution, and what you can learn from Russia is what a revolution is like. You can learn very little about what a communist society would be like. It is, however, immensely significant that, first as practical revolutionists and then as public officials, the Russian communists have relied not upon the spontaneous democracy of the Russian people, but on the discipline, special interest and the noblesse oblige of a specialized class—the loyal and indoctrinated members of the Communist party. In the "transition," on which no time limit has been set, I believe, the cure for class government and the coercive state is strictly homeopathic.

There is also the question of why I selected Mr. Cole's books rather than the much more closely reasoned "Constitution for the Socialist Commonwealth of Great Britain" by Sidney and Beatrice Webb. I admire that book very much, but I have not been able to convince myself that it is not an intellectual tour de force. Mr. Cole seems to me far more authentically in the spirit of the socialist movement, and therefore, a better witness.

# XX. A New Image

## 1

THE lesson is, I think, a fairly clear one. In the absence of institutions and education by which the environment is so successfully reported that the realities of public life stand out sharply against self-centered opinion, the common interests very largely elude public opinion entirely, and can be managed only by a specialized class whose personal interests reach beyond the locality. This class is irresponsible, for it acts upon information that is not common property, in situations that the public at large does not conceive, and it can be held to account only on the accomplished fact.

The democratic theory by failing to admit that self-centered opinions are not sufficient to procure good government, is involved in perpetual conflict between theory and practice. According to the theory, the full dignity of man requires that his will should be, as Mr. Cole says, expressed "in any and every form of social action." It is supposed that the expression of their will is the consuming passion of men, for they are assumed to possess by instinct the art of government. But as a matter of plain experience, self-determination is only one of the many interests of a human personality. The desire to be the master of one's own destiny is a strong desire, but it has to adjust itself to other equally strong desires, such as the desire for a good life, for peace, for relief from burdens. In the original assumptions of democracy it was held that the expression of each man's will would spontaneously satisfy not only his desire for self-expression, but his desire for a good life, because the instinct to express one's self in a good life was innate.

The emphasis, therefore, has always been on the mechanism for expressing the will. The democratic El Dorado has always been some perfect environment, and some perfect system of voting and representation, where the innate good will and instinctive statesmanship of every man could be translated into action. In limited areas and for brief periods the environment has been so favorable, that is to say so isolated, and so rich in opportunity, that the theory worked well enough to confirm men in thinking that it was sound for all time and everywhere. Then when the isolation ended, and society became complex, and men had to adjust themselves closely to one another, the democrat spent his time trying to devise more perfect units of voting, in the hope that somehow he would, as Mr. Cole says, "get the mechanism right, and adjust it as far as possible to men's social wills." But while the democratic theorist was busy at this, he was far away from the actual interests of human nature. He was absorbed by one interest: self-government. Mankind was interested in all kinds of other things, in order, in its rights, in prosperity, in sights and sounds and in not being bored. In so far as spontaneous democracy does not satisfy their other interests, it seems to most men most of the time to be an empty thing. Because the art of successful self-government is not instinctive, men do not long desire self-government for its own sake. They desire it for the sake of the results. That is why the impulse to self-government is always strongest as a protest against bad conditions.

The democratic fallacy has been its preoccupation with the origin of government rather than with the processes and results. The democrat has always assumed that if political power could be derived in the right way, it would be beneficent. His whole attention has been on the source of power, since he is hypnotized by the belief that the great thing is to express the will of the people, first because expression is the highest interest of man, and second because the will is instinctively good. But no amount of regulation at the source of a river will completely control its behavior, and while democrats have been absorbed in trying to find a good mechanism for originating social power, that is to say a good mechanism of voting and representation, they neglected almost every other interest of men. For no matter how power originates, the crucial interest is in how power is exercised. What determines the quality of civilization is the use made of power. And that use cannot be controlled at the source.

If you try to control government wholly at the source, you inevitably make all the vital decisions invisible. For since there is no instinct which automatically makes political decisions that produce a good life, the men who actually exercise power not only fail to express the will of the people, because on most questions no will exists, but they exercise power according to opinions which are hidden from the electorate.

If, then, you root out of the democratic philosophy the whole assumption in all its ramifications that government is instinctive, and that therefore it can be managed by self-centered opinions, what becomes of the democratic faith in the dignity of man? It takes a fresh lease of life by associating itself with the whole personality instead of with a meager aspect of it. For the traditional democrat risked the dignity of man on one very precarious assumption, that he would exhibit that dignity instinctively in wise laws and good government. Voters did not do that, and so the democrat was forever being made to look a little silly by tough-minded men. But if, instead of hanging human dignity on the one assumption about self-government, you insist that man's dignity requires a standard of living, in which his capacities are properly exercised, the whole problem changes. The criteria which you then apply to government are whether it is producing a certain minimum of health, of decent housing, of material necessities, of education, of freedom, of pleasures, of beauty, not simply whether at the sacrifice of all these things, it vibrates to the self-centered opinions that happen to be floating around in men's minds. In the degree to which these criteria can be made exact and objective, political decision, which is inevitably the concern of comparatively few people, is actually brought into relation with the interests of men.

There is no prospect, in any time which we can conceive, that the whole invisible environment will be so clear to all men that they will spontaneously arrive at sound public opinions on the whole business of government. And even if there were a prospect, it is extremely doubtful whether many of us would wish to be bothered, or would take the time to form an opinion on "any and every form of social action" which affects us. The only prospect which is not visionary is that each of us in his own sphere will act more and more on a realistic picture of the invisible world, and that we shall develop more and more men who are expert in keeping these pictures realistic. Outside the rather narrow range of our own possible attention, social control depends upon devising standards of living and methods of audit by which the acts of public officials and industrial directors are measured. We cannot ourselves inspire or guide all these acts, as the mystical democrat has always imagined. But we can steadily increase our real control over these acts by insisting that all of them shall be plainly recorded, and their results objectively measured. I should say, perhaps, that we can progressively hope to insist. For the working out of such standards and of such audits has only begun.

# PART VII.   NEWSPAPERS

# XXI.  The Buying Public

1

THE idea that men have to go forth and study the world in order to govern it, has played a very minor part in political thought. It could figure very little, because the machinery for reporting the world in any way useful to government made comparatively little progress from the time of Aristotle to the age in which the premises of democracy were established.

Therefore, if you had asked a pioneer democrat where the information was to come from on which the will of the people was to be based, he would have been puzzled by the question. It would have seemed a little as if you had asked him where his life or his soul came from. The will of the people, he almost always assumed, exists at all times; the duty of political science was to work out the inventions of the ballot and representative government. If they were properly worked out and applied under the right conditions, such as exist in the self-contained village or the self-contained shop, the mechanism would somehow overcome the brevity of attention which Aristotle had observed, and the narrowness of its range, which the theory of a self-contained community tacitly acknowledged. We have seen how even at this late date the guild socialists are transfixed by the notion that if only you can build on the right unit of voting and representation, an intricate coöperative commonwealth is possible.

Convinced that the wisdom was there if only you could find it, democrats have treated the problem of making public opinions as a problem in civil liberties.[1] "Who ever knew Truth put to the worse, in a free and open encounter?"[2] Supposing that no one has ever seen it put to the worse, are we to believe then that the truth is generated by the encounter, like fire by rubbing two sticks? Behind this classic doctrine of liberty, which

---

[1] The best study is Prof. Zechariah Chafee's *Freedom of Speech.*

[2] Milton, *Areopagitica,* cited at the opening of Mr. Chafee's book. For comment on this classic doctrine of liberty as stated by Milton, John Stuart Mill, and Mr. Bertrand Russell, see my *Liberty and the News,* Ch. II.

American democrats embodied in their Bill of Rights, there are, in fact, several different theories of the origin of truth. One is a faith that in the competition of opinions, the truest will win because there is a peculiar strength in the truth. This is probably sound if you allow the competition to extend over a sufficiently long time. When men argue in this vein they have in mind the verdict of history, and they think specifically of heretics persecuted when they lived, canonized after they were dead. Milton's question rests also on a belief that the capacity to recognize truth is inherent in all men, and that truth freely put in circulation will win acceptance. It derives no less from the experience, which has shown that men are not likely to discover truth if they cannot speak it, except under the eye of an uncomprehending policeman.

No one can possibly overestimate the practical value of these civil liberties, nor the importance of maintaining them. When they are in jeopardy, the human spirit is in jeopardy, and should there come a time when they have to be curtailed, as during a war, the suppression of thought is a risk to civilization which might prevent its recovery from the effects of war, if the hysterics, who exploit the necessity, were numerous enough to carry over into peace the taboos of war. Fortunately, the mass of men is too tolerant long to enjoy the professional inquisitors, as gradually, under the criticism of men not willing to be terrorized, they are revealed as mean-spirited creatures who nine-tenths of the time do not know what they are talking about.[3]

But in spite of its fundamental importance, civil liberty in this sense does not guarantee public opinion in the modern world. For it always assumes, either that truth is spontaneous, or that the means of securing truth exist when there is no external interference. But when you are dealing with an invisible environment, the assumption is false. The truth about distant or complex matters is not self-evident, and the machinery for assembling information is technical and expensive. Yet political science, and especially democratic political science, has never freed itself from the original assumption of Aristotle's politics sufficiently to restate the premises, so that political thought might come to grips with the problem of how to make the invisible world visible to the citizens of a modern state.

So deep is the tradition, that until quite recently, for example, political science was taught in our colleges as if newspapers did not exist. I am not referring to schools of journalism, for they are trade schools, intended to prepare men and women for a career. I am referring to

---

[3] *Cf.* for example, the publications of the Lusk Committee in New York, and the public statements and prophecies of Mr. Mitchell Palmer, who was Attorney-General of the United States during the period of President Wilson's illness.

political science as expounded to future business men, lawyers, public officials, and citizens at large. In that science a study of the press and the sources of popular information found no place. It is a curious fact. To anyone not immersed in the routine interests of political science, it is almost inexplicable that no American student of government, no American sociologist, has ever written a book on newsgathering. There are occasional references to the press, and statements that it is not, or that it ought to be, "free" and "truthful." But I can find almost nothing else. And this disdain of the professionals finds its counterpart in public opinions. Universally it is admitted that the press is the chief means of contact with the unseen environment. And practically everywhere it is assumed that the press should do spontaneously for us what primitive democracy imagined each of us could do spontaneously for himself, that every day and twice a day it will present us with a true picture of all the outer world in which we are interested.

2

This insistent and ancient belief that truth is not earned, but inspired, revealed, supplied gratis, comes out very plainly in our economic prejudices as readers of newspapers. We expect the newspaper to serve us with truth however unprofitable the truth may be. For this difficult and often dangerous service, which we recognize as fundamental, we expected to pay until recently the smallest coin turned out by the mint. We have accustomed ourselves now to paying two and even three cents on weekdays, and on Sundays, for an illustrated encyclopedia and vaudeville entertainment attached, we have screwed ourselves up to paying a nickel or even a dime. Nobody thinks for a moment that he ought to pay for his newspaper. He expects the fountains of truth to bubble, but he enters into no contract, legal or moral, involving any risk, cost or trouble to himself. He will pay a nominal price when it suits him, will stop paying whenever it suits him, will turn to another paper when that suits him. Somebody has said quite aptly that the newspaper editor has to be re-elected every day.

This casual and one-sided relationship between readers and press is an anomaly of our civilization. There is nothing else quite like it, and it is, therefore, hard to compare the press with any other business or institution. It is not a business pure and simple, partly because the product is regularly sold below cost, but chiefly because the community applies one ethical measure to the press and another to trade or manufacture. Ethically a newspaper is judged as if it were a church or a school. But if you try to compare it with these you fail; the taxpayer pays for the public school, the private school is endowed or supported by tuition fees, there are subsidies and collections for the church. You cannot compare journalism with law, medicine or engineering, for in every one of these professions the consumer pays for the service. A free press, if you judge by the attitude of the readers, means newspapers that are virtually given away.

Yet the critics of the press are merely voicing the moral standards of the community, when they expect such an institution to live on the same plane as that on which the school, the church, and the disinterested professions are supposed to live. This illustrates again the concave character of democracy. No need for artificially acquired information is felt to exist. The information must come naturally, that is to say gratis, if not out of the heart of the citizen, then gratis out of the newspaper. The citizen will pay for his telephone, his railroad rides, his motor car, his entertainment. But he does not pay openly for his news.

He will, however, pay handsomely for the privilege of having someone read about him. He will pay directly to advertise. And he will pay indirectly for the advertisements of other people, because that payment, being concealed in the price of commodities is part of an invisible environment that he does not effectively comprehend. It would be regarded as an outrage to have to pay openly the price of a good ice cream soda for all the news of the world, though the public will pay that and more when it buys the advertised commodities. The public pays for the press, but only when the payment is concealed.

### 3

Circulation is, therefore, the means to an end. It becomes an asset only when it can be sold to the advertiser, who buys it with revenues secured through indirect taxation of the reader.[4] The kind of circulation which the advertiser will buy depends on what he has to sell. It may be "quality" or "mass." On the whole there is no sharp dividing line, for in respect to most commodities sold by advertising, the customers are neither the small class of the very rich nor the very poor. They are the people with enough surplus over bare necessities to exercise discretion in their buying. The paper, therefore, which goes into the homes of the fairly prosperous is by and large the one which offers most to the advertiser. It may also go into the homes of the poor, but

---

[4] "An established newspaper is entitled to fix its advertising rates so that its net receipts from circulation may be left on the credit side of the profit and loss account. To arrive at net receipts, I would deduct from the gross the cost of promotion, distribution, and other expenses incidental to circulation." From an address by Mr. Adolph S. Ochs, publisher of the New York Times, at the Philadelphia Convention of the Associated Advertising Clubs of The World, June 26, 1916. Cited, Elmer Davis, History of The New York Times, 1851–1921, pp. 397–398.

except for certain lines of goods, an analytical advertising agent does not rate that circulation as a great asset, unless, as seems to be the case with certain of Mr. Hearst's properties, the circulation is enormous.

A newspaper which angers those whom it pays best to reach through advertisements is a bad medium for an advertiser. And since no one ever claimed that advertising was philanthropy, advertisers buy space in those publications which are fairly certain to reach their future customers. One need not spend much time worrying about the unreported scandals of the dry-goods merchants. They represent nothing really significant, and incidents of this sort are less common than many critics of the press suppose. The real problem is that the readers of a newspaper, unaccustomed to paying the cost of newsgathering, can be capitalized only by turning them into circulation that can be sold to manufacturers and merchants. And those whom it is most important to capitalize are those who have the most money to spend. Such a press is bound to respect the point of view of the buying public. It is for this buying public that newspapers are edited and published, for without that support the newspaper cannot live. A newspaper can flout an advertiser, it can attack a powerful banking or traction interest, but if it alienates the buying public, it loses the one indispensable asset of its existence.

Mr. John L. Given,[5] formerly of the New York *Evening Sun*, stated in 1914 that out of over two thousand three hundred dailies published in the United States, there were about one hundred and seventy-five printed in cities having over one hundred thousand inhabitants. These constitute the press for "general news." They are the key papers which collect the news dealing with great events, and even the people who do not read any one of the one hundred and seventy-five depend ultimately upon them for news of the outer world. For they make up the great press associations which cooperate in the exchange of news. Each is, therefore, not only the informant of its own readers, but it is the local reporter for the newspapers of other cities. The rural press and the special press, by and large, take their general news from these key papers. And among these there are some very much richer than others, so that for international news, in the main, the whole press of the nation may depend upon the reports of the press associations and the special services of a few metropolitan dailies.

Roughly speaking, the economic support for general newsgathering is in the price paid for advertised goods by the fairly prosperous sections of cities with more than one hundred thousand inhabitants. These buying

---

[5] *Making a Newspaper*, p. 13. This is the best technical book I know, and should be read by everyone who undertakes to discuss the press. Mr. G. B. Diblee, who wrote the volume on *The Newspaper* in the Home University Library, says (p. 253), that "on the press for pressmen I only know of one good book, Mr. Given's."

publics are composed of the members of families, who depend for their income chiefly on trade, merchandising, the direction of manufacture, and finance. They are the clientele among whom it pays best to advertise in a newspaper. They wield a concentrated purchasing power, which may be less in volume than the aggregate for farmers and workingmen; but within the radius covered by a daily newspaper they are the quickest assets.

## 4

They have, moreover, a double claim to attention. They are not only the best customers for the advertiser, they include the advertisers. Therefore the impression made by the newspapers on this public matters deeply. Fortunately this public is not unanimous. It may be "capitalistic" but it contains divergent views on what capitalism is, and how it is to be run. Except in times of danger, this respectable opinion is sufficiently divided to permit of considerable differences of policy. These would be greater still if it were not that publishers are themselves usually members of these urban communities, and honestly see the world through the lenses of their associates and friends.

They are engaged in a speculative business,[6] which depends on the general condition of trade, and more peculiarly on a circulation based not on a marriage contract with their readers, but on free love. The object of every publisher is, therefore, to turn his circulation from a medley of catch-as-catch-can newsstand buyers into a devoted band of constant readers. A newspaper that can really depend upon the loyalty of its readers is as independent as a newspaper can be, given the economics of modern journalism.[7] A body of readers who stay by it through thick and thin is a power greater than any which the individual advertiser can wield, and a power great enough to break up a combination of advertisers. Therefore, whenever you find a newspaper betraying its readers for the sake of an advertiser, you can be fairly certain either that the publisher sincerely shares the views of the advertiser, or that he thinks, perhaps mistakenly, he cannot count upon the support of his readers if he openly resists dictation. It is a question of whether the readers, who do not pay in cash for their news, will pay for it in loyalty.

---

[6] Sometimes so speculative that in order to secure credit the publisher has to go into bondage to his creditors. Information on this point is very difficult to obtain, and for that reason its general importance is often much exaggerated.

[7] "It is an axiom in newspaper publishing—'more readers, more independence of the influence of advertisers; fewer readers and more dependence on the advertiser.' It may seem like a contradiction (yet it is the truth) to assert: the greater the number of advertisers, the less influence they are individually able to exercise with the publisher." Adolph S. Ochs, *cf. supra*.

# XXII. The Constant Reader

1

THE loyalty of the buying public to a newspaper is not stipulated in any bond. In almost every other enterprise the person who expects to be served enters into an agreement that controls his passing whims. At least he pays for what he obtains. In the publishing of periodicals the nearest approach to an agreement for a definite time is the paid subscription, and that is not, I believe, a great factor in the economy of a metropolitan daily. The reader is the sole and the daily judge of his loyalty, and there can be no suit against him for breach of promise or nonsupport.

Though everything turns on the constancy of the reader, there does not exist even a vague tradition to call that fact to the reader's mind. His constancy depends on how he happens to feel, or on his habits. And these depend not simply on the quality of the news, but more often on a number of obscure elements that in our casual relation to the press, we hardly take the trouble to make conscious. The most important of these is that each of us tends to judge a newspaper, if we judge it at all, by its treatment of that part of the news in which we feel ourselves involved. The newspaper deals with a multitude of events beyond our experience. But it deals also with some events within our experience. And by its handling of those events we most frequently decide to like it or dislike it, to trust it or refuse to have the sheet in the house. If the newspaper gives a satisfactory account of that which we think we know, our business, our church, our party, it is fairly certain to be immune from violent criticism by us. What better criterion does the man at the breakfast table possess than that the newspaper version checks up with his own opinion? Therefore, most men tend to hold the newspaper most strictly accountable in their capacity, not of general readers, but of special pleaders on matters of their own experience.

Rarely is anyone but the interested party able to test the accuracy of a report. If the news is local, and if there is competition, the editor knows that he will probably hear from the man who thinks his portrait unfair and inaccurate. But if the news is not local, the corrective diminishes as the subject matter recedes into the distance. The only people who can correct what they think is a false picture of themselves printed in another city are members of groups well enough organized to hire publicity men.

Now it is interesting to note that the general reader of a newspaper has no standing in law if he thinks he is being misled by the news. It is only the aggrieved party who can sue for slander or libel, and he has to prove a material injury to himself. The law embodies the tradition that general news is not a matter of common concern,[1] except as to matter which is vaguely described as immoral or seditious.

But the body of the news, though unchecked as a whole by the disinterested reader, consists of items about which some readers have very definite preconceptions. Those items are the data of his judgment, and news which men read without this personal criterion, they judge by some other standard than their standard of accuracy. They are dealing here with a subject matter which to them is indistinguishable from fiction. The canon of truth cannot be applied. They do not boggle over such news if it conforms to their stereotypes, and they continue to read it if it interests them.[2]

## 2

There are newspapers, even in large cities, edited on the principle that the readers wish to read about themselves. The theory is that if enough people see their own names in the paper often enough, can read about their weddings, funerals, sociables, foreign travels, lodge meetings, school prizes, their fiftieth birthdays, their sixtieth birthdays, their silver weddings, their outings and clambakes, they will make a reliable circulation.

The classic formula for such a newspaper is contained in a letter written by Horace Greeley on April 3, 1860, to "Friend Fletcher" who was about to start a country newspaper:[3]

> "I. Begin with a clear conception that the subject of deepest interest to an average human being is himself; next to that he is most concerned about his neighbors. Asia and the Tongo Islands stand a long way after these in his regard. . . . Do not let a new church be organized, or new members be added to one already existing, a farm be sold, a new house raised, a mill set in motion, a store opened, nor anything of interest to a dozen families occur, without having the fact duly, though briefly, chronicled in your columns. If a farmer cuts a big tree, or grows a mammoth beet, or harvests a bounteous yield of wheat or corn, set forth the fact as concisely and unexceptionally as possible."

The function of becoming, as Mr. Lee puts it, "the printed diary of the home town" is one that every newspaper no matter where it is

---

[1] The reader will not mistake this as a plea for censorship. It might, however, be a good thing if there were competent tribunals, preferably not official ones, where charges of untruthfulness and unfairness in the general news could be sifted. *Cf. Liberty and the News*, pp. 73–76.

[2] Note, for example, how absent is indignation in Mr. Upton Sinclair against socialist papers, even those which are as malignantly unfair to employers as certain of the papers cited by him are unfair to radicals.

[3] Cited, James Melvin Lee, *The History of American Journalism*, p. 405.

published must in some measure fill. And where, as in a great city like New York, the general newspapers circulated broadcast cannot fill it, there exist small newspapers published on Greeley's pattern for sections of the city. In the boroughs of Manhattan and the Bronx there are perhaps twice as many local dailies as there are general newspapers.[4] And they are supplemented by all kinds of special publications for trades, religions, nationalities.

These diaries are published for people who find their own lives interesting. But there are also great numbers of people who find their own lives dull, and wish, like Hedda Gabler, to live a more thrilling life. For them there are published a few whole newspapers, and sections of others, devoted to the personal lives of a set of imaginary people, with whose gorgeous vices the reader can in his fancy safely identify himself. Mr. Hearst's unflagging interest in high society caters to people who never hope to be in high society, and yet manage to derive some enhancement out of the vague feeling that they are part of the life that they read about. In the great cities "the printed diary of the home town" tends to be the printed diary of a smart set.

And it is, as we have already noted, the dailies of the cities which carry the burden of bringing distant news to the private citizen. But it is not primarily their political and social news which holds the circulation. The interest in that is intermittent, and few publishers can bank on it alone. The newspaper, therefore, takes to itself a variety of other features, all primarily designed to hold a body of readers together, who so far as big news is concerned, are not able to be critical. Moreover, in big news the competition in any one community is not very serious. The press services standardize the main events; it is only once in a while that a great scoop is made; there is apparently not a very great reading public for such massive reporting as has made the *New York Times* of recent years indispensable to men of all shades of opinion. In order to differentiate themselves and collect a steady public most papers have to go outside the field of general news. They go to the dazzling levels of society, to scandal and crime, to sports, pictures, actresses, advice to the lovelorn, highschool notes, women's pages, buyer's pages, cooking receipts, chess, whist, gardening, comic strips, thundering partisanship, not because publishers and editors are interested in everything but news, but because they have to find some way of holding on to that alleged host of passionately interested readers, who are supposed by some critics of the press to be clamoring for the truth and nothing but the truth.

The newspaper editor occupies a strange position. His enterprises depend upon indirect taxation levied by his advertisers upon his readers;

---

[4] *Cf.* John L. Given, *Making a Newspaper*, p. 13.

the patronage of the advertisers depends upon the editor's skill in holding together an effective group of customers. These customers deliver judgment according to their private experiences and their stereotyped expectations, for in the nature of things they have no independent knowledge of most news they read. If the judgment is not unfavorable, the editor is at least within range of a circulation that pays. But in order to secure that circulation, he cannot rely wholly upon news of the greater environment. He handles that as interestingly as he can, of course, but the quality of the general news, especially about public affairs, is not in itself sufficient to cause very large numbers of readers to discriminate among the dailies.

This somewhat left-handed relationship between newspapers and public information is reflected in the salaries of newspaper men. Reporting, which theoretically constitutes the foundation of the whole institution, is the most poorly paid branch of newspaper work, and is the least regarded. By and large, able men go into it only by necessity or for experience, and with the definite intention of being graduated as soon as possible. For straight reporting is not a career that offers many great rewards. The rewards in journalism go to specialty work, to signed correspondence which has editorial quality, to executives, and to men with a knack and flavor of their own. This is due, no doubt, to what economists call the rent of ability. But this economic principle operates with such peculiar violence in journalism that newsgathering does not attract to itself anything like the number of trained and able men which its public importance would seem to demand. The fact that the able men take up "straight reporting" with the intention of leaving it as soon as possible is, I think, the chief reason why it has never developed in sufficient measure those corporate traditions that give to a profession prestige and a jealous self-respect. For it is these corporate traditions which engender the pride of craft, which tend to raise the standards of admission, punish breaches of the code, and give men the strength to insist upon their status in society.

### 3

Yet all this does not go to the root of the matter. For while the economics of journalism is such as to depress the value of newsreporting, it is, I am certain, a false determinism which would abandon the analysis at that point. The intrinsic power of the reporter appears to be so great, the number of very able men who pass through reporting is so large, that there must be some deeper reason why, comparatively speaking, so little serious effort has gone into raising the vocation to the level say of medicine, engineering, or law.

Mr. Upton Sinclair speaks for a large body of opinion in America,[5] when he claims that in what he calls "The Brass Check" he has found this deeper reason:

> "The Brass Check is found in your pay envelope every week—you who write and print and distribute our newspapers and magazines. The Brass check is the price of your shame—you who take the fair body of truth and sell it in the market place, who betray the virgin hopes of mankind into the loathsome brothel of Big Business."[6]

It would seem from this that there exists a body of known truth, and a set of well founded hopes, which are prostituted by a more or less conscious conspiracy of the rich owners of newspapers. If this theory is correct, then a certain conclusion follows. It is that the fair body of truth would be inviolate in a press not in any way connected with Big Business. For if it should happen that a press not controlled by, and not even friendly with, Big Business somehow failed to contain the fair body of truth, something would be wrong with Mr. Sinclair's theory.

There is such a press. Strange to say, in proposing a remedy Mr. Sinclair does not advise his readers to subscribe to the nearest radical newspaper. Why not? If the troubles of American journalism go back to the Brass Check of Big Business why does not the remedy lie in reading the papers that do not in any remote way accept the Brass Check? Why subsidize a "National News" with a large board of directors "of all creeds or causes" to print a paper full of facts "regardless of what is injured, the Steel Trust or the I. W. W., the Standard Oil Company or the Socialist Party?" If the trouble is Big Business, that is, the Steel Trust, Standard Oil and the like, why not urge everybody to read I. W. W. or Socialist papers? Mr. Sinclair does not say why not. But the reason is simple. He cannot convince anybody, not even himself, that the anti-capitalist press is the remedy for the capitalist press. He ignores the anti-capitalist press both in his theory of the Brass Check and in his constructive proposal. But if you are diagnosing American journalism you cannot ignore it. If what you care about is "the fair body of truth," you do not commit the gross logical error of assembling all the instances of unfairness and lying you can find in one set of newspapers, ignore all the instances you could easily find in another set, and then assign as the cause of the lying, the one supposedly common characteristic of the press to which you have confined your investigation. If you are going to blame "capitalism" for the faults

---

[5] Mr. Hilaire Belloc makes practically the same analysis for English newspapers. *Cf. The Free Press.*
[6] Upton Sinclair, *The Brass Check. A Study of American Journalism*, p. 436.

of the press, you are compelled to prove that those faults do not exist except where capitalism controls. That Mr. Sinclair cannot do this, is shown by the fact that while in his diagnosis he traces everything to capitalism, in his prescription he ignores both capitalism and anti-capitalism.

One would have supposed that the inability to take any non-capitalist paper as a model of truthfulness and competence would have caused Mr. Sinclair, and those who agree with him, to look somewhat more critically at their assumptions. They would have asked themselves, for example, where is the fair body of truth, that Big Business prostitutes, but anti-Big Business does not seem to obtain? For that question leads, I believe, to the heart of the matter, to the question of what is news.

# XXIII. The Nature of News

## 1

ALL the reporters in the world working all the hours of the day could not witness all the happenings in the world. There are not a great many reporters. And none of them has the power to be in more than one place at a time. Reporters are not clairvoyant, they do not gaze into a crystal ball and see the world at will, they are not assisted by thought-transference. Yet the range of subjects these comparatively few men manage to cover would be a miracle indeed, if it were not a standardized routine.

Newspapers do not try to keep an eye on all mankind.[1] They have watchers stationed at certain places, like Police Headquarters, the Coroner's Office, the County Clerk's Office, City Hall, the White House, the Senate, House of Representatives, and so forth. They watch, or rather in the majority of cases they belong to associations which employ men who watch "a comparatively small number of places where it is made known when the life of anyone . . . departs from ordinary paths, or when events worth telling about occur. For example, John Smith, let it be supposed, becomes a broker. For ten years he pursues the even tenor of his way and except for his customers and his friends no one gives him a thought. To the newspapers he is as if he were not. But in the eleventh year he suffers heavy losses and, at last, his resources all gone, summons his lawyer and arranges for the making of an assignment. The lawyer posts off to the County Clerk's office,

---

[1] See the illuminating chapter in Mr. John L. Given's book, already cited, on "Uncovering the News," Ch. V.

and a clerk there makes the necessary entries in the official docket. Here in step the newspapers. While the clerk is writing Smith's business obituary a reporter glances over his shoulder and a few minutes later the reporters know Smith's troubles and are as well informed concerning his business status as they would be had they kept a reporter at his door every day for over ten years."[2]

When Mr. Given says that the newspapers know "Smith's troubles" and "his business status," he does not mean that they know them as Smith knows them, or as Mr. Arnold Bennett would know them if he had made Smith the hero of a three volume novel. The newspapers know only "in a few minutes" the bald facts which are recorded in the County Clerk's Office. That overt act "uncovers" the news about Smith. Whether the news will be followed up or not is another matter. The point is that before a series of events become news they have usually to make themselves noticeable in some more or less overt act. Generally too, in a crudely overt act. Smith's friends may have known for years that he was taking risks, rumors may even have reached the financial editor if Smith's friends were talkative. But apart from the fact that none of this could be published because it would be libel, there is in these rumors nothing definite on which to peg a story. Something definite must occur that has unmistakable form. It may be the act of going into bankruptcy, it may be a fire, a collision, an assault, a riot, an arrest, a denunciation, the introduction of a bill, a speech, a vote, a meeting, the expressed opinion of a well known citizen, an editorial in a newspaper, a sale, a wage-schedule, a price change, the proposal to build a bridge. . . . There must be a manifestation. The course of events must assume a certain definable shape, and until it is in a phase where some aspect is an accomplished fact, news does not separate itself from the ocean of possible truth.

2

Naturally there is room for wide difference of opinion as to when events have a shape that can be reported. A good journalist will find news oftener than a hack. If he sees a building with a dangerous list, he does not have to wait until it falls into the street in order to recognize news. It was a great reporter who guessed the name of the next Indian Viceroy when he heard that Lord So-and-So was inquiring about climates. There are lucky shots but the number of men who can make them is small. Usually it is the stereotyped shape assumed by an event at an obvious place that uncovers the run of the news. The most obvious place is where people's affairs touch public authority. De minimis

---

[2] *Op. cit.*, p. 57.

non curat lex. It is at these places that marriages, births, deaths, contracts, failures, arrivals, departures, lawsuits, disorders, epidemics and
calamities are made known.

In the first instance, therefore, the news is not a mirror of social conditions, but the report of an aspect that has obtruded itself. The news
does not tell you how the seed is germinating in the ground, but it may
tell you when the first sprout breaks through the surface. It may even tell
you what somebody says is happening to the seed under ground. It may
tell you that the sprout did not come up at the time it was expected. The
more points, then, at which any happening can be fixed, objectified,
measured, named, the more points there are at which news can occur.

So, if some day a legislature, having exhausted all other ways of
improving mankind, should forbid the scoring of baseball games, it
might still be possible to play some sort of game in which the umpire
decided according to his own sense of fair play how long the game
should last, when each team should go to bat, and who should be
regarded as the winner. If that game were reported in the newspapers
it would consist of a record of the umpire's decisions, plus the reporter's
impression of the hoots and cheers of the crowd, plus at best a vague
account of how certain men, who had no specified position on the field
moved around for a few hours on an unmarked piece of sod. The more
you try to imagine the logic of so absurd a predicament, the more clear
it becomes that for the purposes of newsgathering, (let alone the purposes of playing the game) it is impossible to do much without an apparatus and rules for naming, scoring, recording. Because that machinery
is far from perfect, the umpire's life is often a distracted one. Many crucial plays he has to judge by eye. The last vestige of dispute could be
taken out of the game, as it has been taken out of chess when people
obey the rules, if somebody thought it worth his while to photograph
every play. It was the moving pictures which finally settled a real doubt
in many reporters' minds, owing to the slowness of the human eye, as
to just what blow of Dempsey's knocked out Carpentier.

Wherever there is a good machinery of record, the modern news service
works with great precision. There is one on the stock exchange, and the
news of price movements is flashed over tickers with dependable accuracy.
There is a machinery for election returns, and when the counting and tab-
ulating are well done, the result of a national election is usually known on
the night of the election. In civilized communities deaths, births, marriages
and divorces are recorded, and are known accurately except where there is
concealment or neglect. The machinery exists for some, and only some,
aspects of industry and government, in varying degrees of precision for
securities, money and staples, bank clearances, realty transactions, wage
scales. It exists for imports and exports because they pass through a custom
house and can be directly recorded. It exists in nothing like the same
degree for internal trade, and especially for trade over the counter.

It will be found, I think, that there is a very direct relation between the certainty of news and the system of record. If you call to mind the topics which form the principal indictment by reformers against the press, you find they are subjects in which the newspaper occupies the position of the umpire in the unscored baseball game. All news about states of mind is of this character: so are all descriptions of personalities, of sincerity, aspiration, motive, intention, of mass feeling, of national feeling, of public opinion, the policies of foreign governments. So is much news about what is going to happen. So are questions turning on private profit, private income, wages, working conditions, the efficiency of labor, educational opportunity, unemployment,[3] monotony, health, discrimination, unfairness, restraint of trade, waste, "backward peoples," conservatism, imperialism, radicalism, liberty, honor, righteousness. All involve data that are at best spasmodically recorded. The data may be hidden because of a censorship or a tradition of privacy, they may not exist because nobody thinks record important, because he thinks it red tape, or because nobody has yet invented an objective system of measurement. Then the news on these subjects is bound to be debatable, when it is not wholly neglected. The events which are not scored are reported either as personal and conventional opinions, or they are not news. They do not take shape until somebody protests, or somebody investigates, or somebody publicly, in the etymological meaning of the word, makes an *issue* of them.

This is the underlying reason for the existence of the press agent. The enormous discretion as to what facts and what impressions shall be reported is steadily convincing every organized group of people that whether it wishes to secure publicity or to avoid it, the exercise of discretion cannot be left to the reporter. It is safer to hire a press agent who stands between the group and the newspapers. Having hired him, the temptation to exploit his strategic position is very great. "Shortly before the war," says Mr. Frank Cobb, "the newspapers of New York took a census of the press agents who were regularly employed and regularly accredited and found that there were about twelve hundred of them. How many there are now (1919) I do not pretend to know, but what I do know is that many of the direct channels to news have been closed and the information for the public is first filtered through publicity agents. The great corporations have them, the banks have them, the railroads have them, all the organizations of business and of social and political activity have them, and they are the media through which news comes. Even statesmen have them."[4]

---

[3] Think of what guess work went into the Reports of Unemployment in 1921.

[4] Address before the Women's City Club of New York, Dec. 11, 1919. Reprinted, *New Republic*, Dec. 31, 1919, p. 44.

Were reporting the simple recovery of obvious facts, the press agent would be little more than a clerk. But since, in respect to most of the big topics of news, the facts are not simple, and not at all obvious, but subject to choice and opinion, it is natural that everyone should wish to make his own choice of facts for the newspapers to print. The publicity man does that. And in doing it, he certainly saves the reporter much trouble, by presenting him a clear picture of a situation out of which he might otherwise make neither head nor tail. But it follows that the picture which the publicity man makes for the reporter is the one he wishes the public to see. He is censor and propagandist, responsible only to his employers, and to the whole truth responsible only as it accords with the employers' conception of his own interests.

The development of the publicity man is a clear sign that the facts of modern life do not spontaneously take a shape in which they can be known. They must be given a shape by somebody, and since in the daily routine reporters cannot give a shape to facts, and since there is little disinterested organization of intelligence, the need for some formulation is being met by the interested parties.

### 3

The good press agent understands that the virtues of his cause are not news, unless they are such strange virtues that they jut right out of the routine of life. This is not because the newspapers do not like virtue, but because it is not worth while to say that nothing has happened when nobody expected anything to happen. So if the publicity man wishes free publicity he has, speaking quite accurately, to start something. He arranges a stunt: obstructs the traffic, teases the police, somehow manages to entangle his client or his cause with an event that is already news. The suffragists knew this, did not particularly enjoy the knowledge but acted on it, and kept suffrage in the news long after the arguments pro and con were straw in their mouths, and people were about to settle down to thinking of the suffrage movement as one of the established institutions of American life.[5]

Fortunately the suffragists, as distinct from the feminists, had a perfectly concrete objective, and a very simple one. What the vote symbolizes is not simple, as the ablest advocates and the ablest opponents knew. But the right to vote is a simple and familiar right. Now in labor

---

[5] *Cf.* Inez Haynes Irwin, *The Story of the Woman's Party.* It is not only a good account of a vital part of a great agitation, but a reservoir of material on successful, non-revolutionary, non-conspiring agitation under modern conditions of public attention, public interest, and political habit.

disputes, which are probably the chief item in the charges against newspapers, the right to strike, like the right to vote, is simple enough. But the causes and objects of a particular strike are like the causes and objects of the woman's movement, extremely subtle.

Let us suppose the conditions leading up to a strike are bad. What is the measure of evil? A certain conception of a proper standard of living, hygiene, economic security, and human dignity. The industry may be far below the theoretical standard of the community, and the workers may be too wretched to protest. Conditions may be above the standard, and the workers may protest violently. The standard is at best a vague measure. However, we shall assume that the conditions are below par, as par is understood by the editor. Occasionally without waiting for the workers to threaten, but prompted say by a social worker, he will send reporters to investigate, and will call attention to bad conditions. Necessarily he cannot do that often. For these investigations cost time, money, special talent, and a lot of space. To make plausible a report that conditions are bad, you need a good many columns of print. In order to tell the truth about the steel worker in the Pittsburgh district, there was needed a staff of investigators, a great deal of time, and several fat volumes of print. It is impossible to suppose that any daily newspaper could normally regard the making of Pittsburgh Surveys, or even Interchurch Steel Reports, as one of its tasks. News which requires so much trouble as that to obtain is beyond the resources of a daily press.[6]

The bad conditions as such are not news, because in all but exceptional cases, journalism is not a first hand report of the raw material. It is a report of that material after it has been stylized. Thus bad conditions might become news if the Board of Health reported an unusually high death rate in an industrial area. Failing an intervention of this sort, the facts do not become news, until the workers organize and make a demand upon their employers. Even then, if an easy settlement is certain the news value is low, whether or not the conditions themselves are remedied in the settlement. But if industrial relations collapse into a strike or lockout the news value increases. If the stoppage involves a service on which the readers of the newspapers immediately depend, or if it involves a breach of order, the news value is still greater.

The underlying trouble appears in the news through certain easily recognizable symptoms, a demand, a strike, disorder. From the point of

---

[6] Not long ago Babe Ruth was jailed for speeding. Released from jail just before the afternoon game started, he rushed into his waiting automobile, and made up for time lost in jail by breaking the speed laws on his way to the ball grounds. No policeman stopped him, but a reporter timed him, and published his speed the next morning. Babe Ruth is an exceptional man. Newspapers cannot time all motorists. They have to take their news about speeding from the police.

view of the worker, or of the disinterested seeker of justice, the demand, the strike, and the disorder, are merely incidents in a process that for them is richly complicated. But since all the immediate realities lie outside the direct experience both of the reporter, and of the special public by which most newspapers are supported, they have normally to wait for a signal in the shape of an overt act. When that signal comes, say through a walkout of the men or a summons for the police, it calls into play the stereotypes people have about strikes and disorders. The unseen struggle has none of its own flavor. It is noted abstractly, and that abstraction is then animated by the immediate experience of the reader and reporter. Obviously this is a very different experience from that which the strikers have. They feel, let us say, the temper of the foreman, the nerve-racking monotony of the machine, the depressingly bad air, the drudgery of their wives, the stunting of their children, the dinginess of their tenements. The slogans of the strike are invested with these feelings. But the reporter and reader see at first only a strike and some catchwords. They invest these with their feelings. Their feelings may be that their jobs are insecure because the strikers are stopping goods they need in their work, that there will be shortage and higher prices, that it is all devilishly inconvenient. These, too, are realities. And when they give color to the abstract news that a strike has been called, it is in the nature of things that the workers are at a disadvantage. It is in the nature, that is to say, of the existing system of industrial relations that news arising from grievances or hopes by workers should almost invariably be uncovered by an overt attack on production.

You have, therefore, the circumstances in all their sprawling complexity, the overt act which signalizes them, the stereotyped bulletin which publishes the signal, and the meaning that the reader himself injects, after he has derived that meaning from the experience which directly affects him. Now the reader's experience of a strike may be very important indeed, but from the point of view of the central trouble which caused the strike, it is eccentric. Yet this eccentric meaning is automatically the most interesting.[7] To enter imaginatively into the central issues is for the reader to step out of himself, and into very different lives.

It follows that in the reporting of strikes, the easiest way is to let the news be uncovered by the overt act, and to describe the event as the story of interference with the reader's life. That is where his attention is first aroused, and his interest most easily enlisted. A great deal, I think myself the crucial part, of what looks to the worker and the reformer as deliberate misrepresentation on the part of newspapers, is the direct

---

[7] Cf. Ch. XI, "The Enlisting of Interest."

outcome of a practical difficulty in uncovering the news, and the emotional difficulty of making distant facts interesting unless, as Emerson says, we can "perceive [them] to be only a new version of our familiar experience" and can "set about translating [them] at once into our parallel facts."[8]

If you study the way many a strike is reported in the press, you will find, very often, that the issues are rarely in the headlines, barely in the leading paragraphs, and sometimes not even mentioned anywhere. A labor dispute in another city has to be very important before the news account contains any definite information as to what is in dispute. The routine of the news works that way, with modifications it works that way in regard to political issues and international news as well. The news is an account of the overt phases that are interesting, and the pressure on the newspaper to adhere to this routine comes from many sides. It comes from the economy of noting only the stereotyped phase of a situation. It comes from the difficulty of finding journalists who can see what they have not learned to see. It comes from the almost unavoidable difficulty of finding sufficient space in which even the best journalist can make plausible an unconventional view. It comes from the economic necessity of interesting the reader quickly, and the economic risk involved in not interesting him at all, or of offending him by unexpected news insufficiently or clumsily described. All these difficulties combined make for uncertainty in the editor when there are dangerous issues at stake, and cause him naturally to prefer the indisputable fact and a treatment more readily adapted to the reader's interest. The indisputable fact and the easy interest, are the strike itself and the reader's inconvenience.

All the subtler and deeper truths are in the present organization of industry very unreliable truths. They involve judgments about standards of living, productivity, human rights that are endlessly debatable in the absence of exact record and quantitative analysis. And as long as these do not exist in industry, the run of news about it will tend, as Emerson said, quoting from Isocrates, "to make of moles mountains, and of mountains moles."[9] Where there is no constitutional procedure in industry, and no expert sifting of evidence and the claims, the fact that is sensational to the reader is the fact that almost every journalist will seek. Given the industrial relations that so largely prevail, even where there is conference or arbitration, but no independent filtering

---

[8] From his essay entitled *Art and Criticism*. The quotation occurs in a passage cited on page 87 of Professor R. W. Brown's *The Writer's Art*.
[9] *Id., supra.*

of the facts for decision, the issue for the newspaper public will tend
not to be the issue for the industry. And so to try disputes by an appeal
through the newspapers puts a burden upon newspapers and readers
which they cannot and ought not to carry. As long as real law and order
do not exist, the bulk of the news will, unless consciously and coura-
geously corrected, work against those who have no lawful and orderly
method of asserting themselves. The bulletins from the scene of action
will note the trouble that arose from the assertion, rather than the reasons which led to it. The reasons are intangible.


## 4

The editor deals with these bulletins. He sits in his office, reads
them, rarely does he see any large portion of the events themselves. He
must, as we have seen, woo at least a section of his readers every day,
because they will leave him without mercy if a rival paper happens to
hit their fancy. He works under enormous pressure, for the competition
of newspapers is often a matter of minutes. Every bulletin requires a
swift but complicated judgment. It must be understood, put in relation
to other bulletins also understood, and played up or played down
according to its probable interest for the public, as the editor conceives
it. Without standardization, without stereotypes, without routine judgments, without a fairly ruthless disregard of subtlety, the editor would
soon die of excitement. The final page is of a definite size, must be ready
at a precise moment; there can be only a certain number of captions
on the items, and in each caption there must be a definite number of
letters. Always there is the precarious urgency of the buying public, the
law of libel, and the possibility of endless trouble. The thing could not
be managed at all without systematization, for in a standardized product there is economy of time and effort, as well as a partial guarantee
against failure.

It is here that newspapers influence each other most deeply. Thus
when the war broke out, the American newspapers were confronted
with a subject about which they had no previous experience. Certain
dailies, rich enough to pay cable tolls, took the lead in securing news,
and the way that news was presented became a model for the whole
press. But where did that model come from? It came from the English
press, not because Northcliffe owned American newspapers, but because
at first it was easier to buy English correspondence, and because, later,
it was easier for American journalists to read English newspapers than
it was for them to read any others. London was the cable and news center, and it was there that a certain technic for reporting the war was

evolved. Something similar occurred in the reporting of the Russian Revolution. In that instance, access to Russia was closed by military censorship, both Russian and Allied, and closed still more effectively by the difficulties of the Russian language. But above all it was closed to effective news reporting by the fact that the hardest thing to report is chaos, even though it is an evolving chaos. This put the formulating of Russian news at its source in Helsingfors, Stockholm, Geneva, Paris and London, into the hands of censors and propagandists. They were for a long time subject to no check of any kind. Until they had made themselves ridiculous they created, let us admit, out of some genuine aspects of the huge Russian maelstrom, a set of stereotypes so evocative of hate and fear, that the very best instinct of journalism, its desire to go and see and tell, was for a long time crushed.[10]

## 5

Every newspaper when it reaches the reader is the result of a whole series of selections as to what items shall be printed, in what position they shall be printed, how much space each shall occupy, what emphasis each shall have. There are no objective standards here. There are conventions. Take two newspapers published in the same city on the same morning. The headline of one reads: "Britain pledges aid to Berlin against French aggression; France openly backs Poles." The headline of the second is "Mrs. Stillman's Other Love." Which you prefer is a matter of taste, but not entirely a matter of the editor's taste. It is a matter of his judgment as to what will absorb the half hour's attention a certain set of readers will give to his newspaper. Now the problem of securing attention is by no means equivalent to displaying the news in the perspective laid down by religious teaching or by some form of ethical culture. It is a problem of provoking feeling in the reader, of inducing him to feel a sense of personal identification with the stories he is reading. News which does not offer this opportunity to introduce oneself into the struggle which it depicts cannot appeal to a wide audience. The audience must participate in the news, much as it participates in the drama, by personal identification. Just as everyone holds his breath when the heroine is in danger, as he helps Babe Ruth swing his bat, so in subtler form the reader enters into the news. In order that he shall enter he must find a familiar foothold in the story, and this is supplied to him by the use of stereotypes. They tell him that

---

[10] Cf. A *Test of the News,* by Walter Lippmann and Charles Merz, assisted by Faye Lippmann, *New Republic,* August 4, 1920.

if an association of plumbers is called a "combine" it is appropriate to develop his hostility; if it is called a "group of leading business men" the cue is for a favorable reaction.

It is in a combination of these elements that the power to create opinion resides. Editorials reinforce. Sometimes in a situation that on the news pages is too confusing to permit of identification, they give the reader a clue by means of which he engages himself. A clue he must have if, as most of us must, he is to seize the news in a hurry. A suggestion of some sort he demands, which tells him, so to speak, where he, a man conceiving himself to be such and such a person, shall integrate his feelings with the news he reads.

"It has been said" writes Walter Bagehot,[11] "that if you can only get a middleclass Englishman to think whether there are 'snails in Sirius,' he will soon have an opinion on it. It will be difficult to make him think, but if he does think, he cannot rest in a negative, he will come to some decision. And on any ordinary topic, of course, it is so. A grocer has a full creed as to foreign policy, a young lady a complete theory of the sacraments, as to which neither has any doubt whatever."

Yet that same grocer will have many doubts about his groceries, and that young lady, marvelously certain about the sacraments, may have all kinds of doubts as to whether to marry the grocer, and if not whether it is proper to accept his attentions. The ability to rest in the negative implies either a lack of interest in the result, or a vivid sense of competing alternatives. In the case of foreign policy or the sacraments, the interest in the results is intense, while means for checking the opinion are poor. This is the plight of the reader of the general news. If he is to read it at all he must be interested, that is to say, he must enter into the situation and care about the outcome. But if he does that he cannot rest in a negative, and unless independent means of checking the lead given him by his newspaper exists, the very fact that he is interested may make it difficult to arrive at that balance of opinions which may most nearly approximate the truth. The more passionately involved he becomes, the more he will tend to resent not only a different view, but a disturbing bit of news. That is why many a newspaper finds that, having honestly evoked the partisanship of its readers, it can not easily, supposing the editor believes the facts warrant it, change position. If a change is necessary, the transition has to be managed with the utmost skill and delicacy. Usually a newspaper will not attempt so hazardous a performance. It is easier and safer to have the news of that subject taper off and disappear, thus putting out the fire by starving it.

---

[11] On the Emotion of Conviction, *Literary Studies*, Vol. II, p. 172.

# XXIV. News, Truth, and a Conclusion

## 1

A S we begin to make more and more exact studies of the press, much will depend upon the hypothesis we hold. If we assume with Mr. Sinclair, and most of his opponents, that news and truth are two words for the same thing, we shall, I believe, arrive nowhere. We shall prove that on this point the newspaper lied. We shall prove that on that point Mr. Sinclair's account lied. We shall demonstrate that Mr. Sinclair lied when he said that somebody lied, and that somebody lied when he said Mr. Sinclair lied. We shall vent our feelings, but we shall vent them into air.

The hypothesis, which seems to me the most fertile, is that news and truth are not the same thing, and must be clearly distinguished.[1] The function of news is to signalize an event, the function of truth is to bring to light the hidden facts, to set them into relation with each other, and make a picture of reality on which men can act. Only at those points, where social conditions take recognizable and measurable shape, do the body of truth and the body of news coincide. That is a comparatively small part of the whole field of human interest. In this sector, and only in this sector, the tests of the news are sufficiently exact to make the charges of perversion or suppression more than a partisan judgment. There is no defense, no extenuation, no excuse whatever, for stating six times that Lenin is dead, when the only information the paper possesses is a report that he is dead from a source repeatedly shown to be unreliable. The news, in that instance, is not "Lenin Dead" but "Helsingfors Says Lenin Is Dead." And a newspaper can be asked to take the responsibility of not making Lenin more dead than the source of the news is reliable; if there is one subject on which editors are most responsible it is in their judgment of the reliability of the source. But when it comes to dealing, for example, with stories of what the Russian people want, no such test exists.

The absence of these exact tests accounts, I think, for the character of the profession, as no other explanation does. There is a very small body of exact knowledge, which it requires no outstanding ability or training to deal with. The rest is in the journalist's own discretion. Once he departs from the region where it is definitely recorded at the County Clerk's office that John Smith has gone into bankruptcy, all fixed

---

[1] When I wrote *Liberty and the News*, I did not understand this distinction clearly enough to state it, but *cf.* p. 89 ff.

standards disappear. The story of why John Smith failed, his human frail-
ties, the analysis of the economic conditions on which he was ship-
wrecked, all of this can be told in a hundred different ways. There is no
discipline in applied psychology, as there is a discipline in medicine,
engineering, or even law, which has authority to direct the journalist's
mind when he passes from the news to the vague realm of truth. There
are no canons to direct his own mind, and no canons that coerce the
reader's judgment or the publisher's. His version of the truth is only his
version. How can he demonstrate the truth as he sees it? He cannot
demonstrate it, any more than Mr. Sinclair Lewis can demonstrate that
he has told the whole truth about Main Street. And the more he understands his own weaknesses, the more ready he is to admit that where
there is no objective test, his own opinion is in some vital measure constructed out of his own stereotypes, according to his own code, and by the
urgency of his own interest. He knows that he is seeing the world through
subjective lenses. He cannot deny that he too is, as Shelley remarked, a
dome of many-colored glass which stains the white radiance of eternity.

And by this knowledge his assurance is tempered. He may have all
kinds of moral courage, and sometimes has, but he lacks that sustain-
ing conviction of a certain technic which finally freed the physical sciences from theological control. It was the gradual development of an
irrefragable method that gave the physicist his intellectual freedom as
against all the powers of the world. His proofs were so clear, his evidence so sharply superior to tradition, that he broke away finally from
all control. But the journalist has no such support in his own conscience or in fact. The control exercised over him by the opinions of
his employers and his readers, is not the control of truth by prejudice,
but of one opinion by another opinion that it is not demonstrably less
true. Between Judge Gary's assertion that the unions will destroy
American institutions, and Mr. Gomper's assertion that they are agen-
cies of the rights of man, the choice has, in large measure, to be governed by the will to believe.

The task of deflating these controversies, and reducing them to a
point where they can be reported as news, is not a task which the
reporter can perform. It is possible and necessary for journalists to bring
home to people the uncertain character of the truth on which their
opinions are founded, and by criticism and agitation to prod social science into making more usable formulations of social facts, and to prod
statesmen into establishing more visible institutions. The press, in
other words, can fight for the extension of reportable truth. But as social
truth is organized to-day, the press is not constituted to furnish from
one edition to the next the amount of knowledge which the democratic theory of public opinion demands. This is not due to the Brass
Check, as the quality of news in radical papers shows, but to the fact

that the press deals with a society in which the governing forces are so
imperfectly recorded. The theory that the press can itself record those
forces is false. It can normally record only what has been recorded for
it by the working of institutions. Everything else is argument and opinion, and fluctuates with the vicissitudes, the self-consciousness, and the
courage of the human mind.

If the press is not so universally wicked, nor so deeply conspiring, as
Mr. Sinclair would have us believe, it is very much more frail than the
democratic theory has as yet admitted. It is too frail to carry the whole
burden of popular sovereignty, to supply spontaneously the truth which
democrats hoped was inborn. And when we expect it to supply such a
body of truth we employ a misleading standard of judgment. We misunderstand the limited nature of news, the illimitable complexity of
society; we overestimate our own endurance, public spirit, and all-
round competence. We suppose an appetite for uninteresting truths
which is not discovered by any honest analysis of our own tastes.

If the newspapers, then, are to be charged with the duty of translating
the whole public life of mankind, so that every adult can arrive at an
opinion on every moot topic, they fail, they are bound to fail, in any
future one can conceive they will continue to fail. It is not possible to
assume that a world, carried on by division of labor and distribution of
authority, can be governed by universal opinions in the whole population. Unconsciously the theory sets up the single reader as theoretically
omnicompetent, and puts upon the press the burden of accomplishing
whatever representative government, industrial organization, and diplomacy have failed to accomplish. Acting upon everybody for thirty minutes in twenty-four hours, the press is asked to create a mystical force
called Public Opinion that will take up the slack in public institutions.
The press has often mistakenly pretended that it could do just that. It has
at great moral cost to itself, encouraged a democracy, still bound to its
original premises, to expect newspapers to supply spontaneously for every
organ of government, for every social problem, the machinery of information which these do not normally supply themselves. Institutions, having failed to furnish themselves with instruments of knowledge, have
become a bundle of "problems," which the population as a whole, reading the press as a whole, is supposed to solve.

The press, in other words, has come to be regarded as an organ of
direct democracy, charged on a much wider scale, and from day to day,
with the function often attributed to the initiative, referendum, and
recall. The Court of Public Opinion, open day and night, is to lay down
the law for everything all the time. It is not workable. And when you consider the nature of news, it is not even thinkable. For the news, as we
have seen, is precise in proportion to the precision with which the event
is recorded. Unless the event is capable of being named, measured, given

shape, made specific, it either fails to take on the character of news, or it is subject to the accidents and prejudices of observation.

Therefore, on the whole, the quality of the news about modern society is an index of its social organization. The better the institutions, the more all interests concerned are formally represented, the more issues are disentangled, the more objective criteria are introduced, the more perfectly an affair can be presented as news. At its best the press is a servant and guardian of institutions; at its worst it is a means by which a few exploit social disorganization to their own ends. In the degree to which institutions fail to function, the unscrupulous journalist can fish in troubled waters, and the conscientious one must gamble with uncertainties.

The press is no substitute for institutions. It is like the beam of a searchlight that moves restlessly about, bringing one episode and then another out of darkness into vision. Men cannot do the work of the world by this light alone. They cannot govern society by episodes, incidents, and eruptions. It is only when they work by a steady light of their own, that the press, when it is turned upon them, reveals a situation intelligible enough for a popular decision. The trouble lies deeper than the press, and so does the remedy. It lies in social organization based on a system of analysis and record, and in all the corollaries of that principle; in the abandonment of the theory of the omnicompetent citizen, in the decentralization of decision, in the coordination of decision by comparable record and analysis. If at the centers of management there is a running audit, which makes work intelligible to those who do it, and those who superintend it, issues when they arise are not the mere collisions of the blind. Then, too, the news is uncovered for the press by a system of intelligence that is also a check upon the press.

That is the radical way. For the troubles of the press, like the troubles of representative government, be it territorial or functional, like the troubles of industry, be it capitalist, coöperative, or communist, go back to a common source: to the failure of self-governing people to transcend their casual experience and their prejudice, by inventing, creating, and organizing a machinery of knowledge. It is because they are compelled to act without a reliable picture of the world, that governments, schools, newspapers and churches make such small headway against the more obvious failings of democracy, against violent prejudice, apathy, preference for the curious trivial as against the dull important, and the hunger for sideshows and three legged calves. This is the primary defect of popular government, a defect inherent in its traditions, and all its other defects can, I believe, be traced to this one.

# PART VIII.   ORGANIZED INTELLIGENCE

# XXV.   The Entering Wedge

## 1

IF the remedy were interesting, American pioneers like Charles McCarthy, Robert Valentine, and Frederick W. Taylor would not have had to fight so hard for a hearing. But it is clear why they had to fight, and why bureaus of governmental research, industrial audits, budgeting and the like are the ugly ducklings of reform. They reverse the process by which interesting public opinions are built up. Instead of presenting a casual fact, a large screen of stereotypes, and a dramatic identification, they break down the drama, break through the stereotypes, and offer men a picture of facts, which is unfamiliar and to them impersonal. When this is not painful, it is dull, and those to whom it is painful, the trading politician and the partisan who has much to conceal, often exploit the dullness that the public feels, in order to remove the pain that they feel.

## 2

Yet every complicated community has sought the assistance of special men, of augurs, priests, elders. Our own democracy, based though it was on a theory of universal competence, sought lawyers to manage its government, and to help manage its industry. It was recognized that the specially trained man was in some dim way oriented to a wider system of truth than that which arises spontaneously in the amateur's mind. But experience has shown that the traditional lawyer's equipment was not enough assistance. The Great Society had grown furiously and to colossal dimensions by the application of technical knowledge. It was made by engineers who had learned to use exact measurements and quantitative analysis. It could not be governed, men began to discover, by men who thought deductively about rights and wrongs. It could be brought under human control only by the technic which had created it. Gradually, then, the more enlightened directing minds have called in experts who were trained, or had trained themselves, to make parts of this Great Society intelligible to those who manage it. These men are known by all kinds of names, as statisticians, accountants, auditors, industrial counsellors, engineers of many species, scientific managers, personnel administrators, research men, "scientists," and sometimes just as plain private secretaries. They have brought with them each a jargon of his own, as well as filing cabinets, card catalogues, graphs, loose-leaf contraptions, and above all the perfectly sound ideal of an executive who sits before a flat-top desk, one sheet of typewritten paper before him, and decides on matters of policy presented in a form ready for his rejection or approval.

This whole development has been the work, not so much of a spontaneous creative evolution, as of blind natural selection. The statesman, the executive, the party leader, the head of a voluntary association, found that if he had to discuss two dozen different subjects in the course of the day, somebody would have to coach him. He began to clamor for memoranda. He found he could not read his mail. He demanded somebody who would blue-pencil the interesting sentences in the important letters. He found he could not digest the great stacks of type-written reports that grew mellow on his desk. He demanded summaries. He found he could not read an unending series of figures. He embraced the man who made colored pictures of them. He found that he really did not know one machine from another. He hired engineers to pick them, and tell him how much they cost and what they could do. He peeled off one burden after another, as a man will take off first his hat, then his coat, then his collar, when he is struggling to move an unwieldy load.

3

Yet curiously enough, though he knew that he needed help, he was slow to call in the social scientist. The chemist, the physicist, the geologist, had a much earlier and more friendly reception. Laboratories were set up for them, inducements offered, for there was quick appreciation of the victories over nature. But the scientist who has human nature as his problem is in a different case. There are many reasons for this: the chief one, that he has so few victories to exhibit. He has so few, because unless he deals with the historic past, he cannot prove his theories before offering them to the public. The physical scientist can make an hypothesis, test it, revise the hypothesis hundreds of times, and, if after all that, he is wrong, no one else has to pay the price. But the social scientist cannot begin to offer the assurance of a laboratory test, and if his advice is followed, and he is wrong, the consequences may be incalculable. He is in the nature of things far more responsible, and far less certain.

But more than that. In the laboratory sciences the student has conquered the dilemma of thought and action. He brings a sample of the action to a quiet place, where it can be repeated at will, and examined at leisure. But the social scientist is constantly being impaled on a dilemma. If he stays in his library, where he has the leisure to think, he has to rely upon the exceedingly casual and meager printed record that comes to him through official reports, newspapers, and interviews. If he goes out into "the world" where things are happening, he has to serve a long, often wasteful, apprenticeship, before he is admitted to the sanctum where they are being decided. What he cannot do is to dip into action and out again whenever it suits him. There are no privileged listeners. The man of affairs, observing that the social scientist knows only from the outside what he knows, in part at least, from the inside, recognizing that the social scientist's hypothesis is not in the nature of things susceptible of laboratory proof, and that verification is possible only in the "real" world, has developed a rather low opinion of social scientists who do not share his views of public policy.

In his heart of hearts the social scientist shares this estimate of himself. He has little inner certainty about his own work. He only half believes in it, and being sure of nothing, he can find no compelling reason for insisting on his own freedom of thought. What can he actually claim for it, in the light of his own conscience?[1] His data are uncertain, his means of verification lacking. The very best qualities in him are a source of frustration. For if he is really critical and saturated in the scientific spirit, he cannot be doctrinaire, and go to Armageddon against the trustees and the students and the Civic Federation and the conservative press for a theory of which he is not sure. If you are going to Armageddon, you have to battle for the Lord, but the political scientist is always a little doubtful whether the Lord called him.

Consequently if so much of social science is apologetic rather than constructive, the explanation lies in the opportunities of social science, not in "capitalism." The physical scientists achieved their freedom from clericalism by working out a method that produced conclusions of a sort that could not be suppressed or ignored. They convinced themselves and acquired dignity, and knew what they were fighting for. The social scientist will acquire his dignity and his strength when he

---

[1] *Cf.* Charles E. Merriam, *The Present State of the Study of Politics, American Political Science Review,* Vol. XV, No. 2, May, 1921.

has worked out his method. He will do that by turning into opportunity the need among directing men of the Great Society for instruments of analysis by which an invisible and most stupendously difficult environment can be made intelligible.

But as things go now, the social scientist assembles his data out of a mass of unrelated material. Social processes are recorded spasmodically, quite often as accidents of administration. A report to Congress, a debate, an investigation, legal briefs, a census, a tariff, a tax schedule; the material, like the skull of the Piltdown man, has to be put together by ingenious inference before the student obtains any sort of picture of the event he is studying. Though it deals with the conscious life of his fellow citizens, it is all too often distressingly opaque, because the man who is trying to generalize has practically no supervision of the way his data are collected. Imagine medical research conducted by students who could rarely go into a hospital, were deprived of animal experiment, and compelled to draw conclusions from the stories of people who had been ill, the reports of nurses, each of whom had her own system of diagnosis, and the statistics compiled by the Bureau of Internal Revenue on the excess profits of druggists. The social scientist has usually to make what he can out of categories that were uncritically in the mind of an official who administered some part of a law, or who was out to justify, to persuade, to claim, or to prove. The student knows this, and, as a protection against it, has developed that branch of scholarship which is an elaborated suspicion about where to discount his information.

That is a virtue, but it becomes a very thin virtue when it is merely a corrective for the unwholesome position of social science. For the scholar is condemned to guess as shrewdly as he can why in a situation not clearly understood something or other may have happened. But the expert who is employed as the mediator among representatives, and as the mirror and measure of administration, has a very different control of the facts. Instead of being the man who generalizes from the facts dropped to him by the men of action, he becomes the man who prepares the facts for the men of action. This is a profound change in his strategic position. He no longer stands outside, chewing the cud provided by busy men of affairs, but he takes his place in front of decision instead of behind it. To-day the sequence is that the man of affairs finds his facts, and decides on the basis of them; then, some time later, the social scientist deduces excellent reasons why he did or did not decide wisely. This ex post facto relationship is academic in the bad sense of that fine word. The real sequence should be one where the disinterested expert first finds and formulates the facts for the man of action, and later makes what wisdom he can out of comparison between the decision, which he understands, and the facts, which he organized.

•

4

For the physical sciences this change in strategic position began slowly, and then accelerated rapidly. There was a time when the inventor and the engineer were romantic half-starved outsiders, treated as cranks. The business man and the artisan knew all the mysteries of their craft. Then the mysteries grew more mysterious, and at last industry began to depend upon physical laws and chemical combinations that no eye could see, and only a trained mind could conceive. The scientist moved from his noble garret in the Latin Quarter into office buildings and laboratories. For he alone could construct a working image of the reality on which industry rested. From the new relationship he took as much as he gave, perhaps more: pure science developed faster than applied, though it drew its economic support, a great deal of its inspiration, and even more of its relevancy, from constant contact with practical decision. But physical science still labored under the enormous limitation that the men who made decisions had only their commonsense to guide them. They administered without scientific aid a world complicated by scientists. Again they had to deal with facts they could not apprehend, and as once they had to call in engineers, they now have to call in statisticians, accountants, experts of all sorts.

These practical students are the true pioneers of a new social science. They are "in mesh with the driving wheels"[2] and from this practical engagement of science and action, both will benefit radically: action by the clarification of its beliefs; beliefs by a continuing test in action. We are in the earliest beginnings. But if it is conceded that all large forms of human association must, because of sheer practical difficulty, contain men who will come to see the need for an expert reporting of their particular environment, then the imagination has a premise on which to work. In the exchange of technic and result among expert staffs, one can see, I think, the beginning of experimental method in social science. When each school district and budget, and health department, and factory, and tariff schedule, is the material of knowledge for every other, the number of comparable experiences begins to approach the dimensions of genuine experiment. In forty-eight states, and 2400 cities, and 277,000 school houses, 270,000 manufacturing establishments, 27,000 mines and quarries, there is a wealth of experience, if only it were recorded and available. And there is, too, opportunity for trial and error at such slight risk that any reasonable hypothesis might be given a fair test without shaking the foundations of society.

---

[2] Cf. The Address of the President of the American Philosophical Association, Mr. Ralph Barton Perry, Dec. 28, 1920. Published in the Proceedings of the Twentieth Annual Meeting.

standards used to measure it. Instead, then, of asking ourselves whether we believe in competition, we should ask ourselves whether we believe in that for which the competitors compete. No one in his senses expects to "abolish competition," for when the last vestige of emulation had disappeared, social effort would consist in mechanical obedience to a routine, tempered in a minority by native inspiration. Yet no one expects to work out competition to its logical conclusion in a murderous struggle of each against all. The problem is to select the goals of competition and the rules of the game. Almost always the most visible and obvious standard of measurement will determine the rules of the game: such as money, power, popularity, applause, or Mr. Veblen's "conspicuous waste." What other standards of measurement does our civilization normally provide? How does it measure efficiency, productivity, service, for which we are always clamoring?

By and large there are no measures, and there is, therefore, not so much competition to achieve these ideals. For the difference between the higher and the lower motives is not, as men often assert, a difference between altruism and selfishness.[1] It is a difference between acting for easily understood aims, and for aims that are obscure and vague. Exhort a man to make more profit than his neighbor, and he knows at what to aim. Exhort him to render more social service, and how is he to be certain what service is social? What is the test, what is the measure? A subjective feeling, somebody's opinion. Tell a man in time of peace that he ought to serve his country and you have uttered a pious platitude. Tell him in time of war, and the word service has a meaning; it is a number of concrete acts, enlistment, or buying bonds, or saving food, or working for a dollar a year, and each one of these services he sees definitely as part of a concrete purpose to put at the front an army larger and better armed, than the enemy's.

So the more you are able to analyze administration and work out elements that can be compared, the more you invent quantitative measures for the qualities you wish to promote, the more you can turn competition to ideal ends. If you can contrive the right index numbers[2] you can set up a competition between individual workers in a shop; between shops; between factories; between schools;[3] between government departments; between regiments; between divisions; between ships; between states; counties; cities; and the better your index numbers the more useful the competition.

---

[1] Cf. Ch. XII.

[2] I am not using the term index numbers in its purely technical meaning, but to cover any device for the comparative measurement of social phenomena.

[3] See, for example, An Index Number for State School Systems by Leonard P. Ayres, Russell Sage Foundation, 1920. The principle of the quota was very successfully applied in the Liberty Loan Campaigns, and under very much more difficult circumstances by the Allied Maritime Transport Council.

6

The possibilities that lie in the exchange of material are evident. Each department of government is all the time asking for information that may already have been obtained by another department, though perhaps in a somewhat different form. The State Department needs to know, let us say the extent of the Mexican oil reserves, their relation to the rest of the world's supply, the present ownership of Mexican oil lands, the importance of oil to warships now under construction or planned, the comparative costs in different fields. How does it secure such information to-day? The information is probably scattered through the Departments of Interior, Justice, Commerce, Labor, and Navy. Either a clerk in the State Department looks up Mexican oil in a book of reference, which may or may not be accurate, or somebody's private secretary telephones somebody else's private secretary, asks for a memorandum, and in the course of time a darkey messenger arrives with an armful of unintelligible reports. The Department should be able to call on its own intelligence bureau to assemble the facts in a way suited to the diplomatic problem up for decision. And these facts the diplomatic intelligence bureau would obtain from the central clearing house.[4]

This establishment would pretty soon become a focus of information of the most extraordinary kind. And the men in it would be made aware of what the problems of government really are. They would deal with problems of definition, of terminology, of statistical technic, of logic; they would traverse concretely the whole gamut of the social sciences. It is difficult to see why all this material, except a few diplomatic and military secrets, should not be open to the scholars of the country. It is there that the political scientist would find the real nuts to crack and the real researches for his students to make. The work need not all be done in Washington, but it could be done in reference to Washington. The central agency would, thus, have in it the makings of a national university. The staff could be recruited there for the bureaus from among college graduates. They would be working on theses selected after consultation between the curators of the national university and teachers scattered over the country. If the association was as flexible as it ought to be, there would be, as a supplement to the permanent staff, a steady turnover of temporary and specialist appointments from the universities, and exchange lecturers called out from Washington. Thus the training and the recruiting of the staff would go together. A part of the research itself would be done by students, and political science in the universities would be associated with politics in America.

---

[4] There has been a vast development of such services among the trade associations. The possibilities of a perverted use were revealed by the New York Building Trades investigation of 1921.

### 7

In its main outlines the principle is equally applicable to state governments, to cities, and to rural counties. The work of comparison and interchange could take place by federations of state and city and county bureaus. And within those federations any desirable regional combination could be organized. So long as the accounting systems were comparable, a great deal of duplication would be avoided. Regional coördination is especially desirable. For legal frontiers often do not coincide with the effective environments. Yet they have a certain basis in custom that it would be costly to disturb. By coördinating their information several administrative areas could reconcile autonomy of decision with coöperation. New York City, for example, is already an unwieldy unit for good government from the City Hall. Yet for many purposes, such as health and transportation, the metropolitan district is the true unit of administration. In that district, however, there are large cities, like Yonkers, Jersey City, Patterson, Elizabeth, Hoboken, Bayonne. They could not all be managed from one center, and yet they should act together for many functions. Ultimately perhaps some such flexible scheme of local government as Sidney and Beatrice Webb have suggested may be the proper solution.[5] But the first step would be a coördination, not of decision and action, but of information and research. Let the officials of the various municipalities see their common problems in the light of the same facts.

### 8

It would be idle to deny that such a network of intelligence bureaus in politics and industry might become a dead weight and a perpetual irritation. One can easily imagine its attraction for men in search of soft jobs, for pedants, for meddlers. One can see red tape, mountains of papers, questionnaires ad nauseam, seven copies of every document, endorsements, delays, lost papers, the use of form 136 instead of form 29b, the return of the document because pencil was used instead of ink, or black ink instead of red ink. The work could be done very badly. There are no fool-proof institutions.

But if one could assume that there was circulation through the whole system between government departments, factories, offices, and the universities; a circulation of men, a circulation of data and of criticism, the risks of dry rot would not be so great. Nor would it be true to say that these

---

[5] "The Reorganization of Local Government" (Ch. IV), in A *Constitution for the Socialist Commonwealth of Great Britain*.

intelligence bureaus will complicate life. They will tend, on the contrary, to simplify, by revealing a complexity now so great as to be humanly unmanageable. The present fundamentally invisible system of government is so intricate that most people have given up trying to follow it, and because they do not try, they are tempted to think it comparatively simple. It is, on the contrary, elusive, concealed, opaque. The employment of an intelligence system would mean a reduction of personnel per unit of result, because by making available to all the experience of each, it would reduce the amount of trial and error; and because by making the social process visible, it would assist the personnel to self-criticism. It does not involve a great additional band of officials, if you take into account the time now spent vainly by special investigating committees, grand juries, district attorneys, reform organizations, and bewildered office holders, in trying to find their way through a dark muddle.

If the analysis of public opinion and of the democratic theories in relation to the modern environment is sound in principle, then I do not see how one can escape the conclusion that such intelligence work is the clue to betterment. I am not referring to the few suggestions contained in this chapter. They are merely illustrations. The task of working out the technic is in the hands of men trained to do it, and not even they can to-day completely foresee the form, much less the details. The number of social phenomena which are now recorded is small, the instruments of analysis are very crude, the concepts often vague and uncriticized. But enough has been done to demonstrate, I think, that unseen environments can be reported effectively, that they can be reported to divergent groups of people in a way which is neutral to their prejudice, and capable of overcoming their subjectivism.

If that is true, then in working out the intelligence principle men will find the way to overcome the central difficulty of self-government, the difficulty of dealing with an unseen reality. Because of that difficulty, it has been impossible for any self-governing community to reconcile its need for isolation with the necessity for wide contact, to reconcile the dignity and individuality of local decision with security and wide coordination, to secure effective leaders without sacrificing responsibility, to have useful public opinions without attempting universal public opinions on all subjects. As long as there was no way of establishing common versions of unseen events, common measures for separate actions, the only image of democracy that would work, even in theory, was one based on an isolated community of people whose political faculties were limited, according to Aristotle's famous maxim, by the range of their vision.

But now there is a way out, a long one to be sure, but a way. It is fundamentally the same way as that which has enabled a citizen of Chicago, with no better eyes or ears than an Athenian, to see and hear over great distances. It is possible to-day, it will become more possible when more labor has gone into it, to reduce the discrepancies between the conceived environment and the effective environment. As that is done, federalism will work more and more by consent, less and less by coercion. For while federalism is the only possible method of union among self-governing groups,[6] federalism swings either towards imperial centralization or towards parochial anarchy wherever the union is not based on correct and commonly accepted ideas of federal matters. These ideas do not arise spontaneously. They have to be pieced together by generalization based on analysis, and the instruments for that analysis have to be invented and tested by research.

No electoral device, no manipulation of areas, no change in the system of property, goes to the root of the matter. You cannot take more political wisdom out of human beings than there is in them. And no reform, however sensational, is truly radical, which does not consciously provide a way of overcoming the subjectivism of human opinion based on the limitation of individual experience. There are systems of government, of voting, and representation which extract more than others. But in the end knowledge must come not from the conscience but from the environment with which that conscience deals. When men act on the principle of intelligence they go out to find the facts and to make their wisdom. When they ignore it, they go inside themselves and find only what is there. They elaborate their prejudice, instead of increasing their knowledge.

## XXVII. The Appeal to the Public

### 1

IN real life no one acts on the theory that he can have a public opinion on every public question, though this fact is often concealed where a person thinks there is no public question because he has no public opinion. But in the theory of our politics we continue to think more literally than Lord Bryce intended, that "the action of Opinion is continuous,"[1] even though "its action . . . deals with broad principles only."[2] And then because we try to think of ourselves having continuous opinions, without being altogether certain what a broad principle

---

[6] Cf. H. J. Laski, The Foundations of Sovereignty, and other Essays, particularly the Essay of this name, as well as the Problems of Administrative Areas, The Theory of Popular Sovereignty, and The Pluralistic State.

[1] Modern Democracies, Vol. I, p. 159.

[2] Id., footnote, p. 158.

is, we quite naturally greet with an anguished yawn an argument that seems to involve the reading of more government reports, more statistics, more curves and more graphs. For all these are in the first instance just as confusing as partisan rhetoric, and much less entertaining.

The amount of attention available is far too small for any scheme in which it was assumed that all the citizens of the nation would, after devoting themselves to the publications of all the intelligence bureaus, become alert, informed, and eager on the multitude of real questions that never do fit very well into any broad principle. I am not making that assumption. Primarily, the intelligence bureau is an instrument of the man of action, of the representative charged with decision, of the worker at his work, and if it does not help them, it will help nobody in the end. But in so far as it helps them to understand the environment in which they are working, it makes what they do visible. And by that much they become more responsible to the general public.

The purpose, then, is not to burden every citizen with expert opinions on all questions, but to push that burden away from him towards the responsible administrator. An intelligence system has value, of course, as a source of general information, and as a check on the daily press. But that is secondary. Its real use is as an aid to representative government and administration both in politics and industry. The demand for the assistance of expert reporters in the shape of accountants, statisticians, secretariats, and the like, comes not from the public, but from men doing public business, who can no longer do it by rule of thumb. It is in origin and in ideal an instrument for doing public business better, rather than an instrument for knowing better how badly public business is done.

2

As a private citizen, as a sovereign voter, no one could attempt to digest these documents. But as one party to a dispute, as a committee-man in a legislature, as an officer in government, business, or a trade union, as a member of an industrial council, reports on the specific matter at issue will be increasingly welcome. The private citizen interested in some cause would belong, as he does now, to voluntary societies which employed a staff to study the documents, and make reports that served as a check on officialdom. There would be some study of this material by newspaper men, and a good deal by experts and by political scientists. But the outsider, and every one of us is an outsider to all but a few aspects of modern life, has neither time, nor attention, nor interest, nor the equipment for specific judgment. It is on the men inside, working under conditions that are sound, that the daily administrations of society must rest.

The general public outside can arrive at judgments about whether these conditions are sound only on the result after the event, and on the procedure before the event. The broad principles on which the action of public opinion can be continuous are essentially principles of procedure. The outsider can ask experts to tell him whether the relevant facts were duly considered; he cannot in most cases decide for himself what is relevant or what is due consideration. The outsider can perhaps judge whether the groups interested in the decision were properly heard, whether the ballot, if there was one, was honestly taken, and perhaps whether the result was honestly accepted. He can watch the procedure when the news indicates that there is something to watch. He can raise a question as to whether the procedure itself is right, if its normal results conflict with his ideal of a good life.[3] But if he tries in every case to substitute himself for the procedure, to bring in Public Opinion like a providential uncle in the crisis of a play, he will confound his own confusion. He will not follow any train of thought consecutively.

For the practice of appealing to the public on all sorts of intricate matters means almost always a desire to escape criticism from those who know by enlisting a large majority which has had no chance to know. The verdict is made to depend on who has the loudest or the most entrancing voice, the most skilful or the most brazen publicity man, the best access to the most space in the newspapers. For even when the editor is scrupulously fair to "the other side," fairness is not enough. There may be several other sides, unmentioned by any of the organized, financed and active partisans.

The private citizen, beset by partisan appeals for the loan of his Public Opinion, will soon see, perhaps, that these appeals are not a compliment to his intelligence, but an imposition on his good nature and an insult to his sense of evidence. As his civic education takes account of the complexity of his environment, he will concern himself about the equity and the sanity of procedure, and even this he will in most cases expect his elected representative to watch for him. He will refuse himself to accept the burden of these decisions, and will turn down his thumbs in most cases on those who, in their hurry to win, rush from the conference table with the first dope for the reporters.

Only by insisting that problems shall not come up to him until they have passed through a procedure, can the busy citizen of a modern state hope to deal with them in a form that is intelligible. For issues, as they are stated by a partisan, almost always consist of an intricate series of facts, as he has observed them, surrounded by a large fatty mass of stereotyped phrases charged with his emotion. According to the fashion

---

[3] Cf. Chapter XX.

of the day, he will emerge from the conference room insisting that what he wants is some soulfilling idea like Justice, Welfare, Americanism, Socialism. On such issues the citizen outside can sometimes be provoked to fear or admiration, but to judgment never. Before he can do anything with the argument, the fat has to be boiled out of it for him.

### 3

That can be done by having the representative inside carry on discussion in the presence of some one, chairman or mediator, who forces the discussion to deal with the analyses supplied by experts. This is the essential organization of any representative body dealing with distant matters. The partisan voices should be there, but the partisans should find themselves confronted with men, not personally involved, who control enough facts and have the dialectical skill to sort out what is real perception from what is stereotype, pattern and elaboration. It is the Socratic dialogue, with all of Socrates's energy for breaking through words to meanings, and something more than that, because the dialectic in modern life must be done by men who have explored the environment as well as the human mind.

There is, for example, a grave dispute in the steel industry. Each side issues a manifesto full of the highest ideals. The only public opinion that is worth respect at this stage is the opinion which insists that a conference be organized. For the side which says its cause is too just to be contaminated by conference there can be little sympathy, since there is no such cause anywhere among mortal men. Perhaps those who object to conference do not say quite that. Perhaps they say that the other side is too wicked; they cannot shake hands with traitors. All that public opinion can do then is to organize a hearing by public officials to hear the proof of wickedness. It cannot take the partisans' word for it. But suppose a conference is agreed to, and suppose there is a neutral chairman who has at his beck and call the consulting experts of the corporation, the union, and, let us say, the Department of Labor.

Judge Gary states with perfect sincerity that his men are well paid and not overworked, and then proceeds to sketch the history of Russia from the time of Peter the Great to the murder of the Czar. Mr. Foster rises, states with equal sincerity that the men are exploited, and then proceeds to outline the history of human emancipation from Jesus of Nazareth to Abraham Lincoln. At this point the chairman calls upon the intelligence men for wage tables in order to substitute for the words "well paid" and "exploited" a table showing what the different classes *are* paid. Does Judge Gary think they are all well paid? He does. Does Mr. Foster think they are all exploited? No, he thinks that groups C, M, and X are exploited. What does he mean by exploited? He means they are not paid a living wage. They are, says Judge Gary. What can a man buy on that wage, asks the chairman. Nothing, says Mr. Foster. Everything he needs, says Judge Gary. The chairman consults the budgets and price statistics of the government.[4] He rules that X can meet an average budget, but that C and M cannot. Judge Gary serves notice that he does not regard the official statistics as sound. The budgets are too high, and prices have come down. Mr. Foster also serves notice of exception. The budget is too low, prices have gone up. The chairman rules that this point is not within the jurisdiction of the conference, that the official figures stand, and that Judge Gary's experts and Mr. Foster's should carry their appeals to the standing committee of the federated intelligence bureaus.

Nevertheless, says Judge Gary, we shall be ruined if we change these wage scales. What do you mean by ruined, asks the chairman, produce your books. I can't, they are private, says Judge Gary. What is private does not interest us, says the chairman, and, therefore, issues a statement to the public announcing that the wages of workers in groups C and M are so-and-so much below the official minimum living wage, and that Judge Gary declines to increase them for reasons that he refuses to state. After a procedure of that sort, a public opinion in the eulogistic sense of the term[5] can exist.

The value of expert mediation is not that it sets up opinion to coerce the partisans, but that it disintegrates partisanship. Judge Gary and Mr. Foster may remain as little convinced as when they started, though even they would have to talk in a different strain. But almost everyone else who was not personally entangled would save himself from being entangled. For the entangling stereotypes and slogans to which his reflexes are so ready to respond are by this kind of dialectic untangled.

4

On many subjects of great public importance, and in varying degree among different people for more personal matters, the threads of memory and emotion are in a snarl. The same word will connote any number of different ideas: emotions are displaced from the images to which they belong to names which resemble the names of these images. In the uncriticized parts of the mind there is a vast amount of association

---

[4] See an article on "The Cost of Living and Wage Cuts," in the *New Republic*, July 27, 1921, by Dr. Leo Wolman, for a brilliant discussion of the naïve use of such figures and "pseudo-principles." The warning is of particular importance because it comes from an economist and statistician who has himself done so much to improve the technic of industrial disputes.

[5] As used by Mr. Lowell in his *Public Opinion and Popular Government*.

by mere clang, contact, and succession. There are stray emotional attachments, there are words that were names and are masks. In dreams, reveries, and panic, we uncover some of the disorder, enough to see how the naïve mind is composed, and how it behaves when not disciplined by wakeful effort and external resistance. We see that there is no more natural order than in a dusty old attic. There is often the same incongruity between fact, idea, and emotion as there might be in an opera house, if all the wardrobes were dumped in a heap and all the scores mixed up, so that Madame Butterfly in a Valkyr's dress waited lyrically for the return of Faust. "At Christmas-tide" says an editorial, "old memories soften the heart. Holy teachings are remembered afresh as thoughts run back to childhood. The world does not seem so bad when seen through the mist of half-happy, half-sad recollections of loved ones now with God. No heart is untouched by the mysterious influence. . . . The country is honeycombed with red propaganda—but there is a good supply of ropes, muscles and lampposts . . . while this world moves the spirit of liberty will burn in the breast of man."

The man who found these phrases in his mind needs help. He needs a Socrates who will separate the words, cross-examine him until he has defined them, and made words the names of ideas. Made them mean a particular object and nothing else. For these tense syllables have got themselves connected in his mind by primitive association, and are bundled together by his memories of Christmas, his indignation as a conservative, and his thrills as the heir to a revolutionary tradition. Sometimes the snarl is too huge and ancient for quick unravelling. Sometimes, as in modern psychotherapy, there are layers upon layers of memory reaching back to infancy, which have to be separated and named.

The effect of naming, the effect, that is, of saying that the labor groups C and M, but not X, are underpaid, instead of saying that Labor is Exploited, is incisive. Perceptions recover their identity, and the emotion they arouse is specific, since it is no longer reinforced by large and accidental connections with everything from Christmas to Moscow. The disentangled idea with a name of its own, and an emotion that has been scrutinized, is ever so much more open to correction by new data in the problem. It had been imbedded in the whole personality, had affiliations of some sort with the whole ego: a challenge would reverberate through the whole soul. After it has been thoroughly criticized, the idea is no longer *me* but *that*. It is objectified, it is at arm's length. Its fate is not bound up with my fate, but with the fate of the outer world upon which I am acting.

5

Re-education of this kind will help to bring our public opinions into grip with the environment. That is the way the enormous censoring, stereotyping, and dramatizing apparatus can be liquidated. Where there is no difficulty in knowing what the relevant environment is, the critic, the teacher, the physician, can unravel the mind. But where the environment is as obscure to the analyst as to his pupil, no analytic technic is sufficient. Intelligence work is required. In political and industrial problems the critic as such can do something, but unless he can count upon receiving from expert reporters a valid picture of the environment, his dialectic cannot go far.

Therefore, though here, as in most other matters, "education" is the supreme remedy, the value of this education will depend upon the evolution of knowledge. And our knowledge of human institutions is still extraordinarily meager and impressionistic. The gathering of social knowledge is, on the whole, still haphazard; not, as it will have to become, the normal accompaniment of action. And yet the collection of information will not be made, one may be sure, for the sake of its ultimate use. It will be made because modern decision requires it to be made. But as it is being made, there will accumulate a body of data which political science can turn into generalization, and build up for the schools into a conceptual picture of the world. When that picture takes form, civic education can become a preparation for dealing with an unseen environment.

As a working model of the social system becomes available to the teacher, he can use it to make the pupil acutely aware of how his mind works on unfamiliar facts. Until he has such a model, the teacher cannot hope to prepare men fully for the world they will find. What he can do is to prepare them to deal with that world with a great deal more sophistication about their own minds. He can, by the use of the case method, teach the pupil the habit of examining the sources of his information. He can teach him, for example, to look in his newspaper for the place where the dispatch was filed, for the name of the correspondent, the name of the press service, the authority given for the statement, the circumstances under which the statement was secured. He can teach the pupil to ask himself whether the reporter saw what he describes, and to remember how that reporter described other events in the past. He can teach him the character of censorship, of the idea of privacy, and furnish him with knowledge of past propaganda. He can, by the proper use of history, make him aware of the stereotype, and can educate a habit of introspection about the imagery evoked by printed words. He can, by courses in comparative history and anthropology, produce a life-long realization of the way codes impose a special pattern upon the imagination. He can teach men to catch themselves making allegories, dramatizing relations, and personifying abstractions. He can show the pupil how he identifies himself with these allegories, how he becomes interested, and how he selects the attitude, heroic, romantic, economic which he adopts while holding a particular opinion. The study of error is not only in the highest degree prophylactic, but it serves as a stimulating introduction to the study of truth. As our minds become more deeply aware of their own subjectivism, we find a zest in objective method that is not otherwise there. We see vividly, as normally we should not, the enormous mischief and casual cruelty of our prejudices. And the destruction of a prejudice, though painful at first, because of its connection with our self-respect, gives an immense relief and a fine pride when it is successfully done. There is a radical enlargement of the range of attention. As the current categories dissolve, a hard, simple version of the world breaks up. The scene turns vivid and full. There follows an emotional incentive to hearty appreciation of scientific method, which otherwise it is not easy to arouse, and is impossible to sustain. Prejudices are so much easier and more interesting. For if you teach the principles of science as if they had always been accepted, their chief virtue as a discipline, which is objectivity, will make them dull. But teach them at first as victories over the superstitions of the mind, and the exhilaration of the chase and of the conquest may carry the pupil over that hard transition from his own self-bound experience to the phase where his curiosity has matured, and his reason has acquired passion.

# XXVIII. The Appeal to Reason

## 1

I HAVE written, and then thrown away, several endings to this book. Over all of them there hung that fatality of last chapters, in which every idea seems to find its place, and all the mysteries, that the writer has not forgotten, are unravelled. In politics the hero does not live happily ever after, or end his life perfectly. There is no concluding chapter, because the hero in politics has more future before him than there is recorded history behind him. The last chapter is merely a place where the writer imagines that the polite reader has begun to look furtively at his watch.

## 2

When Plato came to the point where it was fitting that he should sum up, his assurance turned into stage-fright as he thought how absurd it would sound to say what was in him about the place of reason in politics. Those sentences in book five of the *Republic* were hard even for Plato to speak; they are so sheer and so stark that men can neither forget them nor live by them. So he makes Socrates say to Glaucon that he will be broken and drowned in laughter for telling "what is the least change which will enable a state to pass into the truer form,"[1] because the thought he "would fain have uttered if it had not seemed too extravagant" was that "until philosophers are kings, or the kings and princes of this world have the spirit and power of philosophy, and political greatness and wisdom meet in one . . . cities will never cease from ill,—no, nor the human race . . ."

Hardly had he said these awful words, when he realized they were a counsel of perfection, and felt embarrassed at the unapproachable grandeur of his idea. So he hastens to add that, of course, "the true pilot" will be called "a prater, a star-gazer, a good-for-nothing."[2] But this wistful admission, though it protects him against whatever was the Greek equivalent for the charge that he lacked a sense of humor, furnished a humiliating tailpiece to a solemn thought. He becomes defiant and warns Adeimantus that he must "attribute the uselessness" of philosophers "to the fault of those who will not use them, and not to themselves. The pilot should not humbly beg the sailors to be commanded by him—that is not the order of nature." And with this haughty gesture, he hurriedly picked up the tools of reason, and disappeared into the Academy, leaving the world to Machiavelli.

Thus, in the first great encounter between reason and politics, the strategy of reason was to retire in anger. But meanwhile, as Plato tells us, the ship is at sea. There have been many ships on the sea, since Plato wrote, and to-day, whether we are wise or foolish in our belief, we could no longer call a man a true pilot, simply because he knows how to "pay attention to the year and seasons and sky and stars and winds, and whatever else belongs to his art."[3] He can dismiss nothing which is necessary to make that ship sail prosperously. Because there are mutineers aboard, he cannot say: so much the worse for us all . . . it is not in the order of nature that I should handle a mutiny . . . it is not in the order of philosophy that I should consider mutiny . . . I know how to navigate . . . I do not know how to navigate a ship full of sailors . . . and if they do not see that I am the man to steer, I cannot help it. We shall all go on the rocks, they to be punished for their sins; I, with the assurance that I knew better. . . .

3

Whenever we make an appeal to reason in politics, the difficulty in this parable recurs. For there is an inherent difficulty about using the method of reason to deal with an unreasoning world. Even if you assume

---

[1] *Republic*, Bk. V, 473. Jowett transl.
[2] Bk. VI, 488–489.
[3] Bk. VI, 488–489.

with Plato that the true pilot knows what is best for the ship, you have to recall that he is not so easy to recognize, and that this uncertainty leaves a large part of the crew unconvinced. By definition the crew does not know what he knows, and the pilot, fascinated by the stars and winds, does not know how to make the crew realize the importance of what he knows. There is no time during mutiny at sea to make each sailor an expert judge of experts. There is no time for the pilot to consult his crew and find out whether he is really as wise as he thinks he is. For education is a matter of years, the emergency a matter of hours. It would be altogether academic, then, to tell the pilot that the true remedy is, for example, an education that will endow sailors with a better sense of evidence. You can tell that only to shipmasters on dry land. In the crisis, the only advice is to use a gun, or make a speech, utter a stirring slogan, offer a compromise, employ any quick means available to quell the mutiny, the sense of evidence being what it is. It is only on shore where men plan for many voyages, that they can afford to, and must for their own salvation, deal with those causes that take a long time to remove. They will be dealing in years and generations, not in emergencies alone. And nothing will put a greater strain upon their wisdom than the necessity of distinguishing false crises from real ones. For when there is panic in the air, with one crisis tripping over the heels of another, actual dangers mixed with imaginary scares, there is no chance at all for the constructive use of reason, and any order soon seems preferable to any disorder.

It is only on the premise of a certain stability over a long run of time that men can hope to follow the method of reason. This is not because mankind is inept, or because the appeal to reason is visionary, but because the evolution of reason on political subjects is only in its beginnings. Our rational ideas in politics are still large, thin generalities, much too abstract and unrefined for practical guidance, except where the aggregates are large enough to cancel out individual peculiarity and exhibit large uniformities. Reason in politics is especially immature in predicting the behavior of individual men, because in human conduct the smallest initial variation often works out into the most elaborate differences. That, perhaps, is why when we try to insist solely upon an appeal to reason in dealing with sudden situations, we are broken and drowned in laughter.

4

For the rate at which reason, as we possess it, can advance itself is slower than the rate at which action has to be taken. In the present state of political science there is, therefore, a tendency for one situation to change into another, before the first is clearly understood, and so to make much political criticism hindsight and little else.

Both in the discovery of what is unknown, and in the propagation of that which has been proved, there is a time-differential, which ought to, in a much greater degree than it ever has, occupy the political philosopher. We have begun, chiefly under the inspiration of Mr. Graham Wallas, to examine the effect of an invisible environment upon our opinions. We do not, as yet, understand, except a little by rule of thumb, the element of time in politics, though it bears most directly upon the practicability of any constructive proposal.[4] We can see, for example, that somehow the relevancy of any plan depends upon the length of time the operation requires. Because on the length of time it will depend whether the data which the plan assumes as given, will in truth remain the same.[5] There is a factor here which realistic and experienced men do take into account, and it helps to mark them off somehow from the opportunist, the visionary, the philistine and the pedant.[6] But just how the calculation of time enters into politics we do not know at present in any systematic way.

Until we understand these matters more clearly, we can at least remember that there is a problem of the utmost theoretical difficulty and practical consequence. It will help us to cherish Plato's ideal, without sharing his hasty conclusion about the perversity of those who do not listen to reason. It is hard to obey reason in politics, because you are trying to make two processes march together, which have as yet a different gait and a different pace. Until reason is subtle and particular, the immediate struggle of politics will continue to require an amount of native wit, force, and unprovable faith, that reason can neither provide nor control, because the facts of life are too undifferentiated for its powers of understanding. The methods of social science are so little perfected that in many of the serious decisions and most of the casual ones, there is as yet no choice but to gamble with fate as intuition prompts.

But we can make a belief in reason one of those intuitions. We can use our wit and our force to make footholds for reason. Behind our pictures of the world, we can try to see the vista of a longer duration of events, and wherever it is possible to escape from the urgent present, allow this longer time to control our decisions. And yet, even when there is this will to let the future count, we find again and again that we do not know for certain

---

[4] *Cf.* H. G. Wells in the opening chapters of *Mankind in the Making.*

[5] The better the current analysis in the intelligence work of any institution, the less likely, of course, that men will deal with tomorrow's problems in the light of yesterday's facts.

[6] Not all, but some of the differences between reactionaries, conservatives, liberals, and radicals are due, I think, to a different intuitive estimate of the rate of change in social affairs.

how to act according to the dictates of reason. The number of human problems on which reason is prepared to dictate is small.

### 5

There is, however, a noble counterfeit in that charity which comes from self-knowledge and an unarguable belief that no one of our gregarious species is alone in his longing for a friendlier world. So many of the grimaces men make at each other go with a flutter of their pulse, that they are not all of them important. And where so much is uncertain, where so many actions have to be carried out on guesses, the demand upon the reserves of mere decency is enormous, and it is necessary to live as if good will would work. We cannot prove in every instance that it will, nor why hatred, intolerance, suspicion, bigotry, secrecy, fear, and lying are the seven deadly sins against public opinion. We can only insist that they have no place in the appeal to reason, that in the longer run they are a poison; and taking our stand upon a view of the world which outlasts our own predicaments, and our own lives, we can cherish a hearty prejudice against them.

We can do this all the better if we do not allow frightfulness and fanaticism to impress us so deeply that we throw up our hands peevishly, and lose interest in the longer run of time because we have lost faith in the future of man. There is no ground for this despair, because all the *ifs* on which, as James said, our destiny hangs, are as pregnant as they ever were. What we have seen of brutality, we have seen, and because it was strange, it was not conclusive. It was only Berlin, Moscow, Versailles in 1914 to 1919, not Armageddon, as we rhetorically said. The more realistically men have faced out the brutality and the hysteria, the more they have earned the right to say that it is not foolish for men to believe, because another great war took place, that intelligence, courage, and effort cannot ever contrive a good life for all men.

Great as was the horror, it was not universal. There were corrupt, and there were incorruptible. There was muddle and there were miracles. There was huge lying. There were men with the will to uncover it. It is no judgment, but only a mood, when men deny that what some men have been, more men, and ultimately enough men, might be. You can despair of what has never been. You can despair of ever having three heads, though Mr. Shaw has declined to despair even of that. But you cannot despair of the possibilities that could exist by virtue of any human quality which a human being has exhibited. And if amidst all the evils of this decade, you have not seen men and women, known moments that you would like to multiply, the Lord himself cannot help you.

# Index

Absolutism, 86
Acquisition, 14
Adams, Henry, 60
Adams, H. F., 31
Adams, John, 150
Adams, J. Q., 156
Adler, Alfred, 96
Advertising, 175, 176
Advertisements, 175
Alien, 38
Allegory, 87
Alsace-Lorraine, 79, 116
Amendment of constitutions, 75
America—historical integration, 118;
    national will, 105; World War
    experience, 60, 61
American civilization, 60
American marines and the
    Dalmatian coast, 9
"American rights," 110
Americanism, 47; as a symbol, 112
Americanization, 47
Ames, Fisher, 147
Anemia, 27
Anglo-Saxon, 80
Apprehension, 44
Aristotle, 139; on slavery, 53
Armies, 22–23
Art, moving pictures and master-
    pieces, 90; stereotyped shapes
    and, 45, 46
Artists, pioneering, 91
Asquith, Margot, 4, 29
Attention, distractions of city life, 40;
    time and attention given to news-
    papers, 31
Attrition, 21, 22
Authorities, 121, 122
Automatism, 41, 104
Ayres, L. P., 209

Backward people, 81
Bagehot, Walter, 128, 193
Baseball game, unscored, 185
Beard, C. A., 119, 145
Behavior, 14, 96
Belgian priests, 55
Belgium, 116
Belloc, Hilaire, 182
Berenson, Bernard, 46
Bergson, Henri, 88
Berman, Louis, 96
Berthelot, M., 18
Bierstadt, E. H., 47
Big Business, 65; newspapers and,
    182
Blind spots, 57, 61
Bolshevism, 67; Einstein theory and,
    85, 86
Boundaries, 74
Bowley, Professor, 82
Brandegee, Senator, 10
"Brass Check, The," 182, 195
Brawl, 44
Brest-Litovsk, 114, 115, 116
British Admiralty, 9
British working class, 83–84
Brown, R. W., 190
Brutality, 224
Bryce, Lord, 58, 122, 123, 124,
    213
Buncombe, 128, 138
Bureaus, intelligence, 206; see also
    Intelligence bureaus
Burr, Aaron, 152
Bury, J. B., 58, 59
Buying public, 172, 176

Cabinet, 208; intelligence bureaus
    for, 207
Camouflage, 129

Cannon, W. B., 96

Capitalism, 162; newspaper and, 182

Captains of industry, 65

Castelnau, General de, 19

Casualties of the war, 131

Catholic feudal society, 166

Catholics and Germans, 55

Cause and effect, 85

Censorship, 16; military, 23; privacy and, 18

Chafee, Zechariah, 172

Change of name, 48

Characters, 94, 96, 98

Charnwood's Lincoln, 4

Chesterton, G. K., 12

Christmas, 218

City, life distracting, 40, 41; trolley-car company and, 79

City States of Greece and Italy, 144

Civil liberties, 172, 173

Clang, 40

Class consciousness, 14, 100

Class interest, 102

Classification, 83; of persons, 49

Clearness, speed, words, and, 35

Clemenceau, Georges, 45

Clothes, 47

Coal, time element in, 78

Cobb, Frank, 186

Codes, 35; facts and, 67–68; moral, 66; their enemies, 63

Coercion, 160; Cole's, 161

Cointet, Major, 21, 22

Cole, G. D. H., 160, 161

Collective mind, 51

Collectivism, 62

College societies, 28

Commercial code, 68

Common will, crystallizing, 118

Commune, 161

Communication, barriers, 26

Communism, 102, 123

Community, self-contained, 142

Competition, 208, 209

Conditioned response, 111

Confederation, 118

Confederation, Articles of, 150

Conflict, 142

Confusion of mind, 217

Congress, 156; ignorance of facts, 156–157; opinion, creation, 158

Congressional investigations, 157

Congressmen, 135

Conscience, 14

Consciousness, 39

Consent, creation of, 135

Consistency, 44

Conspiracy of silence, 129

Constant reader, 178

Constitution, U. S., Jefferson and, 153; making, 150, 152

Constitutions, amending, 75

Contact and opportunity, 24

Coöperation, 126

Corporations, 23, 24

Cosmas's map of the universe, 2–3

Cosmopolitans, 30

Courts, 203

Credibility of witness, 43

Creel, George, War propaganda, 24, 25

Croly, Herbert, 98

Crowd, aimlessness, 125; psychology, 97

Cuba, 81

Czechoslovakia, 132

Dalmatian coast, 9

Daniels, Josephus, 9

Dante, 46, 79, 143

Davis, Elmer, 175

Davis, M. W., 67

Decision, 126; mass, 127

Definiteness, 44

Deimling, General von, 18, 19

Democracy, 16; circumscribed field, 147; functional, 165, 166; government as an instinct, 141; industrial, 80; new theory of, 163; old dogma, 136; philosophy, 145;

public opinion made a mystery, 138; revolution in, 136; two visions, 124; unseen environments, 146

Democratic ideal, 146

Democratic theory, 122, 124

Democrats, 106; pioneer, 141

"Deserving Democrats," 109

Determinism, 103, 104

Devils, 5

Dewey, John, on the problem of apprehension, 44

Diblee, G. B., 176

Dignity, 28, 139, 162, 170

Diplomatists, 204; Ruritanian propaganda and, 71

Direct action, limit, 125

Direct primary, 127

Discrimination, 38, 39

Dispositions, 96, 103

Dogmatist, 67

Douaumont, 20

Duration, 76

Eastern front, 73

Economic determinism, 101, 102, 103

Economic mythology, 64

Economic situation, 27; opinion and, 100

Education, 219, 221; moral, 98

Effect and cause, 85

Einstein, Professor, 58

Einstein theory and Bolshevism, 85, 86

Emerson, R. W., 190

Emotion, memory and, 217; rousing by substitution, 111

Empathy, 89

English Guild Socialists, 17, 141, 160

English press, 191

Enhancement, 14

Entering wedge, 198

Environment, difficulties of our access, 42; indirectly known, 2

Error, study of, 219

Erzberger, Matthias, 57

Eternal principles and the World War, 72

Europe as symbol, 118

Evidence, 68

Evolution, 58, 60

Expertness, 63

Experts, 121, 199, 201, 205

Eyewitness, 43

Factions, 99

Factory, 163

Facts, facing, 16; moral codes and, 67, 68; unseen, 17; weighing properly, 84

Faith in man, 224

Faith ladder, 84

Family Tradition, 28

Family tree, 80

Far Eastern Affairs, Division of, 204

Farmers and democracy, 145

Fatigue, mental, 40

Fear of facing facts, 16

Fears, 86

Federal party, 152

Federalism, 213; voluntary, 151

Fences, mending, 135

Ferenczi, S., 39

Fictions, 7, 8, 10

Fictitious personality, 3

Fighting motif, 89

Flume, 70

Foch, Ferdinand, 129

Force, rule of, 150; see also Coercion

Ford, H. J., 139, 140, 147, 152, 154

Foreign affairs, 132

Foreign policy, 147

Form, 28

Foster, W. Z., 216

Fourteen Points, 113, 114, 115, 117

France as symbol, 118

Franco-Prussian war, 116

Freedom of speech, 172

Freight rates, 132
French General Staff and war news, 18, 22
Freud, Sigmund, 86
Freudians, 14
Functions, 165, 166
Future, illusiveness, 80

Gary, Judge, 216, 217
Genealogy, 80
General news, 176, 178–179, 180, 193
Gennep, A. von, 45
Geography, practical, 74
Germans, 45, 66; Belgian priests legend, 55; killing, 21; in Siberia, 74
Given, J. L., 176, 180, 183
Good will, 207, 224
Goodrich, C. L., 80
Göttingen, psychology experiment, 45
Government, as an instinct, 141; inner circle, 124; most momentous question of, 137; natural, inborn art, 139, 140; natural writ, 163; system of checks and balances, 150
Grasty, Charles, 74
Great Society, 13, 30, 198, 199
Great War. See World War
Greece, city states of, 144
Greeley, Horace, 179, 180
Griffiths, Mr., 51
Group Mind, 16, 51
Guild Socialism, 17, 141, 159
Guildsmen, 162

Hamilton, Alexander, 119; Burr and, 152; on governing body, 139; on lack of state coöperation, 150; statecraft, 152
Hanscom, E. D., 85
Harding, W. G., 106, 107
Harmony, 143
Hart, A. B., 137

Harvey, George, on American motives, 105
Hatred, 98
Headlines, 192
Hearst, W. R., 176, 180
Herd instinct, 28
Hermit, 122
Hero-worship, 5
Hierarchy, political, 124, 125, 127; social, 27, 29
High society, 29; newspapers and, 180
Hindsight, 2, 222
Historic rights and wrongs, 79
History, popular, and time confusions, 79
Hobbes, Thomas, 97, 142
Hotchkiss and Franken questionnaire, 31
House of Representatives, 152–153
Housing shortage, 132
Huerta, Adela, 109
Hughes, C. E., on the European war, 110; speech of July 31, 1916, 107
Human dignity, 139, 162, 170
Human figure, 46
Human nature, 67, 68, 103, 104; complexity, 104
Human relations, harmonious, 110
Huns, 56
Hysteria, 224

Ideal, 57
Ideas, circulation, 26; circulation limits, 24; varying susceptibility, 111–112
Illusions, 130
Imitation, social, 29
Imperialism, 63
Impulses, 97
Income, communication and, 26; economic position and, 27, 28
Independence, 122, 147; intelligence bureaus, 207

Indirect costs, 131
Industrial conditions and newspapers, 188
Industrial democracy, 80, 163; factory as unit, 163
Industrial dialectic, 216
Industrial system, 159
Information, 219
Initiative, 126
Inner circle, 124
Instinct, 103
Instinct of the herd, 28
Institutions and the press, 197
Intelligence, organized, 198; organizations, 203
Intelligence bureaus, clearing house of, 210; conditions of affectiveness, 207; coördination, 208; exchange of material, 210; funds, tenure, etc., 207, 208; need at Washington, 206; objections, 212; purpose, 214; state, city and county, 211
Intelligence work, 203, 219
Interest, enlisting, 87; transfer of, 105
"Interested," 166
Intervention, 109
Intuition, 88, 138
Ireland, 79
Irwin, Inez H., 187
Issue, 127
Italian Irredenta, 116
Italy, city states of, 144
Integration, 118

Jackson, Andrew, 154
James, E. L., 36
James, Henry, 75
James, William (the first), 75
James, William, 8, 44, 65, 75, 76, 125, 224; on discriminations and time perspective, 76–77; on the faith ladder, 84; on instinct, 103
Japan, 38

Japanese and the Eastern front in the war, 73
Jastrow, Joseph, 96, 97
Jean Paul. See Richter, J. P. L.
Jefferson, Thomas, 119, 139, 145; constitution and, 153
Jekyll, Dr., 96
Joffre, General, 4, 5, 7; as editor of war news, 18; at Verdun, 18, 19
Jones, Ernest, 39
Journalism, 17, 142; see also Newspapers
Journalists, 195
Judgment, 30
Jung, C. G., 40, 41

Kempf, E. J., 15, 96, 97
Killing, 66, 98
King, Senator, of Utah, 74
Knox, Senator, 10

Labor, 84
Labor disputes and the newspapers, 187–188
Labor Movement, 84
Laissez-faire, 62, 63
Lamp post, four men at, 12
Landscapes, 48
Lansdowne, Lord, 114
Lansing, Robert, 143
Langenhove, F. van, 45, 55
Language, condensation, 35; inadequacy, 36
Laski, H. J., 127, 213
Last chapters, 220
Leaders, 127; advantages, 135; policy with the mass, 133; propaganda, 135; rank and file and, 127–128; social, 28–29; wise, 134
League of Nations, 10, 11; American opinion, 106
LeBon, Gustave, 97, 107
Lee, J. M., 179
Lee, Vernon, 89
Legislation, 127; see also Congress

Lenin, Nicolai, 101, 102
Lewis, G. C., 121
Lewis, Sinclair, 6, 92, 195
Liberty, 172
"Liberty and the News," 194
Lincoln, Abraham, 108
Lippmann, Faye, 192
Lippmann, Walter, 192
Littell, Philip, 65
Locard, Edmond, 43
Logrolling, 158
London, 191
Long, C. E., 40
Lowell, A. Lawrence, 125
Lucidity of mind, 38
Ludendorff, General, 131
*Lusitania*, 110
Lusk Committee, 173

McCarthy, Charles, 198
McCormick, Senator, 10
McDougall, William, 103
Machiavelli, Niccolo, 143, 144, 160
Machine, political, 123; reason for,
    125
Machinery of knowledge, 197, 206
Madison, James, 99, 145, 151
Magazines, 34, 42
Magic period, 39
"Main Street," 92, 195
*Manchester Guardian*, 37
Marriott, W. K., 143
Martin, E. D., 97, 133
Marx, Karl, 101, 102
Marxism, 57
Mass, leaders and the, 133; right-
    eousness of, 139
Mastery, 14
Mather, Increase, 85
Mechanical invention, 59
Melting Pot pageant, 47
Mental confusion, 217
Mental fatigue, 40
Mentality, low, 42

Merriam, C. E., 200
Merz, Charles, 192
Metaphors, 87
Mexico, 37, 109
Michels, R., 123
Mill, J. S., 172
Milton, John, 172, 173
Mitchell, Wesley, 61
Monroe Doctrine, 147
Moral codes, 66; particular view of
    facts and, 68
Moral education, 98
Morale, 114, 130
Moralist and dogmatist, 67
Moving pictures, 9, 50, 76, 90, 185
Münsterberg, Hugo, 43
Mutinies, military, 131
Mutiny at sea, 221
Mystery and public opinion, 138
Myth, 67

Names, 87, 111; changing, 48
National soul, 51
National university, 210
National Will, 16
Negroes, 29, 81
New, Senator, 10
New York City, writ of administra-
    tion, 211
*New York Times*, 180
News, guess work, 186; lack of exact
    tests, 194; machinery of record,
    185; nature of, 183; reader's inter-
    est, 192; system of record and,
    186; truth distinguished from,
    194; uncovering, 183; unpaid for,
    174
Newsgathering, 174, 181
Newspapers, 17; accuracy, 178;
    casual relation of the public to,
    174; circulation, 175, 176, 177;
    concealed payment for, 175, 176;
    constant reader, 178; diary and
    personal patter, 179; editor's posi-

tion, 180, 181, 191; influence on one another, 191; institutions and, 197; investigations of industrial conditions, 188; misrepresentation, 189; political science and, 173, 174; publishing as a business, 177; radical, 182; salaries of reporters, etc., 181; time and attention given to, 31; truth and, 196; unique position, 174
Nivelle, General, 22, 131
Noise, 40
Northcliffe, Lord, 191

Observation, 43; experiment as to, 45; trained, 58; untrained, 48
Ochs, A. S., 175, 177
Officeholders, 154, 206
Oliver, F. S., 143
Oliver's Hamilton, 4
Omnicompetent citizen, 148, 154, 197
Opinion, 68; property and, 100
Opportunity and contact, 24
Organization, political, 123
Organizations of research and reference, 203
Organized intelligence, 198
Ostrogorski, M., 123
Outside public, 215
Oversoul, 125

Pageant of the Melting Pot, 47
Pain, 14
Palmer, A. Mitchell, 173
Paris, 26
Party politics, 156
Patriotic code, 68
Patronage, 123, 150, 155
Patterson, F. T., 90, 92
Pax, 55
Peace terms, 115
Peel, Sir Robert, 107
Pellé, General, 18, 19

People, voice of the, 139, 140
Perry, R. B., 202
Personality of, 49; distinctions in self, 95; fictitious, 3; symbolic, 5, 6
Persuasion, 136
Pétain, General, 131
Philosophy of life, 49, 65
Photographs, 50
Pictures, 13, 14, 16, 17, 50, 88, 89, 90
Pierrefeu, Jean de, 4, 7, 18, 131
Pittsburgh Survey, 188
Plato's cave, 2
Plato's Republic, 143, 220
Pleasure, 14
Plots, 70
Pluralism, new forms, 160
Policy, incidence, 131, 132, 134; new, 133
Political assumptions, 141
Political behavior, 11
Political life complexity, 11, 12
Political science, 17, 196; newspapers and, 173, 174
Political theories, 138
Political wisdom, innate, 139
Political world, 15, 16
Politicians, fence-mending, 134, 135; professional, 126
Politics, ancient theory, 141; fighting motif in, 90; ideologies, 92; organization, 122, 123; reason and, 220
Popular will, 105
Preconceptions, 49
Prejudice, 65, 138, 220
Present, the, 76
Presidency, 156, 157
Press. See Newspapers
Press agents, 186, 187
Press associations, 176
Privacy, 24; censorship and, 18
Private affairs, 23, 24; public affairs and, 29
Privileged, 123, 150, 158

Progress, 60; American idea, 59;
    idea, 58
Propaganda, 14, 136; government
    during the World War, 24; lead-
    ers and, 135; war news, 22
Property, unequal distribution, 100
Proportional representation, 127
Propriety, 28
Protection, 14
Prussia, 116
Pseudo-environment, 8, 13, 14, 15
Psychoanalysts, 14, 15
Psychology, behavior and character,
    96; new, 15
Public the, as judge in intricate mat-
    ters, 215
Public affairs, 16; private and, 29
Public office, 154, 155
Public opinion, 15, 16, 196; civil lib-
    erty and, 172, 173; codified ver-
    sion of facts and, 69; continuous
    opinions, 213; defective organiza-
    tion, 17; distance of the event
    from, 24; economic situation as
    cause, 100; lack of literature on,
    137; making a mystery of, 138;
    Sir Robert Peel on, 107; symbol-
    ism, 6
Public spirit, 148
Publicity men, 186
Pugnacity, 90

Quota, 209

Races, 79, 80
Rank and file, 127, 133
Rapid transit, 26
Realism and romanticism, 91
Reason, appeal to, 220
Reasoning, untrained, 85
Recording machinery, 185
Referendum, 126
*Relativismus*, 58
Relativity, 58

Repington diaries, 4
Reporting, 141, 142; *New York Times*,
    180; places where news is
    obtained, 183; salaries, 181
Reports, 214
Representative government, 17, 156,
    214; new theory, guild socialism,
    162
Representatives, functional, 165
Repressed cravings, 97
Republican schism of, 108
Republicans, 106
Research and reference organiza-
    tions, 203
Respectability, 28
Response, 39, 40
Revolution, 134; democratic, 136;
    mechanical (1820–50), 59
Rhineland, 116
Richter, J. P. L., 36
Rights and duties, 143
Rights of humanity, 117
Robinson, J. H., 77
Rogers, J. E., 31
Romanticism and realism, 91
Roosevelt, Theodore, 108, 109
Ross, E. A., 29, 123
Rotation in office, 148, 155, 156
Rousseau, J. J., 145
Ruritania, 71
Russell, Bertrand, 172
Russia, 102, 103, 113, 168
Russian news, 192
Ruth, Babe, 188

Saar valley, 116
Sack, A. J., 74
Sagas, 93
St. Ambrose, 2
Salem, Mass., 26
Samples, 82, 83, 84
Scandal, 70
Scholars, 58
Scientists, 199

Scott, W. D., 31
Scriptures, 2
Secrecy, 23
Secret treaties, 114
Self-centered man, 137
Self-contained community, 142
Self-defense, 66
Self-determination, 147
Self-government, 147; human dignity and, 170; men's interest in, 169
Self-interest, 93, 99
Self-respect, 52
Self-sufficiency, 149
Selves, different, 95
Senate, 9
Servant question, 83
Sexual motif, 89
Shaw, G. B., 14, 62, 224
Sheffield, England, 82
Shelley, P. B., 195
Sherrington, C. S., 43
Shop, 163
Silence, conspiracy of, 129
Sinclair, Upton, 179, 194; "The Brass Check," 182
Slavery, Aristotle on, 53
Smart set, 180
Social analysts, 15
Social contact, 16
Social hierarchy, 27, 29
Social leaders, 28, 29
Social Purpose, 16
Social rank, 27, 28
Social science, experimental method, 202
Social scientists, 199; strategic position, 201
Social sets, 27, 28, 29
Socialism, 100, 101, 102
Society, Great, 13, 30, 198, 199; High, 29, 30; variety, 12
Socrates, 220
Socratic dialogue, 216, 218

Space, inability to conceive, 73, 74
Speed, words, clearness, and, 35
Starving Russian children, 111, 112
State, Secretary of, 204
Statehood, 118
Statesmen, 134
Statistics, 82
Steel industry, 182, 188, 216
Stereotypes, 43; as personal defenses, 52; character, 49; detection, 71; facts and, 61; human and personal, 87; maintenance, value, 49; the perfect, 54; systematizing, 57
Stories, varying with character of hearer, 93
Strachey's Queen Victoria, 4
Strife, 142, 145
Strikes and the newspapers, 188
Struggle, 90
Strunsky, Simeon, on H. G. Wells, 77
Success, 60, 64
Suffragists, 187
Superlative, 60
Superstition, 7, 39, 86
Susceptibilities, 42
Suspense, 90
Symbolic personality, 5
Symbols, 5, 6, 112; character, 119, 120; hierarchy, 117; leaders' use of, 128; power and value, 128–129

Taft, W. H., 74
Taste, 28
Taylor, F. W., 198
Taylor, H. O., 2
Teachers, 108
Technical knowledge, 198
Telegraphy, 35
Tennyson, Alfred, on evolution, 59
Teutons, 79
Thinking, difficult conditions, 40; effective, 31

Timber, 78
Time, as element in social problems, 78; attention and time given to newspapers, 31; confusions in history, 79; control of future, 75; factor in politics, 223; presumption about, 75
Time-conception, 76
Time perspective, 76, 77, 78
Tocqueville, Alexis de, 145
Tolerance, 69
Townships, 145, 148
Trade associations, 210
Trades Union Congress, 84
Transportation, city problem, 79
Travel, stories of, 54
Trotter, W., 28
Trust in others, 121, 122
Trusts, 65, 160
Truth, 172, 173; news distinguished from, 194

Union, Hamilton and the, 152
Union League Club, 38
Unity, 129, 130
Unseen environment, 212
Unsuccessful, the, 65

Vagueness, 110
Valentine, Robert, 198
Veblen, Thorstein, 100
Verdun, 18, 19
Victoria, Queen, 4
Victory, 61
Virgil, 46, 79
Virginian, 118
Visualization, 35, 50, 88
Voice of the people, 139, 140
Voting, 106, 107; by functions, 167; method of securing homogeneous vote, 108; preferential, 127; reasons, election of 1920, 120
Vox populi, 140

Wallus, Graham, 13, 51, 223
War, 98
War news, editing in the field, 18
Washington, D.C., need of intelligence bureaus, 206
Washington, George, 152, 153
*Washington Post*, 9
Webb, Sidney and Beatrice, 168, 211
Wells, H. G., 223; on history, 77
White, W. Alanson, 36
White, Wm. Allen, 60
Wilcox, D. F., 31, 33
Will, expression of, 169, 170
Will of the people, 105
Will-making, 75
Wilson, Sir Henry, 129
Wilson, Woodrow, 107; Fourteen Points, 113, 114, 115, 117; Hughes' attack on policies of, 108–109; on American motives, 105; phrases, 117; realization of moral crisis of the war, 114; secret treaties and, 114
Window-pane, cracked, 7
Wolman, Leo, 217
Woman's party, 187
Words, Franco-English exchange, 37; speed, clearness, and, 35
Working class, 83
World, political, 15, 16
World made safe for democracy, 117
World War, American view, 73; America's experience, 60, 61; casualties, 131; crisis and Wilson's part, 113; government's propaganda, 24; treaties concluding, 71
Wright, P. S., 129, 130, 131

Yap, 26
Yes or no, 119, 125

Zurich Association Studies, 40

A CATALOG OF SELECTED
**DOVER BOOKS**
IN ALL FIELDS OF INTEREST

# A CATALOG OF SELECTED DOVER
# BOOKS IN ALL FIELDS OF INTEREST

CONCERNING THE SPIRITUAL IN ART, Wassily Kandinsky. Pioneering work by father of abstract art. Thoughts on color theory, nature of art. Analysis of earlier masters. 12 illustrations. 80pp. of text. 5⅜ x 8½.                                    23411-8

ANIMALS: 1,419 Copyright-Free Illustrations of Mammals, Birds, Fish, Insects, etc., Jim Harter (ed.). Clear wood engravings present, in extremely lifelike poses, over 1,000 species of animals. One of the most extensive pictorial sourcebooks of its kind. Captions. Index. 284pp. 9 x 12.                                    23766-4

CELTIC ART: The Methods of Construction, George Bain. Simple geometric techniques for making Celtic interlacements, spirals, Kells-type initials, animals, humans, etc. Over 500 illustrations. 160pp. 9 x 12. (Available in U.S. only.)                                    22923-8

AN ATLAS OF ANATOMY FOR ARTISTS, Fritz Schider. Most thorough reference work on art anatomy in the world. Hundreds of illustrations, including selections from works by Vesalius, Leonardo, Goya, Ingres, Michelangelo, others. 593 illustrations. 192pp. 7⅛ x 10¼.                                    20241-0

CELTIC HAND STROKE-BY-STROKE (Irish Half-Uncial from "The Book of Kells"): An Arthur Baker Calligraphy Manual, Arthur Baker. Complete guide to creating each letter of the alphabet in distinctive Celtic manner. Covers hand position, strokes, pens, inks, paper, more. Illustrated. 48pp. 8¼ x 11.                                    24336-2

EASY ORIGAMI, John Montroll. Charming collection of 32 projects (hat, cup, pelican, piano, swan, many more) specially designed for the novice origami hobbyist. Clearly illustrated easy-to-follow instructions insure that even beginning papercrafters will achieve successful results. 48pp. 8¼ x 11.                                    27298-2

THE COMPLETE BOOK OF BIRDHOUSE CONSTRUCTION FOR WOOD-WORKERS, Scott D. Campbell. Detailed instructions, illustrations, tables. Also data on bird habitat and instinct patterns. Bibliography. 3 tables. 63 illustrations in 15 figures. 48pp. 5¼ x 8½.                                    24407-5

BLOOMINGDALE'S ILLUSTRATED 1886 CATALOG: Fashions, Dry Goods and Housewares, Bloomingdale Brothers. Famed merchants' extremely rare catalog depicting about 1,700 products: clothing, housewares, firearms, dry goods, jewelry, more. Invaluable for dating, identifying vintage items. Also, copyright-free graphics for artists, designers. Co-published with Henry Ford Museum & Greenfield Village. 160pp. 8¼ x 11.                                    25780-0

HISTORIC COSTUME IN PICTURES, Braun & Schneider. Over 1,450 costumed figures in clearly detailed engravings–from dawn of civilization to end of 19th century. Captions. Many folk costumes. 256pp. 8⅜ x 11¾.                                    23150-X

CATALOG OF DOVER BOOKS

STICKLEY CRAFTSMAN FURNITURE CATALOGS, Gustav Stickley and L. & J. G. Stickley. Beautiful, functional furniture in two authentic catalogs from 1910. 594 illustrations, including 277 photos, show settles, rockers, armchairs, reclining chairs, bookcases, desks, tables. 183pp. 6½ x 9¼.                                      23838-5

AMERICAN LOCOMOTIVES IN HISTORIC PHOTOGRAPHS: 1858 to 1949, Ron Ziel (ed.). A rare collection of 126 meticulously detailed official photographs, called "builder portraits," of American locomotives that majestically chronicle the rise of steam locomotive power in America. Introduction. Detailed captions. xi+ 129pp. 9 x 12.                                      27393-8

AMERICA'S LIGHTHOUSES: An Illustrated History, Francis Ross Holland, Jr. Delightfully written, profusely illustrated fact-filled survey of over 200 American lighthouses since 1716. History, anecdotes, technological advances, more. 240pp. 8 x 10¾.
25576-X

TOWARDS A NEW ARCHITECTURE, Le Corbusier. Pioneering manifesto by founder of "International School." Technical and aesthetic theories, views of industry, economics, relation of form to function, "mass-production split" and much more. Profusely illustrated. 320pp. 6⅛ x 9¼. (Available in U.S. only.)                      25023-7

HOW THE OTHER HALF LIVES, Jacob Riis. Famous journalistic record, exposing poverty and degradation of New York slums around 1900, by major social reformer. 100 striking and influential photographs. 233pp. 10 x 7⅞.                22012-5

FRUIT KEY AND TWIG KEY TO TREES AND SHRUBS, William M. Harlow. One of the handiest and most widely used identification aids. Fruit key covers 120 deciduous and evergreen species; twig key 160 deciduous species. Easily used. Over 300 photographs. 126pp. 5⅜ x 8½.                                      20511-8

COMMON BIRD SONGS, Dr. Donald J. Borror. Songs of 60 most common U.S. birds: robins, sparrows, cardinals, bluejays, finches, more–arranged in order of increasing complexity. Up to 9 variations of songs of each species.
Cassette and manual 99911-4

ORCHIDS AS HOUSE PLANTS, Rebecca Tyson Northen. Grow cattleyas and many other kinds of orchids–in a window, in a case, or under artificial light. 63 illustrations. 148pp. 5⅜ x 8½.                                      23261-1

MONSTER MAZES, Dave Phillips. Masterful mazes at four levels of difficulty. Avoid deadly perils and evil creatures to find magical treasures. Solutions for all 32 exciting illustrated puzzles. 48pp. 8¼ x 11.                                      26005-4

MOZART'S DON GIOVANNI (DOVER OPERA LIBRETTO SERIES), Wolfgang Amadeus Mozart. Introduced and translated by Ellen H. Bleiler. Standard Italian libretto, with complete English translation. Convenient and thoroughly portable–an ideal companion for reading along with a recording or the performance itself. Introduction. List of characters. Plot summary. 121pp. 5¼ x 8½.      24944-1

TECHNICAL MANUAL AND DICTIONARY OF CLASSICAL BALLET, Gail Grant. Defines, explains, comments on steps, movements, poses and concepts. 15-page pictorial section. Basic book for student, viewer. 127pp. 5⅜ x 8½.      21843-0

THE CLARINET AND CLARINET PLAYING, David Pino. Lively, comprehensive work features suggestions about technique, musicianship, and musical interpretation, as well as guidelines for teaching, making your own reeds, and preparing for public performance. Includes an intriguing look at clarinet history. "A godsend," *The Clarinet,* Journal of the International Clarinet Society. Appendixes. 7 illus. 320pp. 5⅜ x 8½. 40270-3

HOLLYWOOD GLAMOR PORTRAITS, John Kobal (ed.). 145 photos from 1926-49. Harlow, Gable, Bogart, Bacall; 94 stars in all. Full background on photographers, technical aspects. 160pp. 8⅜ x 11¼. 23352-9

THE ANNOTATED CASEY AT THE BAT: A Collection of Ballads about the Mighty Casey/Third, Revised Edition, Martin Gardner (ed.). Amusing sequels and parodies of one of America's best-loved poems: Casey's Revenge, Why Casey Whiffed, Casey's Sister at the Bat, others. 256pp. 5⅜ x 8½. 28598-7

THE RAVEN AND OTHER FAVORITE POEMS, Edgar Allan Poe. Over 40 of the author's most memorable poems: "The Bells," "Ulalume," "Israfel," "To Helen," "The Conqueror Worm," "Eldorado," "Annabel Lee," many more. Alphabetic lists of titles and first lines. 64pp. 5³⁄₁₆ x 8¼. 26685-0

PERSONAL MEMOIRS OF U. S. GRANT, Ulysses Simpson Grant. Intelligent, deeply moving firsthand account of Civil War campaigns, considered by many the finest military memoirs ever written. Includes letters, historic photographs, maps and more. 528pp. 6⅛ x 9¼. 28587-1

ANCIENT EGYPTIAN MATERIALS AND INDUSTRIES, A. Lucas and J. Harris. Fascinating, comprehensive, thoroughly documented text describes this ancient civilization's vast resources and the processes that incorporated them in daily life, including the use of animal products, building materials, cosmetics, perfumes and incense, fibers, glazed ware, glass and its manufacture, materials used in the mummification process, and much more. 544pp. 6⅛ x 9¼. (Available in U.S. only.) 40446-3

RUSSIAN STORIES/RUSSKIE RASSKAZY: A Dual-Language Book, edited by Gleb Struve. Twelve tales by such masters as Chekhov, Tolstoy, Dostoevsky, Pushkin, others. Excellent word-for-word English translations on facing pages, plus teaching and study aids, Russian/English vocabulary, biographical/critical introductions, more. 416pp. 5⅜ x 8½. 26244-8

PHILADELPHIA THEN AND NOW: 60 Sites Photographed in the Past and Present, Kenneth Finkel and Susan Oyama. Rare photographs of City Hall, Logan Square, Independence Hall, Betsy Ross House, other landmarks juxtaposed with contemporary views. Captures changing face of historic city. Introduction. Captions. 128pp. 8¼ x 11. 25790-8

AIA ARCHITECTURAL GUIDE TO NASSAU AND SUFFOLK COUNTIES, LONG ISLAND, The American Institute of Architects, Long Island Chapter, and the Society for the Preservation of Long Island Antiquities. Comprehensive, well-researched and generously illustrated volume brings to life over three centuries of Long Island's great architectural heritage. More than 240 photographs with authoritative, extensively detailed captions. 176pp. 8¼ x 11. 26946-9

NORTH AMERICAN INDIAN LIFE: Customs and Traditions of 23 Tribes, Elsie Clews Parsons (ed.). 27 fictionalized essays by noted anthropologists examine religion, customs, government, additional facets of life among the Winnebago, Crow, Zuni, Eskimo, other tribes. 480pp. 6⅛ x 9¼. 27377-6

FRANK LLOYD WRIGHT'S DANA HOUSE, Donald Hoffmann. Pictorial essay of residential masterpiece with over 160 interior and exterior photos, plans, elevations, sketches and studies. 128pp. 9¼ x 10¾. 29120-0

THE MALE AND FEMALE FIGURE IN MOTION: 60 Classic Photographic Sequences, Eadweard Muybridge. 60 true-action photographs of men and women walking, running, climbing, bending, turning, etc., reproduced from rare 19th-century masterpiece. vi + 121pp. 9 x 12. 24745-7

1001 QUESTIONS ANSWERED ABOUT THE SEASHORE, N. J. Berrill and Jacquelyn Berrill. Queries answered about dolphins, sea snails, sponges, starfish, fishes, shore birds, many others. Covers appearance, breeding, growth, feeding, much more. 305pp. 5¼ x 8¼. 23366-9

ATTRACTING BIRDS TO YOUR YARD, William J. Weber. Easy-to-follow guide offers advice on how to attract the greatest diversity of birds: birdhouses, feeders, water and waterers, much more. 96pp. 5³⁄₁₆ x 8¼. 28927-3

MEDICINAL AND OTHER USES OF NORTH AMERICAN PLANTS: A Historical Survey with Special Reference to the Eastern Indian Tribes, Charlotte Erichsen-Brown. Chronological historical citations document 500 years of usage of plants, trees, shrubs native to eastern Canada, northeastern U.S. Also complete identifying information. 343 illustrations. 544pp. 6½ x 9¼. 25951-X

STORYBOOK MAZES, Dave Phillips. 23 stories and mazes on two-page spreads: Wizard of Oz, Treasure Island, Robin Hood, etc. Solutions. 64pp. 8¼ x 11. 23628-5

AMERICAN NEGRO SONGS: 230 Folk Songs and Spirituals, Religious and Secular, John W. Work. This authoritative study traces the African influences of songs sung and played by black Americans at work, in church, and as entertainment. The author discusses the lyric significance of such songs as "Swing Low, Sweet Chariot," "John Henry," and others and offers the words and music for 230 songs. Bibliography. Index of Song Titles. 272pp. 6½ x 9¼. 40271-1

MOVIE-STAR PORTRAITS OF THE FORTIES, John Kobal (ed.). 163 glamor, studio photos of 106 stars of the 1940s: Rita Hayworth, Ava Gardner, Marlon Brando, Clark Gable, many more. 176pp. 8⅜ x 11¼. 23546-7

BENCHLEY LOST AND FOUND, Robert Benchley. Finest humor from early 30s, about pet peeves, child psychologists, post office and others. Mostly unavailable elsewhere. 73 illustrations by Peter Arno and others. 183pp. 5⅜ x 8½. 22410-4

YEKL and THE IMPORTED BRIDEGROOM AND OTHER STORIES OF YIDDISH NEW YORK, Abraham Cahan. Film Hester Street based on *Yekl* (1896). Novel, other stories among first about Jewish immigrants on N.Y.'s East Side. 240pp. 5⅜ x 8½. 22427-9

SELECTED POEMS, Walt Whitman. Generous sampling from *Leaves of Grass*. Twenty-four poems include "I Hear America Singing," "Song of the Open Road," "I Sing the Body Electric," "When Lilacs Last in the Dooryard Bloom'd," "O Captain! My Captain!"–all reprinted from an authoritative edition. Lists of titles and first lines. 128pp. 5³⁄₁₆ x 8¼. 26878-0

THE BEST TALES OF HOFFMANN, E. T. A. Hoffmann. 10 of Hoffmann's most important stories: "Nutcracker and the King of Mice," "The Golden Flowerpot," etc. 458pp. 5⅜ x 8½. 21793-0

FROM FETISH TO GOD IN ANCIENT EGYPT, E. A. Wallis Budge. Rich detailed survey of Egyptian conception of "God" and gods, magic, cult of animals, Osiris, more. Also, superb English translations of hymns and legends. 240 illustrations. 545pp. 5⅜ x 8½. 25803-3

FRENCH STORIES/CONTES FRANÇAIS: A Dual-Language Book, Wallace Fowlie. Ten stories by French masters, Voltaire to Camus: "Micromegas" by Voltaire; "The Atheist's Mass" by Balzac; "Minuet" by de Maupassant; "The Guest" by Camus, six more. Excellent English translations on facing pages. Also French-English vocabulary list, exercises, more. 352pp. 5⅜ x 8½. 26443-2

CHICAGO AT THE TURN OF THE CENTURY IN PHOTOGRAPHS: 122 Historic Views from the Collections of the Chicago Historical Society, Larry A. Viskochil. Rare large-format prints offer detailed views of City Hall, State Street, the Loop, Hull House, Union Station, many other landmarks, circa 1904-1913. Introduction. Captions. Maps. 144pp. 9⅜ x 12¼. 24656-6

OLD BROOKLYN IN EARLY PHOTOGRAPHS, 1865-1929, William Lee Younger. Luna Park, Gravesend race track, construction of Grand Army Plaza, moving of Hotel Brighton, etc. 157 previously unpublished photographs. 165pp. 8⅞ x 11¾. 23587-4

THE MYTHS OF THE NORTH AMERICAN INDIANS, Lewis Spence. Rich anthology of the myths and legends of the Algonquins, Iroquois, Pawnees and Sioux, prefaced by an extensive historical and ethnological commentary. 36 illustrations. 480pp. 5⅜ x 8½. 25967-6

AN ENCYCLOPEDIA OF BATTLES: Accounts of Over 1,560 Battles from 1479 B.C. to the Present, David Eggenberger. Essential details of every major battle in recorded history from the first battle of Megiddo in 1479 B.C. to Grenada in 1984. List of Battle Maps. New Appendix covering the years 1967-1984. Index. 99 illustrations. 544pp. 6½ x 9¼. 24913-1

SAILING ALONE AROUND THE WORLD, Captain Joshua Slocum. First man to sail around the world, alone, in small boat. One of great feats of seamanship told in delightful manner. 67 illustrations. 294pp. 5⅜ x 8½. 20326-3

ANARCHISM AND OTHER ESSAYS, Emma Goldman. Powerful, penetrating, prophetic essays on direct action, role of minorities, prison reform, puritan hypocrisy, violence, etc. 271pp. 5⅜ x 8½. 22484-8

MYTHS OF THE HINDUS AND BUDDHISTS, Ananda K. Coomaraswamy and Sister Nivedita. Great stories of the epics; deeds of Krishna, Shiva, taken from puranas, Vedas, folk tales; etc. 32 illustrations. 400pp. 5⅜ x 8½. 21759-0

THE TRAUMA OF BIRTH, Otto Rank. Rank's controversial thesis that anxiety neurosis is caused by profound psychological trauma which occurs at birth. 256pp. 5⅜ x 8½. 27974-X

A THEOLOGICO-POLITICAL TREATISE, Benedict Spinoza. Also contains unfinished Political Treatise. Great classic on religious liberty, theory of government on common consent. R. Elwes translation. Total of 421pp. 5⅜ x 8½. 20249-6

MY BONDAGE AND MY FREEDOM, Frederick Douglass. Born a slave, Douglass became outspoken force in antislavery movement. The best of Douglass' autobiographies. Graphic description of slave life. 464pp. 5⅜ x 8½. 22457-0

FOLLOWING THE EQUATOR: A Journey Around the World, Mark Twain. Fascinating humorous account of 1897 voyage to Hawaii, Australia, India, New Zealand, etc. Ironic, bemused reports on peoples, customs, climate, flora and fauna, politics, much more. 197 illustrations. 720pp. 5⅜ x 8½. 26113-1

THE PEOPLE CALLED SHAKERS, Edward D. Andrews. Definitive study of Shakers: origins, beliefs, practices, dances, social organization, furniture and crafts, etc. 33 illustrations. 351pp. 5⅜ x 8½. 21081-2

THE MYTHS OF GREECE AND ROME, H. A. Guerber. A classic of mythology, generously illustrated, long prized for its simple, graphic, accurate retelling of the principal myths of Greece and Rome, and for its commentary on their origins and significance. With 64 illustrations by Michelangelo, Raphael, Titian, Rubens, Canova, Bernini and others. 480pp. 5⅜ x 8½. 27584-1

PSYCHOLOGY OF MUSIC, Carl E. Seashore. Classic work discusses music as a medium from psychological viewpoint. Clear treatment of physical acoustics, auditory apparatus, sound perception, development of musical skills, nature of musical feeling, host of other topics. 88 figures. 408pp. 5⅜ x 8½. 21851-1

THE PHILOSOPHY OF HISTORY, Georg W. Hegel. Great classic of Western thought develops concept that history is not chance but rational process, the evolution of freedom. 457pp. 5⅜ x 8½. 20112-0

THE BOOK OF TEA, Kakuzo Okakura. Minor classic of the Orient: entertaining, charming explanation, interpretation of traditional Japanese culture in terms of tea ceremony. 94pp. 5⅜ x 8½. 20070-1

LIFE IN ANCIENT EGYPT, Adolf Erman. Fullest, most thorough, detailed older account with much not in more recent books, domestic life, religion, magic, medicine, commerce, much more. Many illustrations reproduce tomb paintings, carvings, hieroglyphs, etc. 597pp. 5⅜ x 8½. 22632-8

SUNDIALS, Their Theory and Construction, Albert Waugh. Far and away the best, most thorough coverage of ideas, mathematics concerned, types, construction, adjusting anywhere. Simple, nontechnical treatment allows even children to build several of these dials. Over 100 illustrations. 230pp. 5⅜ x 8½. 22947-5

THEORETICAL HYDRODYNAMICS, L. M. Milne-Thomson. Classic exposition of the mathematical theory of fluid motion, applicable to both hydrodynamics and aerodynamics. Over 600 exercises. 768pp. 6⅛ x 9¼. 68970-0

SONGS OF EXPERIENCE: Facsimile Reproduction with 26 Plates in Full Color, William Blake. 26 full-color plates from a rare 1826 edition. Includes "The Tyger," "London," "Holy Thursday," and other poems. Printed text of poems. 48pp. 5¼ x 7. 24636-1

OLD-TIME VIGNETTES IN FULL COLOR, Carol Belanger Grafton (ed.). Over 390 charming, often sentimental illustrations, selected from archives of Victorian graphics—pretty women posing, children playing, food, flowers, kittens and puppies, smiling cherubs, birds and butterflies, much more. All copyright-free. 48pp. 9¼ x 12¼. 27269-9

PERSPECTIVE FOR ARTISTS, Rex Vicat Cole. Depth, perspective of sky and sea, shadows, much more, not usually covered. 391 diagrams, 81 reproductions of drawings and paintings. 279pp. 5⅜ x 8½. 22487-2

DRAWING THE LIVING FIGURE, Joseph Sheppard. Innovative approach to artistic anatomy focuses on specifics of surface anatomy, rather than muscles and bones. Over 170 drawings of live models in front, back and side views, and in widely varying poses. Accompanying diagrams. 177 illustrations. Introduction. Index. 144pp. 8⅜ x11¼. 26723-7

GOTHIC AND OLD ENGLISH ALPHABETS: 100 Complete Fonts, Dan X. Solo. Add power, elegance to posters, signs, other graphics with 100 stunning copyright-free alphabets: Blackstone, Dolbey, Germania, 97 more–including many lower-case, numerals, punctuation marks. 104pp. 8⅛ x 11. 24695-7

HOW TO DO BEADWORK, Mary White. Fundamental book on craft from simple projects to five-bead chains and woven works. 106 illustrations. 142pp. 5⅜ x 8. 20697-1

THE BOOK OF WOOD CARVING, Charles Marshall Sayers. Finest book for beginners discusses fundamentals and offers 34 designs. "Absolutely first rate . . . well thought out and well executed."–E. J. Tangerman. 118pp. 7¾ x 10⅝. 23654-4

ILLUSTRATED CATALOG OF CIVIL WAR MILITARY GOODS: Union Army Weapons, Insignia, Uniform Accessories, and Other Equipment, Schuyler, Hartley, and Graham. Rare, profusely illustrated 1846 catalog includes Union Army uniform and dress regulations, arms and ammunition, coats, insignia, flags, swords, rifles, etc. 226 illustrations. 160pp. 9 x 12. 24939-5

WOMEN'S FASHIONS OF THE EARLY 1900s: An Unabridged Republication of "New York Fashions, 1909," National Cloak & Suit Co. Rare catalog of mail-order fashions documents women's and children's clothing styles shortly after the turn of the century. Captions offer full descriptions, prices. Invaluable resource for fashion, costume historians. Approximately 725 illustrations. 128pp. 8⅜ x 11¼. 27276-1

THE 1912 AND 1915 GUSTAV STICKLEY FURNITURE CATALOGS, Gustav Stickley. With over 200 detailed illustrations and descriptions, these two catalogs are essential reading and reference materials and identification guides for Stickley furniture. Captions cite materials, dimensions and prices. 112pp. 6½ x 9¼. 26676-1

EARLY AMERICAN LOCOMOTIVES, John H. White, Jr. Finest locomotive engravings from early 19th century: historical (1804–74), main-line (after 1870), special, foreign, etc. 147 plates. 142pp. 11⅜ x 8¼. 22772-3

THE TALL SHIPS OF TODAY IN PHOTOGRAPHS, Frank O. Braynard. Lavishly illustrated tribute to nearly 100 majestic contemporary sailing vessels: Amerigo Vespucci, Clearwater, Constitution, Eagle, Mayflower, Sea Cloud, Victory, many more. Authoritative captions provide statistics, background on each ship. 190 black-and-white photographs and illustrations. Introduction. 128pp. 8⅞ x 11¾. 27163-3

LITTLE BOOK OF EARLY AMERICAN CRAFTS AND TRADES, Peter Stockham (ed.). 1807 children's book explains crafts and trades: baker, hatter, cooper, potter, and many others. 23 copperplate illustrations. 140pp. 4⅝ x 6.    23336-7

VICTORIAN FASHIONS AND COSTUMES FROM HARPER'S BAZAR, 1867–1898, Stella Blum (ed.). Day costumes, evening wear, sports clothes, shoes, hats, other accessories in over 1,000 detailed engravings. 320pp. 9⅜ x 12¼.  22990-4

GUSTAV STICKLEY, THE CRAFTSMAN, Mary Ann Smith. Superb study surveys broad scope of Stickley's achievement, especially in architecture. Design philosophy, rise and fall of the Craftsman empire, descriptions and floor plans for many Craftsman houses, more. 86 black-and-white halftones. 31 line illustrations. Introduction 208pp. 6½ x 9¼.    27210-9

THE LONG ISLAND RAIL ROAD IN EARLY PHOTOGRAPHS, Ron Ziel. Over 220 rare photos, informative text document origin ( 1844) and development of rail service on Long Island. Vintage views of early trains, locomotives, stations, passengers, crews, much more. Captions. 8⅞ x 11¾.    26301-0

VOYAGE OF THE LIBERDADE, Joshua Slocum. Great 19th-century mariner's thrilling, first-hand account of the wreck of his ship off South America, the 35-foot boat he built from the wreckage, and its remarkable voyage home. 128pp. 5⅜ x 8½.    40022-0

TEN BOOKS ON ARCHITECTURE, Vitruvius. The most important book ever written on architecture. Early Roman aesthetics, technology, classical orders, site selection, all other aspects. Morgan translation. 331pp. 5⅜ x 8½.    20645-9

THE HUMAN FIGURE IN MOTION, Eadweard Muybridge. More than 4,500 stopped-action photos, in action series, showing undraped men, women, children jumping, lying down, throwing, sitting, wrestling, carrying, etc. 390pp. 7⅞ x 10⅝.    20204-6 Clothbd.

TREES OF THE EASTERN AND CENTRAL UNITED STATES AND CANADA, William M. Harlow. Best one-volume guide to 140 trees. Full descriptions, woodlore, range, etc. Over 600 illustrations. Handy size. 288pp. 4½ x 6⅜.    20395-6

SONGS OF WESTERN BIRDS, Dr. Donald J. Borror. Complete song and call repertoire of 60 western species, including flycatchers, juncoes, cactus wrens, many more–includes fully illustrated booklet.    Cassette and manual 99913-0

GROWING AND USING HERBS AND SPICES, Milo Miloradovich. Versatile handbook provides all the information needed for cultivation and use of all the herbs and spices available in North America. 4 illustrations. Index. Glossary. 236pp. 5⅜ x 8½.    25058-X

BIG BOOK OF MAZES AND LABYRINTHS, Walter Shepherd. 50 mazes and labyrinths in all–classical, solid, ripple, and more–in one great volume. Perfect inexpensive puzzler for clever youngsters. Full solutions. 112pp. 8⅛ x 11.    22951-3

PIANO TUNING, J. Cree Fischer. Clearest, best book for beginner, amateur. Simple repairs, raising dropped notes, tuning by easy method of flattened fifths. No previous skills needed. 4 illustrations. 201pp. 5⅜ x 8½. 23267-0

HINTS TO SINGERS, Lillian Nordica. Selecting the right teacher, developing confidence, overcoming stage fright, and many other important skills receive thoughtful discussion in this indispensible guide, written by a world-famous diva of four decades' experience. 96pp. 5⅜ x 8½. 40094-8

THE COMPLETE NONSENSE OF EDWARD LEAR, Edward Lear. All nonsense limericks, zany alphabets, Owl and Pussycat, songs, nonsense botany, etc., illustrated by Lear. Total of 320pp. 5⅜ x 8½. (Available in U.S. only.) 20167-8

VICTORIAN PARLOUR POETRY: An Annotated Anthology, Michael R. Turner. 117 gems by Longfellow, Tennyson, Browning, many lesser-known poets. "The Village Blacksmith," "Curfew Must Not Ring Tonight," "Only a Baby Small," dozens more, often difficult to find elsewhere. Index of poets, titles, first lines. xxiii + 325pp. 5⅜ x 8¼. 27044-0

DUBLINERS, James Joyce. Fifteen stories offer vivid, tightly focused observations of the lives of Dublin's poorer classes. At least one, "The Dead," is considered a masterpiece. Reprinted complete and unabridged from standard edition. 160pp. 5³⁄₁₆ x 8¼. 26870-5

GREAT WEIRD TALES: 14 Stories by Lovecraft, Blackwood, Machen and Others, S. T. Joshi (ed.). 14 spellbinding tales, including "The Sin Eater," by Fiona McLeod, "The Eye Above the Mantel," by Frank Belknap Long, as well as renowned works by R. H. Barlow, Lord Dunsany, Arthur Machen, W. C. Morrow and eight other masters of the genre. 256pp. 5⅜ x 8½. (Available in U.S. only.) 40436-6

THE BOOK OF THE SACRED MAGIC OF ABRAMELIN THE MAGE, translated by S. MacGregor Mathers. Medieval manuscript of ceremonial magic. Basic document in Aleister Crowley, Golden Dawn groups. 268pp. 5⅜ x 8½. 23211-5

NEW RUSSIAN-ENGLISH AND ENGLISH-RUSSIAN DICTIONARY, M. A. O'Brien. This is a remarkably handy Russian dictionary, containing a surprising amount of information, including over 70,000 entries. 366pp. 4½ x 6⅛. 20208-9

HISTORIC HOMES OF THE AMERICAN PRESIDENTS, Second, Revised Edition, Irvin Haas. A traveler's guide to American Presidential homes, most open to the public, depicting and describing homes occupied by every American President from George Washington to George Bush. With visiting hours, admission charges, travel routes. 175 photographs. Index. 160pp. 8¼ x 11. 26751-2

NEW YORK IN THE FORTIES, Andreas Feininger. 162 brilliant photographs by the well-known photographer, formerly with *Life* magazine. Commuters, shoppers, Times Square at night, much else from city at its peak. Captions by John von Hartz. 181pp. 9¼ x 10¾. 23585-8

INDIAN SIGN LANGUAGE, William Tomkins. Over 525 signs developed by Sioux and other tribes. Written instructions and diagrams. Also 290 pictographs. 111pp. 6⅛ x 9¼. 22029-X

CATALOG OF DOVER BOOKS

ANATOMY: A Complete Guide for Artists, Joseph Sheppard. A master of figure drawing shows artists how to render human anatomy convincingly. Over 460 illustrations. 224pp. 8⅜ x 11¼. 27279-6

MEDIEVAL CALLIGRAPHY: Its History and Technique, Marc Drogin. Spirited history, comprehensive instruction manual covers 13 styles (ca. 4th century through 15th). Excellent photographs; directions for duplicating medieval techniques with modern tools. 224pp. 8⅜ x 11¼. 26142-5

DRIED FLOWERS: How to Prepare Them, Sarah Whitlock and Martha Rankin. Complete instructions on how to use silica gel, meal and borax, perlite aggregate, sand and borax, glycerine and water to create attractive permanent flower arrangements. 12 illustrations. 32pp. 5⅜ x 8½. 21802-3

EASY-TO-MAKE BIRD FEEDERS FOR WOODWORKERS, Scott D. Campbell. Detailed, simple-to-use guide for designing, constructing, caring for and using feeders. Text, illustrations for 12 classic and contemporary designs. 96pp. 5⅜ x 8½. 25847-5

SCOTTISH WONDER TALES FROM MYTH AND LEGEND, Donald A. Mackenzie. 16 lively tales tell of giants rumbling down mountainsides, of a magic wand that turns stone pillars into warriors, of gods and goddesses, evil hags, powerful forces and more. 240pp. 5⅜ x 8½. 29677-6

THE HISTORY OF UNDERCLOTHES, C. Willett Cunnington and Phyllis Cunnington. Fascinating, well-documented survey covering six centuries of English undergarments, enhanced with over 100 illustrations: 12th-century laced-up bodice, footed long drawers (1795), 19th-century bustles, 19th-century corsets for men, Victorian "bust improvers," much more. 272pp. 5⅜ x 8¼. 27124-2

ARTS AND CRAFTS FURNITURE: The Complete Brooks Catalog of 1912, Brooks Manufacturing Co. Photos and detailed descriptions of more than 150 now very collectible furniture designs from the Arts and Crafts movement depict davenports, settees, buffets, desks, tables, chairs, bedsteads, dressers and more, all built of solid, quarter-sawed oak. Invaluable for students and enthusiasts of antiques, Americana and the decorative arts. 80pp. 6½ x 9¼. 27471-3

WILBUR AND ORVILLE: A Biography of the Wright Brothers, Fred Howard. Definitive, crisply written study tells the full story of the brothers' lives and work. A vividly written biography, unparalleled in scope and color, that also captures the spirit of an extraordinary era. 560pp. 6⅛ x 9¼. 40297-5

THE ARTS OF THE SAILOR: Knotting, Splicing and Ropework, Hervey Garrett Smith. Indispensable shipboard reference covers tools, basic knots and useful hitches; handsewing and canvas work, more. Over 100 illustrations. Delightful reading for sea lovers. 256pp. 5⅜ x 8½. 26440-8

FRANK LLOYD WRIGHT'S FALLINGWATER: The House and Its History, Second, Revised Edition, Donald Hoffmann. A total revision–both in text and illustrations–of the standard document on Fallingwater, the boldest, most personal architectural statement of Wright's mature years, updated with valuable new material from the recently opened Frank Lloyd Wright Archives. "Fascinating"–*The New York Times*. 116 illustrations. 128pp. 9¼ x 10¾. 27430-6

## CATALOG OF DOVER BOOKS

PHOTOGRAPHIC SKETCHBOOK OF THE CIVIL WAR, Alexander Gardner. 100 photos taken on field during the Civil War. Famous shots of Manassas Harper's Ferry, Lincoln, Richmond, slave pens, etc. 244pp. 10⅝ x 8¼. 22731-6

FIVE ACRES AND INDEPENDENCE, Maurice G. Kains. Great back-to-the-land classic explains basics of self-sufficient farming. The one book to get. 95 illustrations. 397pp. 5⅜ x 8½. 20974-1

SONGS OF EASTERN BIRDS, Dr. Donald J. Borror. Songs and calls of 60 species most common to eastern U.S.: warblers, woodpeckers, flycatchers, thrushes, larks, many more in high-quality recording. Cassette and manual 99912-2

A MODERN HERBAL, Margaret Grieve. Much the fullest, most exact, most useful compilation of herbal material. Gigantic alphabetical encyclopedia, from aconite to zedoary, gives botanical information, medical properties, folklore, economic uses, much else. Indispensable to serious reader. 161 illustrations. 888pp. 6½ x 9¼. 2-vol. set. (Available in U.S. only.) Vol. I: 22798-7
Vol. II: 22799-5

HIDDEN TREASURE MAZE BOOK, Dave Phillips. Solve 34 challenging mazes accompanied by heroic tales of adventure. Evil dragons, people-eating plants, blood-thirsty giants, many more dangerous adversaries lurk at every twist and turn. 34 mazes, stories, solutions. 48pp. 8¼ x 11. 24566-7

LETTERS OF W. A. MOZART, Wolfgang A. Mozart. Remarkable letters show bawdy wit, humor, imagination, musical insights, contemporary musical world; includes some letters from Leopold Mozart. 276pp. 5⅜ x 8½. 22859-2

BASIC PRINCIPLES OF CLASSICAL BALLET, Agrippina Vaganova. Great Russian theoretician, teacher explains methods for teaching classical ballet. 118 illustrations. 175pp. 5⅜ x 8½. 22036-2

THE JUMPING FROG, Mark Twain. Revenge edition. The original story of The Celebrated Jumping Frog of Calaveras County, a hapless French translation, and Twain's hilarious "retranslation" from the French. 12 illustrations. 66pp. 5⅜ x 8½. 22686-7

BEST REMEMBERED POEMS, Martin Gardner (ed.). The 126 poems in this superb collection of 19th- and 20th-century British and American verse range from Shelley's "To a Skylark" to the impassioned "Renascence" of Edna St. Vincent Millay and to Edward Lear's whimsical "The Owl and the Pussycat." 224pp. 5⅜ x 8½. 27165-X

COMPLETE SONNETS, William Shakespeare. Over 150 exquisite poems deal with love, friendship, the tyranny of time, beauty's evanescence, death and other themes in language of remarkable power, precision and beauty. Glossary of archaic terms. 80pp. 5³⁄₁₆ x 8¼. 26686-9

THE BATTLES THAT CHANGED HISTORY, Fletcher Pratt. Eminent historian profiles 16 crucial conflicts, ancient to modern, that changed the course of civilization. 352pp. 5⅜ x 8½. 41129-X

THE WIT AND HUMOR OF OSCAR WILDE, Alvin Redman (ed.). More than 1,000 ripostes, paradoxes, wisecracks: Work is the curse of the drinking classes; I can resist everything except temptation; etc. 258pp. 5⅜ x 8½.                    20602-5

SHAKESPEARE LEXICON AND QUOTATION DICTIONARY, Alexander Schmidt. Full definitions, locations, shades of meaning in every word in plays and poems. More than 50,000 exact quotations. 1,485pp. 6½ x 9¼. 2-vol. set.
Vol. 1: 22726-X
Vol. 2: 22727-8

SELECTED POEMS, Emily Dickinson. Over 100 best-known, best-loved poems by one of America's foremost poets, reprinted from authoritative early editions. No comparable edition at this price. Index of first lines. 64pp. 5³⁄₁₆ x 8¼.        26466-1

THE INSIDIOUS DR. FU-MANCHU, Sax Rohmer. The first of the popular mystery series introduces a pair of English detectives to their archnemesis, the diabolical Dr. Fu-Manchu. Flavorful atmosphere, fast-paced action, and colorful characters enliven this classic of the genre. 208pp. 5³⁄₁₆ x 8¼.        29898-1

THE MALLEUS MALEFICARUM OF KRAMER AND SPRENGER, translated by Montague Summers. Full text of most important witchhunter's "bible," used by both Catholics and Protestants. 278pp. 6⅝ x 10.        22802-9

SPANISH STORIES/CUENTOS ESPAÑOLES: A Dual-Language Book, Angel Flores (ed.). Unique format offers 13 great stories in Spanish by Cervantes, Borges, others. Faithful English translations on facing pages. 352pp. 5⅜ x 8½.        25399-6

GARDEN CITY, LONG ISLAND, IN EARLY PHOTOGRAPHS, 1869–1919, Mildred H. Smith. Handsome treasury of 118 vintage pictures, accompanied by carefully researched captions, document the Garden City Hotel fire (1899), the Vanderbilt Cup Race (1908), the first airmail flight departing from the Nassau Boulevard Aerodrome (1911), and much more. 96pp. 8⅞ x 11¾.        40669-5

OLD QUEENS, N.Y., IN EARLY PHOTOGRAPHS, Vincent F. Seyfried and William Asadorian. Over 160 rare photographs of Maspeth, Jamaica, Jackson Heights, and other areas. Vintage views of DeWitt Clinton mansion, 1939 World's Fair and more. Captions. 192pp. 8⅞ x 11.        26358-4

CAPTURED BY THE INDIANS: 15 Firsthand Accounts, 1750-1870, Frederick Drimmer. Astounding true historical accounts of grisly torture, bloody conflicts, relentless pursuits, miraculous escapes and more, by people who lived to tell the tale. 384pp. 5⅜ x 8½.        24901-8

THE WORLD'S GREAT SPEECHES (Fourth Enlarged Edition), Lewis Copeland, Lawrence W. Lamm, and Stephen J. McKenna. Nearly 300 speeches provide public speakers with a wealth of updated quotes and inspiration–from Pericles' funeral oration and William Jennings Bryan's "Cross of Gold Speech" to Malcolm X's powerful words on the Black Revolution and Earl of Spenser's tribute to his sister, Diana, Princess of Wales. 944pp. 5⅜ x 8⅜.        40903-1

THE BOOK OF THE SWORD, Sir Richard F. Burton. Great Victorian scholar/adventurer's eloquent, erudite history of the "queen of weapons"–from prehistory to early Roman Empire. Evolution and development of early swords, variations (sabre, broadsword, cutlass, scimitar, etc.), much more. 336pp. 6⅛ x 9¼.
25434-8

# CATALOG OF DOVER BOOKS

AUTOBIOGRAPHY: The Story of My Experiments with Truth, Mohandas K. Gandhi. Boyhood, legal studies, purification, the growth of the Satyagraha (nonviolent protest) movement. Critical, inspiring work of the man responsible for the freedom of India. 480pp. 5⅜ x 8½. (Available in U.S. only.) 24593-4

CELTIC MYTHS AND LEGENDS, T. W. Rolleston. Masterful retelling of Irish and Welsh stories and tales. Cuchulain, King Arthur, Deirdre, the Grail, many more. First paperback edition. 58 full-page illustrations. 512pp. 5⅜ x 8½. 26507-2

THE PRINCIPLES OF PSYCHOLOGY, William James. Famous long course complete, unabridged. Stream of thought, time perception, memory, experimental methods; great work decades ahead of its time. 94 figures. 1,391pp. 5⅜ x 8½. 2-vol. set.
Vol. I: 20381-6    Vol. II: 20382-4

THE WORLD AS WILL AND REPRESENTATION, Arthur Schopenhauer. Definitive English translation of Schopenhauer's life work, correcting more than 1,000 errors, omissions in earlier translations. Translated by E. F. J. Payne. Total of 1,269pp. 5⅜ x 8½. 2-vol. set.    Vol. 1: 21761-2    Vol. 2: 21762-0

MAGIC AND MYSTERY IN TIBET, Madame Alexandra David-Neel. Experiences among lamas, magicians, sages, sorcerers, Bonpa wizards. A true psychic discovery. 32 illustrations. 321pp. 5⅜ x 8½. (Available in U.S. only.) 22682-4

THE EGYPTIAN BOOK OF THE DEAD, E. A. Wallis Budge. Complete reproduction of Ani's papyrus, finest ever found. Full hieroglyphic text, interlinear transliteration, word-for-word translation, smooth translation. 533pp. 6½ x 9¼. 21866-X

MATHEMATICS FOR THE NONMATHEMATICIAN, Morris Kline. Detailed, college-level treatment of mathematics in cultural and historical context, with numerous exercises. Recommended Reading Lists. Tables. Numerous figures. 641pp. 5⅜ x 8½. 24823-2

PROBABILISTIC METHODS IN THE THEORY OF STRUCTURES, Isaac Elishakoff. Well-written introduction covers the elements of the theory of probability from two or more random variables, the reliability of such multivariable structures, the theory of random function, Monte Carlo methods of treating problems incapable of exact solution, and more. Examples. 502pp. 5⅜ x 8½. 40691-1

THE RIME OF THE ANCIENT MARINER, Gustave Doré, S. T. Coleridge. Doré's finest work; 34 plates capture moods, subtleties of poem. Flawless full-size reproductions printed on facing pages with authoritative text of poem. "Beautiful. Simply beautiful."—*Publisher's Weekly.* 77pp. 9¼ x 12. 22305-1

NORTH AMERICAN INDIAN DESIGNS FOR ARTISTS AND CRAFTSPEOPLE, Eva Wilson. Over 360 authentic copyright-free designs adapted from Navajo blankets, Hopi pottery, Sioux buffalo hides, more. Geometrics, symbolic figures, plant and animal motifs, etc. 128pp. 8⅜ x 11. (Not for sale in the United Kingdom.) 25341-4

SCULPTURE: Principles and Practice, Louis Slobodkin. Step-by-step approach to clay, plaster, metals, stone; classical and modern. 253 drawings, photos. 255pp. 8⅛ x 11. 22960-2

THE INFLUENCE OF SEA POWER UPON HISTORY, 1660–1783, A. T. Mahan. Influential classic of naval history and tactics still used as text in war colleges. First paperback edition. 4 maps. 24 battle plans. 640pp. 5⅜ x 8½. 25509-3

# CATALOG OF DOVER BOOKS

THE STORY OF THE TITANIC AS TOLD BY ITS SURVIVORS, Jack Winocour (ed.). What it was really like. Panic, despair, shocking inefficiency, and a little heroism. More thrilling than any fictional account. 26 illustrations. 320pp. 5⅜ x 8½.
20610-6

FAIRY AND FOLK TALES OF THE IRISH PEASANTRY, William Butler Yeats (ed.). Treasury of 64 tales from the twilight world of Celtic myth and legend: "The Soul Cages," "The Kildare Pooka," "King O'Toole and his Goose," many more. Introduction and Notes by W. B. Yeats. 352pp. 5⅜ x 8½.
26941-8

BUDDHIST MAHAYANA TEXTS, E. B. Cowell and others (eds.). Superb, accurate translations of basic documents in Mahayana Buddhism, highly important in history of religions. The Buddha-karita of Asvaghosha, Larger Sukhavativyuha, more. 448pp. 5⅜ x 8½.
25552-2

ONE TWO THREE . . . INFINITY: Facts and Speculations of Science, George Gamow. Great physicist's fascinating, readable overview of contemporary science: number theory, relativity, fourth dimension, entropy, genes, atomic structure, much more. 128 illustrations. Index. 352pp. 5⅜ x 8½.
25664-2

EXPERIMENTATION AND MEASUREMENT, W. J. Youden. Introductory manual explains laws of measurement in simple terms and offers tips for achieving accuracy and minimizing errors. Mathematics of measurement, use of instruments, experimenting with machines. 1994 edition. Foreword. Preface. Introduction. Epilogue. Selected Readings. Glossary. Index. Tables and figures. 128pp. 5⅜ x 8½.    40451-X

DALÍ ON MODERN ART: The Cuckolds of Antiquated Modern Art, Salvador Dalí. Influential painter skewers modern art and its practitioners. Outrageous evaluations of Picasso, Cézanne, Turner, more. 15 renderings of paintings discussed. 44 calligraphic decorations by Dalí. 96pp. 5⅜ x 8½. (Available in U.S. only.)
29220-7

ANTIQUE PLAYING CARDS: A Pictorial History, Henry René D'Allemagne. Over 900 elaborate, decorative images from rare playing cards (14th–20th centuries): Bacchus, death, dancing dogs, hunting scenes, royal coats of arms, players cheating, much more. 96pp. 9¼ x 12¼.
29265-7

MAKING FURNITURE MASTERPIECES: 30 Projects with Measured Drawings, Franklin H. Gottshall. Step-by-step instructions, illustrations for constructing handsome, useful pieces, among them a Sheraton desk, Chippendale chair, Spanish desk, Queen Anne table and a William and Mary dressing mirror. 224pp. 8⅛ x 11¼.
29338-6

THE FOSSIL BOOK: A Record of Prehistoric Life, Patricia V. Rich et al. Profusely illustrated definitive guide covers everything from single-celled organisms and dinosaurs to birds and mammals and the interplay between climate and man. Over 1,500 illustrations. 760pp. 7½ x 10⅛.
29371-8

Paperbound unless otherwise indicated. Available at your book dealer, online at **www.doverpublications.com**, or by writing to Dept. GI, Dover Publications, Inc., 31 East 2nd Street, Mineola, NY 11501. For current price information or for free catalogues (please indicate field of interest), write to Dover Publications or log on to **www.doverpublications.com** and see every Dover book in print. Dover publishes more than 500 books each year on science, elementary and advanced mathematics, biology, music, art, literary history, social sciences, and other areas.